The Dakota Conflict
and Its Leaders,
1862–1865

ALSO BY PAUL WILLIAMS
AND FROM McFARLAND

Rebel Guerrillas: Mosby, Quantrill and Anderson (2018)

*Frontier Forts Under Fire:
The Attacks on Fort William Henry (1757)
and Fort Phil Kearny (1866)* (2017)

*Jackson, Crockett and Houston on the American Frontier:
From Fort Mims to the Alamo, 1813–1836* (2016)

*Custer and the Sioux, Durnford and the Zulus:
Parallels in the American and British Defeats
at the Little Bighorn (1876) and Isandlwana (1879)* (2015)

*The Last Confederate Ship at Sea:
The Wayward Voyage of the CSS* Shenandoah,
October 1864–November 1865 (2015)

The Dakota Conflict and Its Leaders, 1862–1865

Little Crow, Henry Sibley and Alfred Sully

PAUL WILLIAMS

McFarland & Company, Inc., Publishers
Jefferson, North Carolina

LIBRARY OF CONGRESS CATALOGUING-IN-PUBLICATION DATA

Names: Williams, Paul, 1946– author.
Title: The Dakota Conflict and its leaders, 1862-1865 : Little Crow, Henry Sibley and Alfred Sully / Paul Williams.
Other titles: Little Crow, Henry Sibley and Alfred Sully
Description: Jefferson, North Carolina : McFarland & Company, Inc., Publishers, 2020 | Includes bibliographical references and index.
Identifiers: LCCN 2020018844 | ISBN 9781476680699 (paperback) ∞
ISBN 9781476639314 (ebook)
Subjects: LCSH: Dakota War, Minnesota, 1862. | Dakota Indians—Wars, 1862–1865. | Dakota Indians—Minnesota—History—19th century. | Little Crow, –1863. | Sibley, Henry Hastings, 1811–1891. | Sully, Alfred, 1821–1879.
Classification: LCC E83.876 .W4849 2020 | DDC 973.7—dc23
LC record available at https://lccn.loc.gov/2020018844

BRITISH LIBRARY CATALOGUING DATA ARE AVAILABLE

ISBN (print) 978-1-4766-8069-9
ISBN (ebook) 978-1-4766-3931-4

© 2020 The Estate of Paul Williams. All rights reserved

No part of this book may be reproduced or transmitted in any form or by any means, electronic or mechanical, including photocopying or recording, or by any information storage and retrieval system, without permission in writing from the publisher.

On the cover: Little Crow (1862), Henry H. Sibley (1862), Alfred H. Sully (1862), by J.E. Whitney (1822–1886), courtesy of Minnesota Historical Society

Printed in the United States of America

McFarland & Company, Inc., Publishers
Box 611, Jefferson, North Carolina 28640
www.mcfarlandpub.com

Acknowledgments

I wish to thank a number of helpful organizations in the writing of this book, in particular the Minnesota Historical Society, St. Paul; the South Dakota Historical Society, Pierre; the North Dakota Historical Society, Bismarck; Cornell University, Ithaca, New York; University of Oklahoma, Norman; and the Library of Congress, Washington, D.C. I would also like to thank those other authors dating from the Dakota uprising of 1862 to the present day who probed the facts and folklore behind the war and the resulting punitive military expeditions to Dakota Territory.

Table of Contents

Acknowledgments   v

Preface   1

1. Don't Try and Cross the River There   5
2. Popularity Is His God   13
3. Subsisted on a Tall Grass   25
4. You Know Not What You Are Doing   34
5. A Dreadful Scene   40
6. We Laughed in Spite of Our Danger   57
7. We Shall Need More Guns   81
8. I Have a Great Many Prisoners, Women and Children   93
9. They Will Never Get My Live Body   102
10. Maniacs or Wild Beasts   113
11. Five Minutes Would Dispose of a Case   121
12. The Shot That Killed Him   140
13. The Girl I Left Behind Me   146
14. The Results Are Entirely Satisfactory   164
15. An Indian Campaign Is Approved   180
16. Am I Free, Indeed Free?   196
17. They Fear It Is Only a Trap   213
18. The Indian No Longer Has a Country   224

Appendix: Timeline of the Dakota War of 1862–1865	229
Chapter Notes	233
Bibliography	241
Index	247

Preface

For as long as I can remember I've been fascinated with the story of the American frontier, from the arrival of the English settlers at Jamestown in 1607. The U.S. government declared the frontier closed in 1890. No doubt this was news to many who still lived an isolated, rugged life in crude homes on the plains and mountains of the American West. Wounded Knee in 1890 is generally considered to be the last frontier Indian fight, or massacre, if you prefer. But further conflict took place after that desolate affair.

As a child, I begged and borrowed books on American history. One year I requested one as a Christmas gift. I wasn't fussy—the Civil War, the Alamo or perhaps the Indian Wars would do. But what appeared beneath the Christmas tree was a brand-new bicycle, a pleasant surprise, my parents thought. They looked on in wonder as I bypassed the bike and rummaged through the brightly wrapped presents. Where was that book? *Not there!* I was miffed, to say the least.

My innate curiosity was fueled by Hollywood. The Disney version of Davy Crockett at the Alamo caused a phenomenon and the worldwide sale of coonskin caps. On TV I saw Errol Flynn die at the Little Big Horn, a hero, the last man down. I was appalled when a writer in *TV Week* wrote a critique of *They Died with Their Boots On*. He denounced the real Custer as a "personal glory seeker who blundered into a battle with more Indians than he could handle." Aged 13 at the time, I wrote to the reviewer a passionate defense of my hero. He published my letter and wrote a reply titled *"TV Week*'s Last Stand." He insisted he had it right and questioned the validity of my research—with good reason, as I learned with the passage of time. My 2015 book *Custer and The Sioux, Durnford and the Zulus* takes a more balanced view. By then I had learned that Errol Flynn was not, after all, George A. Custer. I read that Raoul Walsh, the director, said his bio-epic "depicted Custer as he should have been, rather than the way he was." Patriotic films like *Boots* and *Sergeant York* helped pave the way for America's entry into World War II.

For me, Walt Disney inspired more than an interest in the Alamo. I loved animated films like *Peter Pan*. As an adult I embarked on a career in animated film production while never losing sight of my hobbies: classic cars and military history. My first history book, about Australian outlaws, was published in 2007. In 2015, McFarland published *The Last Confederate Ship at Sea*, which reveals the true story behind the cruise of the CSS *Shenandoah*, written at the behest of relatives of a key participant. Following this, I had books published about Custer, Fort Mims and the Alamo, Confederate guerrillas and frontier forts.

But amidst all this there was a dark shadow not touched by Hollywood. I read a brief account in Paul Wellman's *Death on the Prairie*. Far less known than Custer, Sitting Bull and Crazy Horse are the names Little Crow, Sibley, and Sully.

Yet these people are linked with the most vicious Indian war in the history of the West. In Minnesota, during six hot summer weeks in 1862, hundreds of white settlers died by bullet, knife and tomahawk. Overshadowed by the coinciding War Between the States, the Minnesota War, while probed by historians, has remained obscure in the public mind. There was no glorious Last Stand, cavalry guidons fluttering in the breeze as valiant defenders fought to the last bullet, or so the Errol Flynn image goes.

Years ago, I met a young lady who proudly told me she was a "Minnesota Sioux." "Oh," said I. "The Minnesota Sioux carried out a terrible massacre of settlers."

"That's right," she laughed, giving her hands one hard clap. "They strung children upside down and crashed their heads together." She turned and walked off. I looked after her in wonder. There was no remorse.

By then, films such as *Soldier Blue* and *Little Big Man* had emerged. These films portrayed, in graphic terms, the massacre of Indians by U.S. troops. In recent years, to satisfy my own curiosity, I decided to delve into the terrible story of the Minnesota Massacre. I would write my own account. But the story is not complete without including the aftermath. Punitive expeditions were sent to the plains, and innocent Indians paid with their lives. The final campaign of 1865 has been dismissed by many as a mere failure, scarcely worth writing about. But taking a close look, I found this expedition to be of great interest. The last shots of the Dakota War were fired when Sitting Bull inspired an attack on Fort Rice.

As I delved, I learned much, becoming interested in the story of Fanny Kelly, briefly mentioned in my book, *Frontier Forts Under Fire*. She was captured by the Dakotas, but saved by Sitting Bull—or so the story goes. And Fanny told a pack of lies, making a false claim of having saved Fort Sully from massacre—so some claimed. And Sitting Bull acted in a cowardly manner in the attack on Fort Rice—so the story goes. This whole saga required a closer look. While researching, I was surprised at how reputable "historians" repeat disparaging assertions about individuals as fact without question. Accusers often had a vested interest in shredding other people's reputations. I feel Sitting Bull suffered smears to his reputation, and Sam Houston of the Texas Revolution also comes to mind. This can be, of course, an oversight. But some writers deliberately falsify facts with selective quotes while omitting other evidence from the same source. One book in recent years claimed that most Alamo defenders fled, to be killed beyond the walls. This publication was an outstanding example of deliberate misrepresentation through very selective quoting from firsthand accounts.

To return to the facts of the Minnesota War: over the years, different treaties removed the Dakotas from their hunting grounds. The United States was obliged to pay annuities in return, and encouraged the traditional hunters to follow the ways of the white man and use the plow. Gradually, the Indians became more dependent on muskets, cooking utensils, sugar, coffee flour, tobacco, and alcohol—goods produced by the whites. The annuity payments were often late, and the Indians became the victims of widespread fraud, many traders and officials enriching themselves at the Dakotas' expense. The voiceless Indians had no control over this.

Things came to a boil in August of 1862 with the killing of five white settlers. Chief Taoyateduta, or Little Crow, quickly emerged as the dominant Dakota leader, and a mass slaughter took place. He had previously traveled to Washington, D.C., and seen with his own eyes the European juggernaut devouring North America. On one hand, feeling might is right, he had wished to stay on best terms with the whites, encouraging farming amongst his people. But he remained a traditional hunter at heart, and it took only one accusation of cowardice for common sense to be thrown to the wind. His pride at stake, Little Crow led his people on a fateful journey that could have only one end.

Generals Henry Sibley and Alfred Sully became the hammers of the Dakota Nation, and another chapter in American history was written in blood.

Note: Period spelling and grammar in quotations are often incorrect, but because the irregularities are so numerous, the customary "[sic]" has been excluded. Author's illustrations are based on period photos, sketches and paintings.

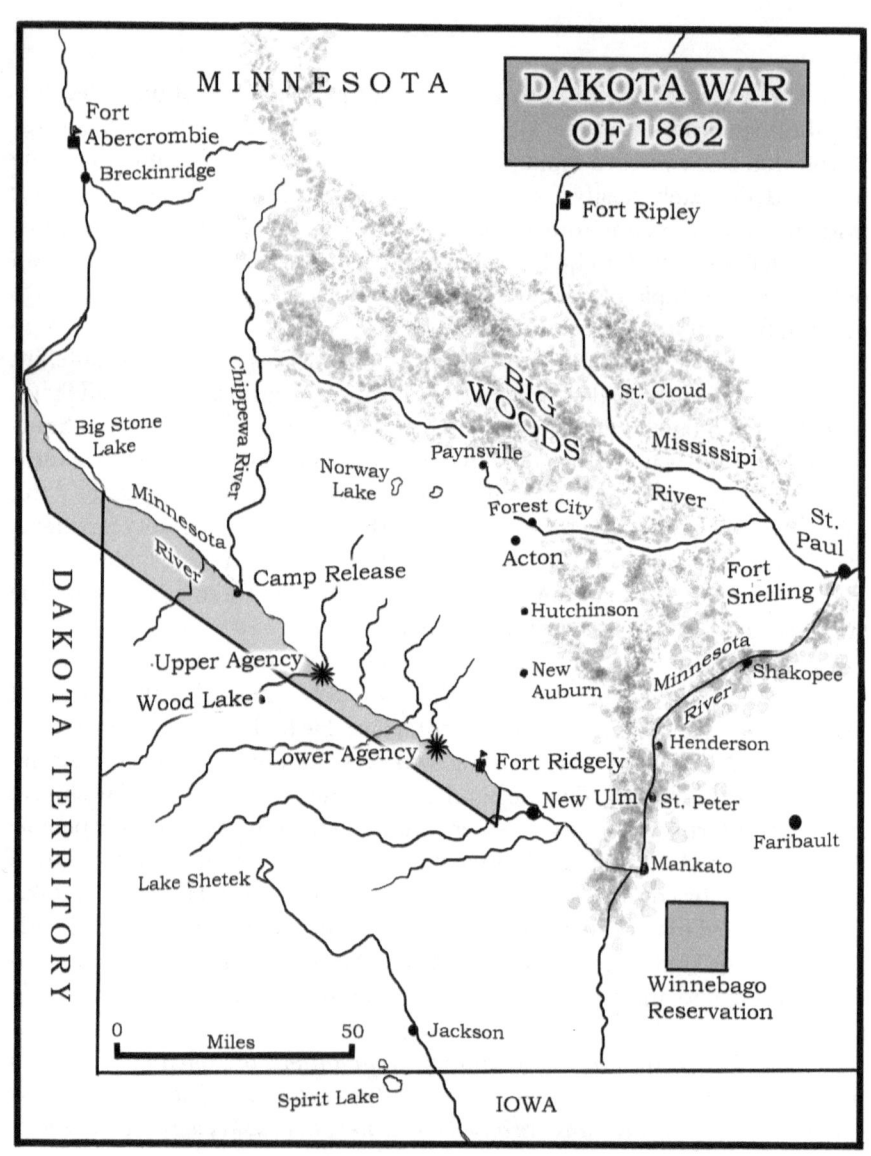

Theater of the Dakota War of 1862 (author's rendition).

1

Don't Try and Cross the River There

Captain John Marsh listened with disbelief. Despite rumblings of discontent from the neighboring Indian reservation, he could scarcely believe what he was being told: the Dakota tribe had gone on the warpath. In recent years, many warriors had forsaken their traditional ways and become peaceful farmers. Many wore the white man's clothing, and some even attended the Christian church.

But on the fine sunny morning of Monday, August 18, 1862, the 32-year-old commander of Fort Ridgely, Minnesota, found himself absorbed by the anxious words of Oliver Martell, owner of the Redwood Ferry. Martell reported hearing gunfire break out at the Redwood, or Lower Dakota Agency. The firing was sometimes irregular and "again it sounded like a hundred or more being discharged simultaneously," he said.[1] The Agency, about 12 miles to the northwest, was a key administration point for the Dakota, or Sioux tribe. Those residing in Minnesota were known as Santees. Their reservation spread for 130 miles along the southern bank of the Minnesota River.

Earlier, the Rev. Sam Hinman had arrived at Martell's ferry with a party of women and children, including his family. Gunfire could be heard. "The Indians were killing every white they saw," he said, and advised Martell to mount a swift horse and ride for Fort Ridgely. The pastor and his party would follow by wagon. Panic-stricken refugees, meanwhile, were gathering on the opposite bank, and Martell's ferry operator bravely stayed behind to bring them across.

As Captain Marsh listened to Martell, a buggy clattered across the fort's dusty parade ground. Post sutler Ben Randall jumped out with similar news heard from settler Joseph Dickinson. He and his family were following by wagon.[2]

Twelve-year-old drummer boy Charley Culver rattled the "long roll" across the parade ground. The soldiers stopped in their tracks, grasped their rifles, and dashed to the sound of the drum. Captain Marsh, meanwhile, hurriedly scribbled a note to Lieutenant Timothy Sheehan, who had marched the day before with 50 men of Company C, Fifth Minnesota Volunteers. They were headed for Fort Ripley, about 140 miles to the north. "It is absolutely necessary that you should return with your command to this post," Marsh wrote. "The Indians are raising hell at the Lower Agency."[3]

About 74 soldiers hurriedly assembled on the Ridgely parade ground, a grossly inadequate force to confront the hundreds of armed warriors on the reservation. Marsh's force included 2nd Lieutenant Thomas Gere, four sergeants, seven corporals, and about 63 privates. Lieutenant Culver was absent, on detachment with six men accompanying 50 "Renville Rangers" under Indian Agent Thomas Galbraith. Despite a recent confrontation with Indians at the Upper Agency, Galbraith had seen fit to leave his post. The rangers were marching to the key post of Fort Snelling, about 65 miles northeast, to join the Union Army, then enmeshed in its titanic struggle with the Confederate States of the South.

As frightened refugees began to arrive by foot, horseback, buggy and carriage, Marsh prepared wagons for an armed expedition. Oliver Martell, with settler Louis La Croix, mounted up and rode back towards the Redwood Ferry. Dead bodies were found during a ride of several miles. "Fresh blood was oozing from the wound in Magner's neck," recalled Martell. This was a recent death; the Indians were close. "So La Croix and I put back to the fort."[4] They soon encountered Captain Marsh leading 46 blue-clad infantry "wagoneers." Each soldier had been issued 40 rounds, and a six-mule team wagon followed with extra ammunition and one day's rations. With Marsh was language interpreter Peter Quinn; both men were riding mules. "I am sure we are going into great danger," Quinn had told Sutler Ben Randall before departing Fort Ridgely. "I do not expect to return alive. Good bye; give my love to all."[5]

"How are things looking up there?" asked Captain Marsh.

"We went as far as Magner's place and found Ed Magner, Smith and another man dead and we could see fire at the agency," Martell replied. "I wouldn't go up there at all. I have no doubt but that the Indians have broken out for good, and you haven't enough men to do any good." Martell went on to describe the ferry crossing, bushed in with willow brush and an old artichoke field. "This is a splendid place for Indians to ambush, and whatever you do, don't try and cross the river there."

Marsh was a lawyer in peacetime. He had seen action as a mere private at Bull Run before becoming an officer, all of which was no preparation for Indian fighting. Dakota warriors did not stand in open ranks and deliver volleys as did regular army Confederates. They fought like rebel guerrillas: concealment, ambush, furtive hit-and-run.

But Marsh could not turn back. Refugees were now streaming past, defenseless settlers, women and children. He gave the order to continue, and the wagons creaked forward. Martell and La Croix rode back to the post where Lieutenant Gere had been left in command with fewer than 25 effective men. And Ridgely was a fort in name only. It had no protective stockade and was poorly situated to fend off an Indian attack.

Marsh led his small command past a deserted home towards a column of dark smoke drifting with the breeze. The burning Magner family cabin, in the last stages of collapse, came into view. There was a rustle in the bush and three men emerged: John Humphrey, John Magill and John Magner. They were relieved beyond belief to see the new arrivals wore blue uniforms rather than breechclouts and war paint. Magill, a soldier on furlough who had been visiting the Magner home, rejoined his comrades in arms. Reassured by all those guns and bayonets, Humphrey and Magner decided to stay with the troops too.

A dead body could be seen lying outside the smoky ruins. John Humphrey moved forward with a few soldiers to find that his father, Dr. Philander Humphrey, was the victim. The Humphrey family had been sheltering at the Magner cabin. "A bullet had pierced the center of his forehead and the fiends had cut his throat," Humphrey recalled. An ax that lay alongside the body indicated that "he went outside the cabin and met them like a brave man." With further horror, Humphrey realized "the smoldering ruins which had fallen into the cellar contained the mortal remains of my mother and brother and sister ... truly I was alone with my dead."[6] The soldiers were moving on, and John, the shattered lone survivor of the Humphrey family, ran after them. He scrambled aboard the supply wagon and sat on a barrel of provisions. He could not understand how such a horrific thing had happened to his virtuous mother. "The atheist, the agnostic, or the nominal Christian can give no reasonable explanation for the fate that befell this Christian woman, and indeed the entire family, excepting one; and it would be equally impossible for such persons to give any sufficient reason why the eldest boy escaped with his life."[7]

Nineteen-year-old John Bishop had only enlisted a few months before, but had already achieved the rank of 5th sergeant. As they advanced, he was not happy with his commanding officer. "I think the great mistake of Captain Marsh was in not deploying two or three men each side of the road, and in advance of the command, after we had commenced finding the dead. In that case the skirmishers might have discovered some of the Indians in the grass as we approached the ferry." A little further on, they found "another citizen, tomahawked and nearly dead," recalled Bishop. "We laid him out on the side of the road." Marsh had a passing refugee, one of many, help the victim back to the fort.

About nine miles from Ridgely, the small command crested Faribault Hill, named for the family who resided at the base. As the wagons clattered down the slope, four more dead bodies were seen alongside the road. Another four were found near a meandering creek in the bottomlands. "These poor souls fleeing for their lives had been shot down from the cover of underbrush and tall course grass which grew rankly in these western river valleys," recalled John Humphrey. The door to the Faribault house flew open and about two dozen desperate women and children dashed out, relieved beyond all measure to see the troops. They had been rounded up with threats of being locked in and burnt alive before the Indians moved on. While they departed with haste towards Fort Ridgely, Marsh continued towards the Redwood ferry, about two miles down the track. More bodies were seen. But where were the offenders? Marsh was yet to come into contact with the enemy—an enemy well aware of his approach.

"There came the hue and cry 'the soldiers are coming, poor unfortunate little band of heroes,'" recalled Cecelia Campbell Stay, 13 years old at the time. She was of a mixed-blood family who had been taken captive by the rebellious warriors. "Just a mouthful for the lion's mouth as mother said. 'Let's go and see how many there are.' So we ran to the hill and saw a handful of glistening bayonets just passing David Faribault's house across the river Mother burst out with 'poor soldiers' 'what foolish soldiers' 'they'll all be killed' come we must get away out of earshot I don't want to hear a shot that kills them."[8]

The troops moved on, and two more bodies were found. From the appearance of their wounds, they had only just been killed. "We could see mounted Indians pursuing parties on the other side of the river," recalled Private William Blodgett, "and in many cases they were overtaken and slain."

It was early afternoon when Marsh arrived at the ferry crossing. The ferryman was dead, having sacrificed his life so that others may live. The soldiers assembled on the riverbank. "The Minnesota River at this point keeps close to the bluffs on the southwest side," recalled Sergeant Bishop. "These bluffs at that time were covered with a thick growth of hazel-brush and small trees, while on the east side was a wide bottom, covered with heavy, high grass." The ferry rocked gently at its moorings, beckoning them to cross. Then "we saw an Indian dressed very gorgeously in feathers and war-paint," recalled Blodgett. "He was standing on a log on the opposite side of the river." Interpreter Quinn peered across and frowned. "I don't know this Indian," he said. "He don't belong here." Bishop told Marsh he recognized White Dog, a Dakota chief from the Upper Agency, over 20 miles upriver—a warning that more than just local tribesmen had gone to war. Quinn called across. What was White Dog doing here? "Only on a visit for a few days," he replied. "The Indians were all at the Lower Agency," he said, about one mile away, waiting for a council. He urged Marsh to board the ferry and cross. There had been trouble with the traders, he said, but the captain could "fix it" and all would be well.[9]

Sergeant Bishop, dipping his cup for a drink, noticed the usually clear water was clouded with twigs and leaves drifting downstream. "Captain Marsh, I believe we are being surrounded by Indians crossing the river above us." Marsh peered up the river as Bishop climbed the graded, sandy edge of the track. Bishop looked upstream to see something moving in a bushy ravine: the swishing tails of many ponies. Quinn called across to White Dog. What were ponies doing there if their owners were waiting at the agency?

"Look out," Quinn yelled as the Indian raised his musket. "At that moment," recalled Blodgett, "the terrible blood-curdling war-whoop of the Sioux, that no white man has ever succeeded in imitating, was sounded. At the same time White Dog discharged his musket and jumped back off the log." In the next instant there was a blast of gun smoke from dozens of concealed firearms. "I felt a sharp pain in my back and side," recalled Blodgett, "and I began to sink down."[10] Men screamed as balls hit home, and nearly half the soldiers dropped where they stood. Quinn, riddled by a dozen shots, fulfilled his prophecy by falling dead, and Marsh was thrown as his mule went down. In the distance, "we heard the first volley," Cecelia recalled. "Mother dropped as tho she was dead with baby Stella on her back, she had fainted."[11]

Bishop, 25 years after the event, wrote that this initial volley came from the opposite bank, but John Humphrey, in a wagon to the rear, stated that the impulsive firing by the Indians "on the side where we were" spoiled a plan to shoot the soldiers midstream on the ferry. Chief Big Eagle, who arrived as the battle smoke cleared, recalled, "The Indians told me that the most of them who fired on Capt. Marsh and his men were on the same side of the river; that only a few shots came from the opposite or south side."[12]

Captain Marsh, regaining his feet, yelled, "Steady, men!" Indians, painted and clad only in breechclouts, charged from the undergrowth behind the command. Marsh ordered the survivors to high ground. From there they delivered a volley at the oncoming tide, but in the next instant the Indians were among them and the fighting was hand-to-hand. A bewildered John Humphrey jumped from the wagon and "joined the survivors and made it to a point to keep about in the middle of them so that I should not fail to keep up. Several soldiers did become separated from us in the confusion and excitement."

Sergeant Bishop, Sergeant Trescott and two others ran for the ferryman's log house alongside the road. Bishop was the only one to make it, the other three being shot down. Bishop dashed between the house and a barn as bullets flew. One ball struck the stock of his rifle, and the ricochet caused a light wound to his thigh. "The charge on [Confederate General John Bell] Hood at Nashville, Dec. 6, 1864, was a quiet promenade for me in comparison to this dash," he recalled years later. Sand flew in front as ill-aimed shotgun pellets splattered the ground.

The Indian started to reload while the sergeant raced to do the same.

The muzzleloaders took time to load, and the life of the winner would be the prize. But the race was cut short when a rifle came up from behind Bishop's left arm. The gun went off and the lethal race ended with the warrior's death. Bishop's savior was Private James Dunn. "Is your gun loaded?" Dunn asked.

"Yes, as soon as I can cap it," Bishop replied.

"You lead, my gun is empty," said Dunn.

They pressed ahead only to find the brush alive with Indians, "who bore down on us." Forced to circle around to the southwest, they soon found themselves in a thicket of scrub and long grass just below the ferry. Here they encountered Captain Marsh and 11 survivors taking shelter. Other men had been cut off, unable to rejoin Marsh. "The Indians surrounded this thicket," Bishop recalled, "yelling and shooting shot and ball in thick and fast, and here we commenced to use our ammunition carefully under cover of brush and grass, to stand the devils off."

By late afternoon, the situation was becoming desperate as they moved back through scrub towards Ridgely. The soldiers had only four rounds per man left. There was no hope of help from any quarter. Their only chance of escape, Marsh thought, was to cross the river and make their way back through the brushwood along the opposite bank. But, according to John Humphrey, this was "in opposition to the judgment of his men."[13] Marsh waded in and started swimming, but in midstream developed difficulties, possibly a cramp. Sergeant Bishop, now the senior man, ordered three strong swimmers, Privates Brennan, Dunn and Van Buren, to the rescue. Brennan reached Marsh as he resurfaced, but could not hold him above water. "I will never forget the look that brave officer gave us just before he sank for the last time," recalled Bishop, and "will never forget how dark the next hour seemed to us, as we crouched underneath the bank of the Minnesota river, and talked over and decided what next best to do." But by then all had become quiet. Marsh's sacrifice had not been in vain. The Indians, seeing soldiers in the water, had thought all survivors were headed for the opposite bank. Most abandoned their positions on the north side and splashed across the river in pursuit.

While the Indians searched in vain, the remains of Marsh's command made their way through long grass and scrub towards what safety the sparsely garrisoned fort could provide. As the sun began to set, smoke drifted from smoldering ruins, and other survivors, some wounded, made their way back by different paths. Two tired and demoralized men with Bishop dropped their muskets as they plodded on. John Humphrey picked the weapons up. Who knows when they would be needed again? The shamefaced soldiers soon retrieved their precious guns with no word spoken.[14] The progress of Bishop's command was hampered by a few wounded, including the sergeant himself, but at least he could make his own way. Private Ole Svendson had to be carried for miles before the exhausted soldiers could bear the weight no longer. After dark he was left behind to make his own way back as best he could.

As the survivors advanced, two stricken white women were discovered in the brush, one of whom had given birth to a baby only one hour before. "Have I found help at last? Am I saved?" she called out. With a baby and women now in tow, it would be an even slower progress. Bishop sent Privates Dunn and Hutchinson forward to alert the garrison. They staggered into the fort through the dark and disclosed the tragic event. A horrified Lieutenant Gere immediately dispatched a rider to get reinforcements from Governor Ramsey at St. Paul and warn settlements along the way.

The post was bustling with refugees, and news of the disaster sent a wave of horror through the crowd. Would the post come under attack? Would any live to see the sun rise? Sobs could be heard from people already traumatized by the day's events. At about 10 that night, Bishop and the remaining survivors made their way back into Fort Ridgely. "Some things we saw that day are too revolting to relate," recalled Bishop. "It chills my blood now to think of them."

Another woman, Mary Hayden, babe in arms, made it in under cover of darkness after hiding in the woods. Then Private Thomas Parsley arrived. He had been separated during the fight. The wounded Svendson made it in. His abandonment was something the command could hardly recall with pride. Private Ezekiel Rose was found a few miles from Henderson township. Two days later, wounded men still came in.

Private Blodgett, shot through the abdomen, had teamed up with wounded Private Edwin Cole during the ferry fight, until Cole moved off by another path. "Just then I heard Comrade Cole cry out as though in great pain, and then heard two Indians laugh and call him a squaw. He continued to beg, so I concluded they were torturing him in some way." Blodgett realized there was nothing he could do to help. "I heard the most sickening sound imaginable. It was a blow with a tomahawk, and poor Cole was no more."[15] Blodgett crawled and staggered through the scrub, subsisting on wild grapes, before gnawing on an old ham bone in an abandoned house.

Here he was discovered by a German civilian, John Fenske, who was spitting blood from an arrow wound. Hit in the back, Fenske had managed to snap off the shaft, but the arrow had punctured one lung. Together the two assisted each other over the last three miles to the fort, arriving in the darkness at about 2 a.m. on Wednesday the 20th. The sentinel on duty could scarcely believe Blodgett when he identified himself. He had seen him fall and he was presumed dead.

The sun was up when William Sutherland made it in. The private had taken a bullet through the right lung, the bullet passing out his back. He had returned by crawling through scrub and drifting downstream on a skiff.

Landing on the wrong bank, he swam back to the north side and stumbled into the fort at about 9 a.m.

From the vantage of hindsight, Marsh's decision to march out and confront the hostiles would be condemned by some. But Sergeant Bishop felt that "no brave officer could have turned back and left those defenseless women and children between that band of Indians and ourselves." The sergeant thought between 200 and 300 civilians fled past them on their way to the fort. "An officer who would order his men back in the face of these facts would deserve to be shot without a trial, and dishonor would have followed him and there would have resulted the murder of many women and children who escaped while we were pressing forward." Had Marsh retreated, the Indians would have taken the fort that night, Bishop felt, "and there would have been nothing to stop them before they reached Fort Snelling."[16]

The fight at Redwood Ferry had seen 24 men killed and five wounded. This was the worst defeat of U.S. troops by a western tribe since 1854, when an ambitious Lieutenant John Grattan had attacked a Dakota camp during a minor dispute over a cow. In the following fight, Grattan died along with 29 other men.[17]

The Redwood Ferry fight saw a well-planned ambush put into effect with little preparation time, which was something unusual for warriors of western tribes. "We did not fight like white men with one officer," recalled Thunder Blanket, but "we all shot as we pleased."[18] Redwood Ferry was a prelude to the Fetterman Fight of 1866, which would see a detachment of 81 men wiped out in a well-executed ambush on the Bozeman Trail. The Indian success at Little Bighorn, by contrast, occurred due to spontaneous events, dubious orders, and a matter of chance.

2

POPULARITY IS HIS GOD

In 1803, France was at war, and Napoleon Bonaparte needed money. The United States had dollars on offer, and the resulting Louisiana Purchase doubled the size of the country. Although the Americans now nominally possessed the vast tract of mountains, valleys, plains and streams, there were others who, not surprisingly, felt the lands were theirs.

In 1805, General James Wilkinson dispatched an expedition of exploration to the upper reaches of the Mississippi River. Lieutenant Zebulon Pike met with Santee Dakota leaders at the confluence of the Mississippi and St. Peter's (later Minnesota) Rivers. He made "Pike's Purchase," a treaty transferring ownership of two local sites from the Indians to the United States. It was only 22 years since the end of the American Revolution, and British America to the north was still considered a threat—with good reason. The War of 1812 was yet to be fought. Work on Fort Saint Anthony was commenced in 1819, and upon its completion in 1825, the robust stone structure was renamed Fort Snelling for its designer and first commanding officer, Colonel Josiah Snelling.

An increasing flow of white settlers arrived, and in 1837 the American government negotiated treaties with the Dakota (or Sioux) and Chippewa (or Ojibwe) tribes for the lands between the Mississippi and St. Croix Rivers—territory that would later be part of the state of Minnesota. The Dakotas, meaning "friends" in their own tongue, were a loose confederation of tribes extending out onto the western plains. The name "Sioux," meaning "snakes" or "enemies," was derived from their longstanding foes, the Chippewas. The Dakotas relinquished their hunting and fishing rights, but would receive annuities in perpetuity. The Chippewas, on the other hand, were to receive payments in money, trade goods and food for a period of 20 years, and reserved the right to hunt and fish within the ceded territory.

These deals were negotiated by Indian agent Lawrence Taliaferro, who, having the natives' best interests at heart, found himself under attack. "How to get rid of me at this Post seems now the main object of Tom-Dick, and Harry," he wrote on July 27, 1838, "so that those who may come after me can

Fort Snelling, Minnesota, became the principal marshaling point for troops to combat the Dakota outbreak of 1862 (author's rendition).

the more easily be bribed or threatened into silence and acquiesced in the diabolical plans afoot to *cheat* & destroy the Indians and a certain class of half Breeds as well as to impose on ignorance—to get a Sett of fraudulent credit accounts allowed."[1]

Minnesota Territory was formed in 1849, and a flow of white settlers arrived by foot, horse and wagon. In 1851, the Santee Dakota leaders agreed to new treaties, which included government assurances of annuity payments and viable reservations that would provide security for the future. Minnesota Territorial Governor Alexander Ramsey and U.S. Commissioner of Indian Affairs Luke Lea negotiated the Treaty of Traverse de Sioux with the Sisseton and Wahpeton bands of the Santee Dakota people, called the Upper Bands. Following weeks of cajoling and intimidation, they relinquished most of their land west of the Mississippi in exchange for an immediate payment of $305,000, and continuing annuities in the form of gold, goods, provisions and education. A reservation would be established along both banks of the upper Minnesota River. But the beguiled chiefs also signed a third set of papers, thinking they were a copy of the originals. Illegally drafted by white traders, these papers transferred much of the $305,000 into their pockets to fulfill "just obligations."

Following similar pressure, the Treaty of Mendota was signed with the

Mdewakanton and Wahpekute people, or Lower Bands of the Santee Dakotas. This treaty had similar terms and conditions, but included a $220,000 deduction for the fur traders. The Lower Bands would also have a reservation along the Minnesota River adjoining that of the Upper Bands. The reservations were promised "in perpetuity." But this perpetuity proved to be a fluid thing. Once before the Senate, "in perpetuity" was altered to "at the discretion of the President," and Ramsey was told to get the required signatures before the treaty's ratification. He used negotiation, withholding food and goods, and threats of military intervention to cajole the chiefs. The Indians had little choice, and reluctantly gave their consent. In 1853 they packed their belongings and began the trek to the new reservations along the Minnesota River, and Fort Ridgely was established to keep the peace.

Not all Dakotas accepted the new treaties. Dissident leader Inkpaduta, meaning "Scarlet Point," led a small party of Wahpekute of the Lower Bands. He was outlawed by his own people following internal feuds, and his father, now deceased, had been accused of murdering a rival chief. The winter of 1856–1857 proved to be particularly severe, with freezing winds and deep snow. Inkpaduta's band begged for food from white settlements in northwestern Iowa. But these settlers were, in many cases, preoccupied with their own survival and turned a cold shoulder to Indian needs. While being forced to steal, one of the band was mauled by a white man's dog. The dog was killed, word got around, and Inkpaduta's camp was invaded by an armed party of 20 white men.[2] They disarmed the Indians, who protested that the weapons were necessary for hunting and basic survival. The following morning, the whites returned to escort the band from the area before returning their weapons, but found the camp deserted.

The Indians traveled north and took retribution in what became known as the Spirit Lake Massacre. During March 8–12, 1857, between 35 and 40 white men, women and children were killed at Spirit Lake, Iowa, and Springfield, Minnesota, and their cabins looted. Most victims were scalped, and four young women were taken captive. Survivors spread the alarm, and wildly exaggerated stories of hundreds of Dakotas on the warpath spread like wildfire. Mankato township had been destroyed by 600 Sioux, the *Chicago Democratic Press* reported. A stagecoach driver named Wagner claimed that 500 to 600 rampaging Indians committed atrocities on women: they "stripped them naked, took their scalps and cut off their breasts." Edward Washburn, a settler living in Blue Earth County, Minnesota, wrote to his father about the hysteria with sarcasm: "We have just learned from authentic sources that every settler in Minnesota Territory, except one [himself], has been murdered!" Washburn added, "Many of the settlers have left the country, and I have seen many women crying with swollen eyes, expecting that their infants and themselves would be scalped by the savages."[3] Timber stockades were hastily erected in various settlements, and troops set out to track the marauders down. But the elusive Inkpaduta kept one step ahead and would remain a thorn in the white man's side for years to come, never to be captured. As settlers fled their homes, innocent Dakotas were murdered in retribution. Two of the women prisoners were killed while in captivity, but the other two were eventually released.

Judge Charles Flandrau had been appointed U.S. Indian Agent for the Dakota tribe. A man of integrity, he had an uphill battle to see the Indians were fairly treated. During June he got wind that one of Inkpaduta's sons, Roaring Cloud, was camped with other members of the guilty band near the Upper Agency. Flandrau set out with an armed force of 12 civilian volunteers and 15 infantry under Lieutenant Alexander Murray from Fort Ridgely. John Other Day, a leading Dakota Christian convert, acted as scout, and located Roaring Cloud's camp on bluffs overlooking the Yellow Medicine River.

In dawn's first light, Murray's infantry were deployed in surrounding ravines, while Flandrau and his mounted volunteers made a direct advance. When the soldiers were seen at 200 yards, a whoop went up and the Indians bolted. Roaring Cloud rushed into a ravine to be confronted by bluecoats. He let blaze with a double-barreled shotgun, but a blast of return fire saw him cut down and his last breath quenched with a bayonet thrust. Flandrau took Roaring Cloud's wife and child prisoner, but Lieutenant Murray felt their presence on the return trip would attract trouble. And he was right. The woman screamed for help while passing through Indian villages, and the word spread. While taking breakfast in Daniel's boarding house, the small force found itself surrounded by a hostile Dakota mob. Giving in to their demands, the soldiers released the woman and child.

Once back at the Upper Agency, Murray sent to Fort Ridgely for reinforcements. Major Thomas Sherman soon arrived with 25 soldiers and Superintendent William Cullen, the director of Minnesota Indian agents. Cullen was once described as "a man of great force of character, self-reliant, original, positive, persuasive, ambitious, and he moved about more like a young elephant than an ordinary man."[4] Perhaps so. But according to Indian Agent Joseph Brown, he did not know the difference between a "Sioux Indian and a snapping turtle."

Under orders from Indian Commissioner James Denver, the "young elephant," now a maturing 45, added fuel to the fire by informing the Dakotas that there would be no annuity payment until the tribesmen themselves had captured or killed Inkpaduta. "Our Great Father has asked us to do a very hard thing," replied Standing Buffalo, "to go and kill men and women who do not belong to our bands." Cullen referred Standing Buffalo's concerns to James Denver by telegraph, but "there will be no yielding" was the reply. The Indians must catch Inkpaduta or fight the U.S. Army.[5] Tempers soared, and a soldier was stabbed. Sherman telegraphed for more troops. "We are on the eve of a general war with all these Indians," he concluded.[6]

But before hostilities erupted, Little Crow arrived from the Lower Agency. This influential Mdewankanton chief waved a calming hand and offered to help bring Inkpaduta to heel. Little Crow was "intelligent, of strong personality, of great physical vigor," a missionary observed, and he "sought attention, speaking at council meetings, always meticulously dressed.... Popularity is his God."[7] White trader James Lynd was a great devotee of Little Crow. He described him as the greatest chief amongst the Dakotas, "dignified and commanding, though at times restless and anxious. He is about five feet ten inches in height, with rather sharp features and a piercing hazel eye." The admiring and unfortunate Lynd would be among the first to die in Little Crow's coming war.

The eldest son of Chief Big Thunder, Taoyateduta (His Red Nation), later to be called Little Crow, was born circa 1810 about 10 miles below the future Fort Snelling site. Despite his destiny as a dominant chief, or possibly because of it, the free-spirited boy grew into a troublesome young man. During the 1830s he moved further west to experience life with other Dakota bands and engaged in gambling, whiskey selling, and womanizing. Polygamy was common amongst the Dakota tribe, and two of his own wives were cast off while he lived amidst the Wahpekutes, and yet another four, all sisters, received similar treatment while he resided with the Wahpetons. In all, he fathered some 22 children—or possibly more.[8]

Upon the death of Big Thunder in 1846, Taoyateduta, now about 36, set out to return east to the auspicious Mdewakanton settlement of Kaposia, not far south of St. Paul, a growing white colony near Fort Snelling. His bloodline, dominant personality and prominence provided support amidst Dakota leaders for him to assume the succession. News spread, and hundreds watched as he passed with his entourage along the river by canoe.

But not all welcomed the prodigal's return. Big Thunder had bequeathed leadership to one of Taoyateduta's half-brothers rather than the wayward elder son, absent for many years. Before an intrigued crowd, the rivals, carrying guns, shouted a warning not to land: "If you do, you shall die." But Taoyateduta stepped ashore. "Shoot, then," he challenged, "where all can see." A gun cracked and the bones in both of Taoyateduta's forearms were shattered by the blast. But an angry shout went up from the crowd. The claimant had shown great courage by coming ashore in the face of loaded guns, and the brothers fled. The bleeding man was taken by canoe upriver to Fort Snelling, where the post surgeon examined the wounds. His recommendation for amputation of both hands met a frosty response.

Taoyateduta returned to Kaposia. Here tribal shamans would weave their magic with words, prayers and herbs. The tribal elders were impressed

Little Crow returned home to claim the leadership of the Mdewakanton Dakota people. Shot through both wrists during a confrontation, he always wore long sleeves to cover the resulting deformity (author's collection).

with his determination. Taoyateduta had faced death unarmed, and now refused to be maimed by a cutting saw in the white surgeon's hands. They would support the man who was, when all was said and done, the traditional leader of the Mdewakanton Dakotas. And best to clear the way for the new regime. Orders went out for the half-brothers to be tracked down and killed.

The gunshot wounds healed, but Taoyateduta never regained full use of his fingers, and his deformed wrists would always be hidden by long sleeves.

And now a change took place. Perhaps the new chief felt the wounds had been a punishment from Wakan Tanka for his former dissolute ways. "I was only a brave then," he said; "I am a chief now."[9] A rebirth required a new image, part of which was the adoption of the new name, Little Crow; traditional for chieftains of his band. This was based on ceremonial attire that included the skin and wings of a raven or crow.[10]

The former whiskey trader now asked Indian Agent Amos Bruce for assistance in ridding his tribe of the alcoholic curse, a cause of endless trouble for Indian and white alike. Little Crow took a 7-month pledge to abstain, and government officials looked on in wonder as his tribe's consumption of alcohol markedly decreased. Little Crow was a man of influence, a man to be watched.

Having made few conversions, missionaries had abandoned Kaposia, but now Little Crow sought their return. A former acquaintance of Little Crow, the Presbyterian pastor Thomas Williamson, arrived in November of 1846 to set up a school and church. Despite often wearing white man's garb and supporting farming as a way of life, the chief did not attend church and retained his Indian identity. Use of the plow, as the white man wished, was for others. He still went hunting for game and dealt with mixed-blood and white fur traders. Williamson doubted the chief's motives. Did he encourage the missionary merely to increase his own prestige with the white community? Little Crow was a wily politician who played a delicate balancing act. While gaining favor with the whites, he kept on side with those Dakotas, the majority, who had no desire to abandon traditional ways.

Minnesota Territory was established in 1849, and in September the Dakotas heard rumors of influential whites plotting behind the scenes once more—a new treaty was in the wind.

Two years of haggling took place, and once boundary lines were settled, Little Crow and other chiefs declared their intention to sign the 1851 Treaties of Mendota and Traverse des Sioux. Not all were happy with this turn of events. Little Crow turned to those in the crowd who looked on with hostile eyes. "It has been said by some of you that the first that signs this treaty you will kill. Now, I am willing to be the first," he said, "but I am not afraid that you will kill me. If you do, it will be all right. A man has to die some time and he cannot die but once ... although I would rather die fighting our enemies. I believe this treaty will be best for the Dakotas, and I will sign it, even if a dog kills me before I lay down the goose quill." The nib was dipped, and Little Crow scratched out his traditional name, "Taoyateduta."[11] The other chiefs lined up and signed. There was no retribution. Perhaps history would have taken a different course if the threat to kill had been carried out that day.

Thus, in 1853, the Dakotas moved to their new reservation along both banks of the Minnesota River "in perpetuity"—a pledge not worth a dime.

In 1857 the Spirit Lake Massacre rent a rift between Indian and white. The whites wanted the culprit brought in, and Little Crow arrived at the Upper Agency to give them a hand. Over three days he persuaded other chiefs to go after Inkpaduta with Dakota braves. Superintendent Cullen happily agreed, but Little Crow's request for soldiers was denied. Major Sherman had no intention of dispatching a small number of troops with many armed warriors. He knew many sympathized with the murderous outlaw. He did, however, contribute supplies. On July 22, Little Crow led 100 Dakotas and six mixed-blood warriors westward. The mixed-blood interpreter Antoine "Joe" Campbell rode with them. Major Sherman was impressed with Little Crow's efforts, feeling he displayed "a fixed determination to bring in the murderers."

In late July, a trail was discovered by Little Crow's scouts. It led to a campsite where, as the party approached, a few dozen men, women and children fled to shelter amidst reeds alongside Lake Herman. Little Crow called out, professing friendship, and two squaws with a child emerged. They listened to Little Crow's reassuring words, then returned to the reeds. Little Crow was not to be trusted, they said. The fugitives prepared for battle and refused to come out. Guns barked and a running fight took place across the plains until a heavy downpour at twilight ended the chase. Three of the fugitives had been killed, another wounded, and two women and a child taken prisoner. One of the those killed was Fire Cloud, another of Inkpaduta's sons. All three killed had taken part in the massacre at Spirit Lake.

Though Inkpaduta was still on the loose, Little Crow felt well satisfied with his success, and led his men back into the Upper Agency on August 4. Superintendent Cullen telegraphed news to Indian Commissioner James Denver. Cullen wanted to pay out the annuities, but Inkpaduta had been the target, Denver replied. The annuities must still be withheld. Despite treaty obligations, Denver felt these payments made the Indians too reliant on handouts. "There seems to be no likelihood of a termination of this pauper system," he wrote, "but with the extinction of the whole race."[12]

Denver took leave to be replaced by Acting Commissioner Charles Mix. He took a different view and ordered the annuities to be distributed in late August. But by then much damage had been done. The whole affair had only heightened distrust between Indian and white.

Military patrols went out in search of the elusive Inkpaduta. During September, Little Crow scouted for a detachment of the Second Artillery as they searched the Coteau des Prairies to the west of Fort Ridgely, but no trace was found. Plans for a bigger military expedition with converging columns were canceled when most troops at Fort Ridgely were ordered to Utah for action against dissident Mormon settlers who refused to accept United States authority.

Educator and reformer Harriet Bishop had taught Dakota children and had no trouble seeing the world through Indian eyes. But she had no time for the perpetrator of Spirit Lake: "Inkpaduta was the vilest wretch un-hung," she recalled. "It had been feared that by his going unpunished would embolden the evil inclined—that the leniency would be a precedent on which they might base future deeds."[13] Inkpaduta's escape from retribution did not go unnoticed by the Dakota people. And many whites feared the consequences. "If you don't punish them," the *Henderson Democrat* cried on May 7, 1857, "within two years will be a general uprising by all the Indians." Apart from timing, the prediction was right.

During early 1858, ninety Indian delegates from 13 western tribes were shipped to Washington, D.C., to negotiate new treaties. Here they could see for themselves the extent and power of the white man's civilization, a juggernaut impossible to resist. On March 13, 1858, Dakota leaders from Minnesota arrived. "I have come a long way and intend, while in your village, to walk the streets as a proud man," Little Crow told Commissioner Charles Mix. Over the next week, the visitors attended the theater, met politicians, and were given a guided tour of the U.S. Penitentiary—perhaps a warning to malcontents who did not see things the white man's way.

March 27 saw the Dakotas begin negotiations, and two days later the feathered and painted warriors entertained their hosts with a ceremonial war dance. Little Crow gave a talk that included an account of his successful attack on Fire Cloud's camp.[14]

On May 11, while negotiations were still underway, Minnesota was admitted to the Union as the 32nd state. Between 1851 and 1858 the white population had climbed from 6,000 to over 150,000.

After three months of argument, pressure and frustration, compromises were reached, and a treaty was signed on June 19, 1858. Three days later, Commissioner Mix had one last meeting with the Dakota leaders, who received patronizing "good conduct" medals. The chiefs had signed away that half of their reservation that lay to the north of the Minnesota River in exchange for increased annuities and goods. Dakotas residing on the ceded land would have to join their kinsman occupying the remaining 130-mile strip along the southern bank.

The treaties of 1851 and 1858 contained inducements for the nomadic warriors to make use of the plow rather than the gun, bow and arrow. Most, however, remained what whites called "blanket Indians"—those who prized wearing blankets about their shoulders and preferred hunting as a way of life. These hard-core hunters had little time for fellow tribesmen who complied. "Cut-hairs" and "breeches Indians," they were called with contempt.[15] There was no way blanket Indians would hand out "good conduct" medals to the whites.

Even before Senate ratification of the new treaty, hundreds of whites moved into the Dakota lands, felling trees, building fences and cabins. Traditional Dakota trails between the Minnesota River and the Big Woods to the north were cut off. This vast tract of elm, oak, and sugar maple provided excellent hunting grounds, as well as a rough divider between the Dakota and their old enemies, the Chippewas.

Urania White and her husband Nathan were among the new arrivals. "We thought we had selected the very heart of this western paradise for our home," recalled Urania. "Truly it was beautiful even in its wild, uncultivated condition, with its gigantic trees in the creek valley, its towering bluffs, and the sweet-scented wild flowers. A babbling brook formed a part of the eastern boundary of our land, and its broad acres of prairie made it desirable enough to have satisfied the wishes of the most fastidious lover of a fine farm." But, she noted, "We had just got settled in our new log house when the Sioux Indians who lived near us began to be uneasy."[16]

On April 27, 1860, John Smitz was shot and killed while building about 10 miles west of New Ulm township, just inside the obscure reservation border. The brave responsible was promptly arrested and put on trial. But, while being escorted to the outhouse, he took to heels, never to be recaptured.

Other frictions erupted, and whites filed claims against the government for compensation following theft and damage by Indians. Such payments would be deducted from the annuities, thus punishing the innocent along with the guilty.[17]

At the same time, bullets were flying and buildings were burning far to the south; it was another racial conflict, but one in which Indians had no involvement. Would "Bleeding Kansas" be admitted to the Union as a free or slave state? The conflict exploded when, on April 12, 1861, Confederate cannon boomed across Charleston Harbor, South Carolina. The federal stronghold of Fort Sumter was under attack; the Civil War had begun.

Out west, corrupt practices within Indian affairs continued unabated. Government inaction fueled frustration and anger. Special Commissioner George E.H. Day was dispatched to investigate. Day traveled 1800 miles by his own mule-drawn wagon, "often sleeping in the woods & generally without any companions." He spoke to both whites and Indians, sifting through facts and hearing stories galling to any honest man. On January 1, 1862, he penned a report to U.S. President Abraham Lincoln that read in part:

> I have discovered numerous violations of law committed by past agents and a superintendent. I think I can establish frauds to the amount of 20 to 100 thousand in or during the four years past.... The Superintendent Major Cullen, alone, has saved, as all his friends say more than 100 thousand in four years out of a salary of two thousand a year and all the agents whose salaries are 15 hundred a year have become rich.... The whole system is defective & must be revised or, your red children, as they call them-

selves, will continue to be wronged & outraged & the just vengeance of heaven will continue to be poured out & visited upon this nation for its abuses and cruelties to the Indian.[18]

But nothing was done. The embattled president had other problems on his mind. The Union had lost the first big battle of the war at Bull Run in July 1861, along with other less critical fights.

By 1862 the Lower Dakota Agency for the Mdewakanton and Wahpekute bands had taken on the appearance of a substantial hamlet. Council Square was bordered by various buildings including a large stone warehouse, Dickinson's boarding house, the Agency headquarters, a carpenter's shop, a large barn, Dr. Humphrey's house, and other private homes and establishments. Spread a little further afield were traders' stores, a sawmill and two Christian churches. "The threats of the 'medicine men' did not stop the Christian Indians from entering the church," recalled mixed-blood Nancy Faribault. "After we all got in and the services began, the men outside began to shoot at the bell as at a target. They shot it several times, and actually cracked it so that it would not ring. Rev. S.R. Riggs was the preacher that day, and he was so affected that he cried before us all."[19]

The less substantial Upper Agency for the Sisseton and Wahpeton bands was situated on high ground to the west side of the Yellow Medicine River, about one mile from its confluence with the Minnesota River. New buildings included a hotel, and a substantial brick warehouse that included the abode of Indian Agent Thomas Galbraith. Several traders' stores had been established in the valley below. Numerous timber bridges had been built across gullies and streams, providing much-improved transport between the two agencies. In total, the entire reservation catered to about 6,000 souls. Many "blanket" Indians, however, spent much time buffalo hunting in the vast Dakota Territory to the west: the present-day states of North and South Dakota, much of Montana and Wyoming, and a part of Nebraska.

The 1856 census indicated 650 mixed-bloods in Minnesota, the result of cross-fertilization between Indian and white, either through marriage or less formal liaisons. Most were living on the reservation, some as Indians, while others gained employment as laborers, interpreters or clerks in white-owned business establishments. But, referred to as "breeds," they lived in a cross-culture shadow. Many full-bloods, both Indian and white, tended to see them as inferior, regardless of accomplishments, who did not properly belong to one world or the other.[20]

On May 20, 1862, President Lincoln took time off from Civil War headaches to sign the Homestead Act. This offered vast tracts of free land to "virtuous yeomen" who would work and build on their 160-acre farms over a period of five years. Those who had money could purchase at $1.25 per acre after an occupation of six months.

The Indians looked on as more wagons rolled into Minnesota, carrying white colonists to occupy their former hunting grounds. More cabins sprang up in the forests, on the plains, and in the river bottomlands. Helen Carrothers and her husband James established themselves north of the Minnesota River, about six miles from the Lower Agency: "My little home was very humble, but it was very dear to me," recalled Helen. "It was built of logs, with a puncheon floor and a bark roof. There was but one small room. There was but one doorway and one small window, with six panes of glass. The door was made from the boards of a dry goods packing box. It was warmed by a cooking stove."[21]

The influx of settlers, combined with Indian crop failures, white trader profiteering, and government tardiness in fulfilling treaty obligations, created a slowly burning fuse.

3

Subsisted on a Tall Grass

On August 11, 1862, a large keg was loaded into a railroad freight car in New York City. Weighing about 220 pounds, this was no ordinary keg. The contents, $71,000 in gold coin, was the annuity payment destined for the Dakota reservation in Minnesota. It required an armed escort of several men—and, not for the first time, it was running late.[1]

The rail did not extend as far as the state capital, St. Paul, and the keg arrived by wagon on August 16. Superintendent Clark Thompson was in town, part of a delegation to settle issues between the Chippewas and Dakotas. Due to "unsettled conditions" at the Dakota Reservation, Thompson wasted no time, and the precious barrel left St. Paul on the 17th. It traveled 125 miles throughout the night, but as the wagon neared Fort Ridgely the following morning, the outbreak erupted at the Lower Agency. "The barbarities committed were beyond description," Thompson reported, "and it is to be hoped that the perpetrators may meet with just retribution. I much fear that if, as is the case of the 'Spirit Lake Massacre,' ... the guilty are not properly punished, it may have an evil influence upon other tribes as well as this, and prove an incentive to further outrages."[2]

The wagon clattered into Fort Ridgely at noon—just as Dakota warriors deployed to greet Captain Marsh at the Redwood Ferry. Had the payment arrived one day earlier, the holocaust would most likely have been averted.

Apart from the late payment, what other events sparked the atrocities of August 18? "Many of the white men often abused the Indians and treated them unkindly," recalled Chief Big Eagle in 1894. "Perhaps they had excuse, but the Indians did not think so. Many of the whites always seemed to say by their manner when they saw an Indian, 'I am better than you,' and the Indians did not like this. There was excuse for this, but the Dakotas did not believe there were better men in the world than they. Then some of the white men abused the Indian women in a certain way and disgraced them, and surely there was no excuse for that."[3]

The Minnesota fuse had been slowly burning as blue and gray soldiers in distant places fought and died by the thousands. But many a young man in

Minnesota wanted to take part. Here was a chance for action and adventure, glory and promotion. Minnesota was slave-free state, and Minnesotans believed the "Sesesh" had no right to leave the Union: once in, never out. And many of these young men came from New England states and overseas countries where slavery was considered an abomination. The Dakotas could not help but notice as young men with fighting spirits formed military companies and marched away. There would be a dearth of worthy opponents should any conflict arise.

The harsh winter of 1861–62 was preceded by a crop failure the previous fall. Future crops looked promising, but as Indians gathered around the agencies awaiting the delayed annuity payment, "The Indians were compelled to ward off starvation by digging roots for food," recalled Urania White. "Three or four weeks previous to the outbreak, we could see squaws almost every day wandering over the prairie in search of the nutritious roots of the plant known to the French voyagers as the 'pomme de terre' [i.e., the potato]."[4]

The missing annuity money was customarily received "so soon as the prairie grass was high enough for pasture," or about the end of June for the Lower Agency, and two weeks later for the Upper Agency. And based on previous experience, the traders' up-front demands would seriously deplete the payout. The appropriation now due had been delayed firstly by Congress, then the Treasury. Gold was scarce in a war-torn country expending millions on the military. Perhaps it would be fitting to renege on the treaty proviso to pay in gold, and send the Civil War–introduced paper greenbacks instead? But traders, their own interests affected, told the Indians that paper money was worth only half that of gold. Wise treasury heads decided to honor the treaty; thus the precious keg had been dispatched.

Thomas Galbraith was an ex-politician appointed by the new Republican regime as Dakota Indian agent. As was usual with Indian agents, he held the honorary rank of major. On June 25, 1862, nearly two months before the outbreak, he had been confronted by the Sisseton and Wahpeton Dakotas at the Upper Agency, his home base. When would the money arrive, and how much? Rumors had circulated that no payment would be forthcoming. Galbraith had little more idea than the Indians themselves. The annuity payment was still bogged down in eastern wartime politics. He assured them, however, that they would receive "very nearly, if not quite, a full payment," but not before July 20, over three weeks away. He soothed ruffled feathers by issuing just enough food, tobacco, powder and shot to ease tensions: "I advised them to go home, and admonished them, not to come back again until I sent for them," he reported. A few days later, Galbraith traveled to the Lower Agency and did likewise with the Mdewakanton and Wahpekute Dakotas in an attempt to keep all happy—for the moment at least. He remained about one week visiting Indian farms, "and urged upon them the necessity of cutting and securing hay for the winter, and watching and keeping the birds from their corn." Galbraith "found in nearly every instance the prospect for good crops very hopeful indeed.... I was led to the belief that we would have no starving Indians to feed the next winter, and little did I dream of the unfortunate and terrible outbreak which in a short time burst upon us."[5]

The Dakotas themselves were split. Little Crow was seen by hardline "blanket" Indians as one of those who had favored selling half the reservation in 1858, thus complying with white demands, and lining his own pockets while doing so. But, on the other hand, those who had taken to tilling the soil felt he was still a traditional hunter at heart. "There was a white man's party and an Indian party," recalled Big Eagle. "Many whites think that Little Crow was the principal chief at this time, but he was not. Wabasha was the principal chief, and he was of the white man's party."[6]

June of 1862 was election time for a new speaker. Wabasha stood aside, and Big Eagle, Little Crow and Traveling Hail put themselves forward. To Little Crow's displeasure, Traveling Hail, backed by Galbraith, won the vote. So, Little Crow reasoned, the way to win favor was to at least appear as one who would toe the Galbraith line. There were more elections yet to come. Little Crow started attending the Episcopal church and took to tilling the soil. He was rewarded by Galbraith with the promise of a new brick house. "The 'farmers' were favored by the government in every way," recalled Big Eagle. "They had houses built for them, some of them even had brick houses, and they were not allowed to suffer. The other Indians did not like this. They were envious of them and jealous, and disliked them

Little Crow, while remaining a warrior at heart, took to wearing the clothing of the whites in order to gain favor with government authorities (Library of Congress).

because they had gone back on the customs of the tribe and because they were favored."[7]

Thomas Galbraith heard that a large party of Yanktonai Dakotas, from further west, were on their way to the Upper Agency. They too wanted to share in the promised pot of gold. If not satisfied, they threatened to kill the contemptible Dakota cut-hairs who had adopted the white man's ways and clothes. Galbraith requested military assistance from Fort Ridgely, and on July 2 a mountain howitzer arrived at the Upper Agency along with 102 infantrymen. But all seemed serene. Mosquitos "are likely to prove our most formidable enemy," Lieutenant Thomas Gere noted in his diary.[8]

Galbraith was absent tending the Lower Agency when, on July 8, interpreter Peter Quinn informed Lieutenant Timothy Sheehan, commanding the detachment, that the Indians wished to talk. "We sold our land to the Great Father, but we don't get the pay for it," Sheehan was told. "The traders are allowed to sit at the pay table, and they take all our money. We wish you to keep the traders away from the pay table, and as we are now hungry we want you to make us the present of a beef."[9] Sheehan replied that the absent Galbraith was in charge of food stores and payments, and the only provisions he had were needed for the troops. But their concerns would be reported to Galbraith upon his return.

An important power amongst the Dakotas was the Soldiers' Lodge, a faction of young, militant warriors who held their own council. They vented grievances and discussed solutions—and saw violence as one way of resolving a problem. It comes as little surprise that Galbraith considered it a dangerous institution. Chief Wabasha, despite being an advocate of the white man's way, was fed up with the traders' constant thrusts into Dakota pockets. Upon invitation, he spoke to the Soldiers' Lodge: "I made a speech in council and told the Indians that I thought it was proper that they should obtain their whole annuities and refuse to pay the traders."[10]

The Soldiers' Lodge decided to obtain goods on credit, if possible, then avoid paying the traders once the money was handed out. This would help balance previous frauds. But this tactic relied on the traders' being denied access to upfront deductions. The traders, however, got wind of the scheme. Indians seeking credit found the door slammed in their faces. Some traitor had talked. The Soldiers' Lodge took retribution against suspected informants. One was pursued and killed in the woods, while the other two were caught within the Agency grounds. Getting off lightly, they were roughed up and had their clothes sliced from them as a public spectacle in the street. The traders were most displeased with the whole affair. "Go to the Soldier's Lodge and get credit," they told all Indians, whether they had been involved in the trouble or not.

A deputation of Dakotas arrived at Fort Ridgely. They wished to speak to Captain Marsh. Through interpreter Quinn they asked that no soldiers be allowed to help the traders collect what they claimed was owing. "The Indians did not think the traders had done right," recalled Big Eagle. "The Indians bought goods of them on credit, and when the government payments came the traders were on hand with their books, which showed that the Indians owed so much and so much, and as the Indians kept no books they could not deny their accounts, but had to pay them, and sometimes the traders got all their money."[11]

Marsh replied that soldiers would be on hand, but only to keep the peace should a disturbance occur. The Indians, well pleased, returned to their villages to spread the good news.

Less pleased were the bookkeepers. Trader William Forbes, according to Little Crow, insulted warriors by telling them they were mere "squaws," not men. Andrew Myrick, who managed his brother's store at the Lower Agency, reportedly said, "You will be sorry. After a while you will come to me and beg for meat and flour to keep you and your wives and children from starving and I will not let you have a thing. You and your wives and children may starve, or eat grass, or your own filth."[12]

The best-known legend of the Dakota War of 1862 was Myrick's having said words along these lines. Some doubt has been cast on this, but the Indians made repeated reference to "eat grass" being said.[13] Robert Hakewaste, or Good Fifth Son, recalled, "They were not going to give us any credit and we were going to eat grass."[14] Three weeks into the war, Little Crow wrote to Colonel Henry Sibley justifying the outbreak: "A.J. Myrick told the Indians that they would eat grass or their own dung."[15] And Big Eagle recalled that Myrick "had refused some hungry Indians credit.... He said to them: 'Go and eat grass.'"[16]

No doubt Myrick said this, as eating grass is, in fact, how many Indians actually survived: "Many days these poor creatures subsisted on a tall grass which they find in the marshes, chewing the roots, and eating wild turnip," recalled Sarah Wakefield, wife of the Upper Agency doctor. "I know that many died of starvation or disease caused by eating improper food."[17]

The traders approached Captain Marsh to revoke his decision. They wanted troops to back up their claims. But "no promises" was the best he was prepared to offer.

Thomas Galbraith "found to my surprise" a few thousand Indians encamped around the Upper Agency when he returned on July 14. "They were afraid there was something wrong," he reported. "They feared they would not get their money, because white men had been telling them so." It is a wonder that Galbraith was surprised. There had been a similar occurrence on June 25. The story had gone around that there would be no money; the government had blown the budget fighting rebels down South, and "the Indians complained of starvation." He did hand out some food, but noted, "I held back, in order to save the provisions, till the last moment."[18]

The soldiers were allowed to distribute peas from a huge private garden, and on the 18th the Indians had "one grand pea dinner," recalled Lieutenant Gere. But marsh grass, peas and wildlife like muskrats could not stave off hunger. Although the Indians remained peaceful, Lieutenant Sheehan sent a rider to Fort Ridgely to request a second howitzer—just in case. No doubt the Indians looked closely as the gun rattled in on July 21. What did this mean? Were the bluecoats preparing to fight?

The following day, a war party of Chippewas from the north killed two Dakotas 18 miles from the Upper Agency. Several hundred Dakotas stripped to breechclouts and donned war paint. The troops looked on in astonishment as the avengers moved off "like so many demons. They poured over the hills armed to the teeth, some stripped to the skin," wrote Lieutenant Gere, who added, "I shall never forget this day." The troops had little idea that a similar throng would soon turn on them. The search was in vain, however, and the warriors returned without enemy scalps. But trouble with the Chippewas was not over yet. During early August they killed a man and his son who were out hunting. Friends took the bodies back to their home village where men, women and children saw what could be expected if caught unawares. Such incidents infuriated the Dakotas. They were out for blood. A dozen braves set out in pursuit, but by the time they returned empty-handed, the Agency was in ashes and hundreds of whites lay dead.

On July 26 the soldiers distributed hard crackers from their own rations while Galbraith carried out a head count that lasted for over 12 hours. This was supposedly for the coming gold distribution, but in reality, it was a sham to give the impression that something positive was being done.

The agent received alarming news. The detested Inkpaduta of Spirit Lake infamy had been seen camped on the Yellow Medicine River. On the 27th, Galbraith instructed Lieutenant Sheehan to go in pursuit with a detachment of 14 men: "You will take said Inkpaduta and all the Indian soldiers with him, prisoners, alive if possible, and deliver them to me at the Agency. If they resist, I advise that they be shot."[19] Guided by a Christian Dakota, Good Voiced Hail, the detachment set out along with four civilian volunteers. Perhaps no one was surprised when they returned empty-handed on August 3. The elusive outlaw chief had flown the coop once more; the whites' impotence at taking retribution had been demonstrated to the Dakotas yet again.

Sheehan and his men barely had time to catch up on badly needed sleep when, on the morning of August 4, two Indian messengers arrived "saying they were coming down to fire a salute … and make one of their demonstrations," reported Lieutenant Gere.[20] According to Galbraith, "not less than four hundred mounted and one hundred and fifty on foot" appeared. They had signaled their arrival so the troops would not expect trouble. But the supposed mere demonstration turned ugly. Not only public space was invaded, recalled Sarah Wakefield: "In a short time they surrounded our house and some came to the door, and rapped violently. I caught up a pistol and went down stairs, opened the door, and enquired as calmly as possible what they wanted. They wished axes, and filled the room and followed me around until I gave them all we had. I expected they would kill me.... But they offered no violence, and departed quietly; all they cared for was food."[21]

Lieutenant Timothy Sheehan assumed command of Fort Ridgely and led the determined defense against two attacks by Dakota warriors (author's collection).

Wood chips flew as a warrior smashed at the timbers of the warehouse door. The Indians "cut down the door of the warehouse," reported Galbraith, "shot down the American flag, and before they could be stopped, had carried over one hundred sacks of flour from the warehouse."[22] The troops, however, "now recovered from their panic," and lined up with muskets cocked and ready to fire. As the ransacking continued, one Indian lunged at Private James Foster and wrenched his gun away. A loud bang split the air as the weapon discharged, and the Indian seized Foster's hair as though about to take his scalp. Sheehan, pistol in hand, ordered the Indian to release the shocked soldier. The Indian complied and Sheehan ordered his men to move back. He could see food was their aim, not slaughter.

Lieutenant Gere, meanwhile, swung into action. Men of Company B trained one howitzer on the warehouse doors and the Indians scrambled to either side. A detachment of 16 men, led by Sheehan, cleared the Indians from the warehouse at bayonet point and occupied the doorway. Flanked by a howitzer and troops, the Indians fell back amidst the numerous flour bags strewn about. As Lieutenant Gere and Sergeant Solon Trescott held the crowd at bay, Sheehan moved hastily to Galbraith's quarters, part of the same building, and demanded that the agent do something *now!*

Galbraith finally emerged and addressed the crowd. He felt giving in to the Indians would encourage further hostility, but Sheehan urged him to distribute food. Galbraith agreed to issue a 2-day supply of flour and pork, along with annuity goods. The chiefs, he said, could return unarmed the following day, when further discussions would be held. The provisions were handed out, but as Galbraith feared, many recipients became stubborn and declined to leave. Sheehan ordered his men to form up in line of battle with the two howitzers defending the warehouse. With reluctance, the muttering and sullen Indians withdrew.[23]

But the Upper Agency was not the only post approached by Indians that day. Nearly 100 warriors approached Fort Ridgely and requested Captain Marsh's permission to hold a "green corn dance" on the parade ground. Marsh agreed, much to the displeasure of 37-year-old regular army Sergeant John Jones. Regular U.S. troops had vacated Fort Ridgely the previous year to be replaced by Minnesota Volunteers. Jones, a Mexican War veteran, had been detailed to stay at Ridgely in charge of the 6-piece cannon battery. Despite having immigrated from England, Jones may well have had a knowledge of Indian tactics superior to that of his commanding officer. In 1763, the Chippewas had used a similar ploy to wipe out the British garrison of 94 men at Fort Michilimackinac in present-day Michigan.[24] Fort Ridgely now had only 30 soldiers and a handful of civilians present.

Jones must have come close to insubordination when, "with all due respect," he refused "to allow those red devils to come in here." He was responsible for protecting government property, he said, and the Dakotas "must stay outside the fort." A disagreement ensued, but the novice captain wilted under the veteran's glare, and he informed the visitors that they must dance alongside the horse pond, outside the post. According to one witness, when the Indians stripped off, they were seen to be covered "in the red and yellow warpaint of the Sioux."[25]

Following their dance, the Indians camped on a rise about a quarter of a mile to the west. After dark, the suspicious Jones had his howitzers manned, trained and loaded, but dawn's first light revealed the rise deserted, with not an Indian in sight. A Frenchman who visited shortly afterwards clamed he had attended an Indian council on August 3, the day before their arrival. A plan had been hatched for the dancers to turn on the garrison and take the fort. Whether or not any assault had really been planned before the big outbreak on August 18 remains a mystery.

With the Rev. Stephen Riggs, Lieutenant Sheehan and others, Galbraith held talks with the chiefs at the Upper Agency the following day. The soldiers were backed up by armed civilians. Word had arrived of much excitement in the Indian camp after dark, and more trouble could be expected.

Little Crow had arrived from the Lower Agency, where to all appearances the situation was calm. Traveling Hail was the nominal Dakota spokesman, but the whites found themselves talking to the dominating Little Crow.

As the government supplies were mostly consumed, the chief suggested that those supplies locked up by traders could be handed out. Or, "When men are hungry, they help themselves." Apparently, interpreter Peter Quinn felt this utterance a threat, and refused to translate it. Galbraith turned to Pastor John Williamson, son of Thomas Williamson, who spoke fluent Dakota and translated Little Crow's words.

Galbraith could not order the traders to hand out their supplies. "What will you do?" he asked them. It was at this time that, according to legend, Myrick said, "So far as I'm concerned, if they are hungry, let them eat grass," or words to that effect, effectively repeating his earlier statement. But evidence is scarce that Myrick was actually at this conference. His store was at the Lower Agency.[26] But there can be no doubt that Myrick had said the fatal words at one point, possibly repeated by other whites over a period of time.

Whatever transpired, Galbraith was most displeased with Quinn's performance. During the day, with negotiations still going, he handed a note to Lieutenant Sheehan: "Sir: Your interpreter, Quinn, is a man whom I cannot trust to communicate or correspond with my Indians. I have therefore to respectfully request that said Quinn be at once ordered to hold no communication, direct or indirect, with any Sioux Indian under my jurisdiction."

According to Sarah Wakefield, the interpreter had told the Indians "to break into the warehouse and help themselves, promising them that he would prevent the soldiers from firing on them."[27] It seems likely that Galbraith had got wind of this. He requested that Quinn be removed to Fort Ridgely.[28] Lieutenant Gere, with Quinn in tow, left at 4 p.m. and arrived in the dark at 3 a.m., tired and saddle sore. Gere also brought instructions for Captain Marsh to attend the Upper Agency and take part in the negotiations. Gere hardly had time for a nap before he was back in the saddle again, setting out with Marsh on the return trip. They arrived at the Upper Agency at 1:30 the following afternoon, August 6. The following day talks resumed, and to keep the peace, Galbraith, under pressure, agreed to release all remaining annuity goods. The Indians were well satisfied as the handout continued over the next two days. Having flexed their muscles, they began to drift off, and by August 10 the forest of tepees had disappeared. The following day the troops slung their muskets and began the trek back to Fort Ridgely. Mrs. Wakefield was "much surprised" to encounter the troops as she returned from a visit to the Lower Agency, "but the Captain assured us there was no longer any need of them, as the Indians had all departed."

"Thus this disagreeable and threatening incident passed off, but, as usual, without the punishment of a single Indian," reported Galbraith, "simply because we had not the power to punish them, and hence we had to adopt the same 'sugar-plumb' policy which had been so often adopted before with the Indians, and especially at the time of the Spirit Lake massacre in 1857."[29]

4

You Know Not What You Are Doing

"Almost every day they were on our backs," recalled New Ulm schoolteacher Rudolph Leonhart, "as they surpass even the slickest Caucasian tramps as beggars. They practice the business with dignity, as if it were the most honorable profession on earth." Rudolph and his family often fed hungry Indians. One, Yomahah, asked him to copy a note professing his friendship for the whites. He was a "good Indian" who should be given aid, said the note. Rudolph supplied the note—later found amidst the carnage in the home of murdered settlers.

Perhaps such events triggered General Philip Sheridan to make his notorious quote that the only "good Indian" was a dead one. Sheridan later denied it, but Lieutenant Charles Nordstrom, present at the time, disagreed.[1]

The settlers around New Ulm noticed little difference in Indian manners and attitudes, but further afield, change was in the air. The Busse family lived on Middle Creek on the north side of the Minnesota River, about midway between the two agencies. Daughter Wilhelmina, one of six children, recalled: "It was at about this time that the conduct of our Indian neighbors changed towards us. They became disagreeable and ill natured." Former friendly acquaintances "passed by sullenly and coldly and often without speaking."[2]

"Indian treachery came to the surface," recalled Urania White. "We frequently saw them on the tops of the bluffs overlooking our dwelling. They seemed to be watching for something. When questioned, they said they were looking for Ojibwas (Chippewas). I think they must have held war meetings or councils, for we often heard drums in the evening on their side of the Minnesota river several weeks before the outbreak."[3] But, considering the Dakota deaths by Chippewa hands, perhaps they were telling the truth.

The Civil War was going badly for the North. President Lincoln put out a call for another 600,000 men. Thomas Galbraith, bursting with patriotism, decided to enlist a company, the Renville Rangers, from the two Dakota Agencies under his control. But, according to Galbraith, there was disunity amongst the recruits. Who should lead them? Who was the one inspirational figure all would accept? Thomas Galbraith, of course. "If you can take charge of us we can all unite," he reported to the Department of the Interior, "otherwise we cannot." Furthermore, "If my services were needed to unite them and get them off, I would cheerfully render them all the aid in my power: that I would go with them to Fort Snelling, and even to Richmond, or wherever else they may be ordered, if I could be relieved of my duties as Sioux agent without injury to the public service." So, without official sanction, "Major" Galbraith, with no military training, took it upon himself to take command of the 50 Renville Rangers for their trek to Fort Snelling. They moved out on August 13, and once there, he "would communicate with the government as to my course."[4]

Their departure was noted by the Indians. But Big Thunder considered them no threat in any case. "His men were nearly all half-breeds," he recalled. "The Indians now thought the whites must be pretty hard up for men to fight the South, or they would not come so far out on the frontier and take half-breeds or anything else to help them."[5] Big Thunder thought little of "half-breeds" because "they had always been the tools of the traders, and aided them to deceive the Indians."[6] Despite Big Thunder's feelings, mixed bloods would fight alongside him in the coming war. And the Renville Rangers, on the other side, would be commended for gallantry, but while fighting under Lieutenant James Gorman, not Thomas Galbraith.

The Indians wondered just what Galbraith was up to. Was it not his job to look after them and hand out the annuity when it arrived? The money had not come, and now he was gone. Questions would be asked. "Didn't this man know that during the past days the starving Indians had assumed a more threatening attitude," asked future militia leader Jacob Nix, "or did he not wish to know?" There were townsfolk who insisted "that the gentleman wished to escape the threatening stormclouds in order to save his own neck."[7] Galbraith later refuted these allegations in the press: "What! Leave my wife and family, all that I love and now own upon the earth if I 'foresaw' the coming storm. None but an *incarnate fiend—a dirty beast*—would ever suggest the like.'"[8]

But perhaps the presence of the Renville Rangers would have deterred the outbreak. Or perhaps their names would have been added to the dead. In any case, they would be much involved in the coming war.

Despite ominous rumblings, it was assumed that peace would prevail. Captain Marsh decided there was no more need for Sheehan's command, Company C, to be on hand at Fort Ridgely. He ordered them to return to Fort Ripley, about 140 miles to the north. They marched at 7 a.m. on Sunday, August 17.[9] Later, Lieutenant Culver and six men of Company B were dispatched to St. Peter, about 30 miles to the east. They were to join the Renville Rangers, already there, and drive them in wagons to Fort Snelling.

As the same time, Little Crow attended the Sunday sermon at the Lower Agency Episcopal Church. If he was to gain white support for a return as elected spokesman for his people, he had to toe the line. He shook hands with Pastor Hinman at the doorway as he and other Indians took their leave.

About 20 Lower Agency warriors, meanwhile, were hunting game in the Big Woods to the north. The party split up. Four warriors—Brown Wing, Killing Ghost, Breaking Up, and Runs Against Something When Crawling—went their own way. "Two of the Indians had on white men's coats," recalled Mrs. Baker, a witness to coming events, "one was quite tall, one was quite small, one was thick and chubby, and all were middle-aged; one had two feathers in his cap, and another had three."[10]

The four Indians searched for game near the home of Robinson Jones at Acton. He lived there with his wife Ann and their two adopted children, 15-year-old Clara and her 18-month-old half brother. Big Eagle later said he heard firsthand from the four Indians involved. They spotted a cluster of hen's eggs in a nest along a fence outside the house. One Indian felt the eggs could well make a tasty treat.

"Don't take them," said a companion, "for they belong to a white man and we may get into trouble."

Incensed, the other man flung them to the ground, the smashed eggs a portent of tragic events about to unfold. "You are a coward," he said. "You are afraid of the white man. You are afraid to take even an egg from him, although you are half-starved. Yes, you are a coward and I will tell everybody so."

The other brave snapped back that he was no coward, and would shoot the white man in the house to prove it. "Are you brave enough to go with me?"

"Yes, I will go with you, and we will see who is the braver of us two."[11]

The Indians entered the home, which also served as a boarding house and post office.

But instead of shooting Jones straight off, they asked for whiskey. He declined, and the mood turned ugly. Jones was surprised. He knew these Indians, and their attitude was out of character. Leaving teenage Clara and her infant brother behind, he dashed half a mile to the home of his son-in-law, Howard Baker, who lived there with his wife and two children. Robinson Jones' wife Ann, Howard's mother, was visiting there. Jones arrived and told them of the strange conduct. But it was not long before the Indians also arrived. For 15 minutes they spoke affably to Jones, who spoke Dakota, and they could speak a little English.

Michigan emigrant Viranus Webster was also present. He and his wife Rosa Ann were staying with the Bakers while they searched for a suitable farm site. After dark, they slept in their covered wagon in the Bakers' yard.

It was decided to hold a shooting match, and a target was set up. The muskets banged, the results compared, and a deal was done to trade one of Bakers' guns, plus three silver dollars, for an Indian musket. While the whites' guns remained unloaded, the Indians rammed powder and ball home. "The next thing I knew I heard the report of a gun and saw Mr. Webster fall," recalled Mrs. Baker. "He stood and fell near the door of the house. Another Indian came to the door and aimed his gun at my husband and fired, but did not kill him; then he shot the other barrel of the gun at him, and then he fell dead."[12] Ann Jones stared out the door, only to be shot. She turned, and as two more shots were fired at her, she fell into "the buttery." Mrs. Baker attempted to escape through a window but slipped. While regaining her footing, she stumbled and fell through the open cellar entrance. Robinson Jones started to run, but another bullet brought him down alongside the wagon in which Mrs. Webster was sheltering. He thrashed about, tearing up handfuls of grass and soil as he died.

Soon all was quiet. The Indians had gone without mutilating the dead, plundering the home or stealing four fine horses in the yard. Mrs. Baker emerged from the cellar and, with her two young children, fled into a thicket of hazel bushes. Viranus Webster was still alive when his wife reached his side. She asked why the Indians had shot him. "I do not know," he replied. "I never saw a Sioux Indian before, and never had anything to do with one." His life slipped away, and the distraught Mrs. Webster joined the Baker survivors in the thicket.

Then an Irishman named Cox appeared along the road. The woman dashed out and begged for help, but he merely grinned and, with a shake of his head, said they were liars. "There have been no Indians here," he said. Mrs. Baker pointed to the bleeding corpses strewn about. "Oh, they only have the nose bleed," he laughed. "It will do them good." The strange man commenced crooning a weird song as he moved off down the road. He was later arrested as an Indian spy and sent to St. Paul, but upon investigation, was released as a harmless lunatic.[13]

The distraught women and children set out through the woods and made their way to the home of Nels Olsen, a few miles to the north. Despite language difficulties, the women got the message across, and in short order Ole Ingerman was galloping for Forest City, 14 miles to the northeast. Word of the tragedy spread, and that night a party rode for Acton. Local settlers, meanwhile, made a shocking discovery by lamplight at the Baker home: the dead bodies of Howard Baker, Ann Jones, Robinson Jones and Viranus Webster. They moved on to the Jones home and discovered the body of young Clara sprawled in the doorway. She lay as she fell, unmolested, the contents of the house still intact. She had been shot while watching the murderous four pass back that way. Her infant brother was found uninjured in bed. Clara was "hurt," the child said, then asked for his supper.

The following morning, Monday, August 18, saw a hasty inquest being held in Acton, Judge A.E. Smith of Meeker County presiding. About 60 people were in attendance, including Mrs. Baker and Mrs. Webster. They told their horrific tales while five coffins were quickly put together on site.

Then a shout went up. Eleven Indians, all mounted, were seen watching from a distance. Men hastily scrambled into saddles and gave chase, their guns at the ready. But the fleet Indian ponies carried their riders to safety, disappearing amidst the shadows and trees. These warriors had heard shooting the night before and had come back with their chief, Island Cloud, to investigate. As the four hunters had not been seen since, they thought they may have been killed by whites.

But the missing men had arrived the night before at the village of Chief Red Middle Voice on Rice Creek, not far from the Lower Agency. "Get your guns!" they cried. "There is war with the whites and we have begun it."[14] There was a buzz of excitement as Indians moved from their tepees and bark huts. They clustered about as the news spread. What to do? Women had been killed. The whites would seek a terrible revenge. All would be blamed, innocent and guilty alike. Indians would be shot on sight, as occurred after Spirit Lake.

Red Middle Voice took the offenders to Chief Shakopee's village eight miles downstream. Shakopee, described as "a tall, scowling ruffian," was of the hunter breed, not inclined to trade a swift Indian pony for a plowman's horse. For him, now was the time to strike those who told lies and did not pay the promised annuities. But other bands would have to join in to make an effective strike. Riders were dispatched to summon leaders like Mankato, Wabasha, and Big Eagle. They were to meet at the village of Little Crow, two miles northwest of the Lower Agency. Although Traveling Hail had been elected head chief, it was Little Crow who had come to the fore in negotiations with the whites. His influence would be crucial in coming events.

Before dawn the chiefs arrived at Little Crow's home, a timber frame structure built for him by the government. A cellar was already being dug for his replacement brick house. But the dream of that new home evaporated as Little Crow sat up in bed and heard of the atrocities. "Why do you come to me for advice?" he said. "Go to the man you elected speaker and let him tell you what to do." But the Indians would have none of that. Traveling Hail was a farming, peacetime man. They needed a war chief now. No doubt Little Crow was pleased to have his status restored.

"War was now declared," Little Crow said, recalled Big Eagle. But Little Crow blackened his face and covered his head as a sign of mourning. He was not in favor of a war against a white tide impossible to resist—and said so. "You are a coward," yelled one warrior.

"Taoyateduta is not a coward," retorted Little Crow, "and he is not a fool. When did he run away from his enemies?" He grasped his accuser's headdress and threw it to the ground. It was Little Crow who had faced pursuing Chippewas, protecting his men, he said, "as a she-bear covers her cubs." He was no coward; he had taken many scalps. "Braves, you are like little children; you know not what you are doing." They were full of the "white man's devil-water [rum]." He added, "See!—the white men are like the locusts when they fly so thick the sky is like a snowstorm ... count your fingers all day long and the white men with guns in their hands will come faster than you can count." Yes, the whites were now fighting each other, but that conflict was far away, and "if you strike at them they will turn on you and devour you and your women and little children just as the locusts in their time fall on the leaves and devour all the leaves in one day.... You will die like the rabbits when the hungry wolves hunt them in the Hard Moon [January]."

But Little Crow knew the warriors' blood was up. They would not be pacified. Years of frustration and deep-seated resentment bubbled to the surface. War was inevitable. "Taoyateduta is not a coward: he will die with you."[15]

"Wabasha, Wacouta, myself and others still talked for peace," recalled Big Thunder, "but nobody would listen to us, and soon the cry was 'Kill the whites and kill all those cut-hairs who will not join us.' A council was held and war was declared. Parties formed and dashed away in the darkness to kill settlers. Then women began to run bullets and the men to clean their guns."[16]

5

A Dreadful Scene

On Monday, August 18, the sun peeked through the morning mist a little before five-thirty, marking the beginning of another warm summer's day. Before long, early risers were preparing for the day's work. Trader James Lynd, formerly a newspaper editor and state senator, was sharing breakfast with an Indian assistant in the establishment of Andrew Myrick. Lynd had been an unsuccessful applicant for the position of Indian agent, but took solace with the pursuit and seduction of young Dakota women.[1] He had, however, taken time off to study and write about other aspects of life within the Dakota tribe. He described Little Crow as "the greatest man" amongst the present chiefs. "He possesses shrewd judgment, great foresight, and a comprehensive mind, together with that greatest of requisites in a statesman, caution."[2]

But now Little Crow had thrown caution to the wind. Lynd looked up to see a Dakota warrior, Much Hail, silhouetted in the doorway. Myrick, the "eat grass" man, was the first target, but he was upstairs at the time. "Now I will kill the dog who would not give me credit," said Much Hail. In the next instant there was a deafening bang and a cloud of acrid smoke filled the room. Lynd reeled and collapsed to the floor. The Indian alongside him also fell, but it was hardly fatal. "My Brother, who had been sitting next to the storekeeper became covered with blood and fainted," recalled Blue Sky Woman.[3]

That single shot served as a signal. A storm of gunfire echoed along the valley towards the Lower Agency. "Like a destructive storm," recalled Blue Sky Woman, "the war struck suddenly and spread rapidly. Everything was confusion. It was difficult to know who was friend and who was foe."

But not for Andrew Myrick. He well knew who his enemies were. He overheard plans to burn him out as braves looted the store below. Despite owning a 16-shot Henry repeater, the trader knew his minutes were numbered unless he could make good his escape. He dropped from the bedroom window to a lower roof adjoining the building's north side. With another leap he hit the ground and dashed for the shelter of nearby cottonwoods. But the rush was short-lived. The hated grass man was later found perforated with bullet holes and arrows, and a nasty gash from a scythe. Farmer Indians had joined the revolt and were now harvesting things other than crops. "Now he was lying on the ground dead, with his mouth stuffed full of grass," recalled Big Eagle, "and the Indians were saying tauntingly: 'Myrick is eating grass himself.'"[4]

The Indians poured into other stores. Traders and their clerks were shot down, clubbed or tomahawked. Others died on the run. The next target would be the main buildings of the Lower Agency, half a mile down the road. There people looked up as gunfire was heard. What could it mean? The recent confrontation with troops had occurred at the Upper Agency. All was peaceful here, and the local Indians friendly. The perplexed residents were given a breathing space while the Indians paused to loot the stores of meat, flour, coffee, sugar and clothing. Once the booty had been piled into wagons, the buildings were set ablaze.

The Indians, in good order, then set out for the Lower Agency. They did not arrive as a screaming horde, but moved in quietly, spreading themselves about. Pastor Hinman, who had shaken hands with Little Crow at his church just the day before, saw the chief stalk past his front gate and asked him what was going on. "He was usually very polite," Hinman recalled, "but now he made no answer, and regarding me with a savage look, went on towards the stable, the next building below." Farms Superintendent August Wagner was next to walk past Hinman's gate. The pastor again asked what was happening. The Indians were bent on stealing horses, Wagner replied. Don't interfere, Hinman warned; it appeared that bad things were afoot. But the determined Wagner continued on. Hinman followed, and saw Wagner and stable hands John Lamb and Lathrop Dickinson confronting the Indians. "What are you doing?" Little Crow asked his braves. "Why don't you shoot these men? What are you waiting for?" One man lunged at an Indian with a pitchfork, and in the next instant all three whites fell amidst a blaze of musket fire.[5]

John Fenske heard the blast and dashed into the barn. In the next instant he felt the thud of an arrow in his back. Despite the wound, he made his way up a ladder into the hayloft, where he lay concealed. Having snapped off the shaft, and huddling under a blanket, he soon made his way through the marauding Indians and across the river. He eventually fell in with Private Blodgett, the badly wounded survivor of Marsh's command, and together they reached Fort Ridgely.

Despite ordering the killings, Little Crow told his half brother, a cut-hair farmer named White Spider, to save what women and children he could. He led John Nairn and Alexander Hunter, along with their families, to a ravine from which they could escape along the road to New Ulm. Mrs. Nairn offered White Spider her wedding ring in gratitude. "No, no, I don't want your ring," he said. "Just look at my face and if anything happens, remember it."

The Reverend Hinman, meanwhile, gathered his family and other refugees. He led them with all haste towards the Redwood ferry, about ¾ of a mile away. Once over the river, he told Martell to ride for Fort Ridgely.

Escapees dashed by horse, vehicle and foot, women with babes in arms, towards the ferry. They were given this last chance to save themselves when the Indians paused to loot rather than pursuing to kill. The ferryman saved many lives that day, but paid the ultimate price. Fort Ridgely was about 12 miles to the southeast. Many of those who crossed must have cursed the army post being built so far away, at the southern tip of the reservation instead of near the two agencies.

Two miles along the road to Fort Ridgely lived David Faribault, a prosperous trader and farmer, and his 25-year-old mixed-blood wife Nancy, the offspring of Lieutenant James McClure and his Dakota wife, Winona. McClure, stationed at Fort Snelling, had been transferred to Florida, where he died in 1837. His well-educated daughter felt "more white than Indian in my tastes and sympathies," and the Faribaults' log farm house was "large and roomy and very well furnished."

Her August 18 experiences were typical of many that fateful day:

> On the very morning of the outbreak my husband and I heard shooting in the direction of the agency, but supposed that the Indians were out shooting wild pigeons. As the shooting increased I went to the door once or twice and looked toward the agency, for there was something unusual about it. My husband was out attending to the milking. All at once a Frenchman named Martell came galloping down the road from the agency, and, seeing me in the door, he called out: 'Oh, Mrs. Faribault, the Indians are killing all the white people at the agency! Run away, run away quick!' He did not stop or slacken his speed, but waved his hand and called out as he passed. There was blood on his shirt, and I presume he was wounded.
>
> My husband and I were not prepared for trouble of this kind. Our best horses and wagons were not at home. We had two horses in the stable and harness for them, but no wagon. My husband told me to get my saddle ready and we would go away on horseback, both of us being good riders. We were getting ready to do this when we saw a wagon, drawn by two yoke of oxen and loaded with people, coming down the road at a good trot. My husband said we would wait and see what these people would say. When they came up to us we saw there were five or six men, three or four women and some children, and they were all in great fright. They asked us to put our horses to their wagon—as they could travel faster than oxen—and to get in with them. This we agreed to do, and soon had the change made. When they were harnessing the horses I ran to the house to try to secure some articles of value, for as yet we had taken nothing but what we had on our backs, and I had many things I did not want to lose. Woman-like, I tried first to save my jewelry, which I kept in a strong drawer. This drawer was swelled and I could not open it, and I was running for an ax to burst it, when my husband said, 'Let it go—they are ready to start.' So I took my dear little daughter, who was eight years old and my only child, and we started for the wagon. Just as I was about to get in—everybody else was in—I looked up the road toward the agency and saw the Indians coming. I was afraid they would overtake the wagon; so I declined to get in, and my husband got out with me, and we took our child and ran for the woods, while the wagon started off, the men lashing the horses.

5. A Dreadful Scene

Just as we started for the woods, Louis Brisbois and his wife and two children, mixed-blood people, came up and went with us. We all hid in the wood. In a few minutes the Indians came up, and somehow they knew we were hidden, and they called out very loudly: 'Oh, Faribault, if you are here, come out; we won't hurt you.' My husband was armed and had determined to sell his life for all it would bring, and I had encouraged him; but now it seemed best that we should come out and surrender, and so we did. The Indians at once disarmed my husband. They seemed a little surprised to see the Brisbois family, and declared they would kill them, as they had not agreed to spare their lives. Poor Mrs. Brisbois ran to me and asked me to save her, and she and her husband got behind me, and I began to beg the Indians not to kill them. My husband asked the Indians what all this meant—what they were doing anyhow. They replied, 'We have killed all the white people at the agency; all the Indians are on the war-path; we are going to kill all the white people in Minnesota; we are not going to hurt you, for you have trusted us with goods, but we are going to kill these Brisbois.' And then one ran up and struck over my shoulder and hit Mrs. Brisbois a cruel blow in the face, saying she had treated them badly at one time. Then I asked them to wait until I got away, as I did not want to see them killed. This stopped them for half a minute, when one said: 'Come to the house.' So we started for the house, and just then two more wagons drawn by oxen and loaded with white people came along the road. All the Indians left us and ran yelling and whooping to kill them.

We went into the house. At the back part of the house was a window, and a little beyond was a corn field. I opened the window and put the Brisbois family out of it, and they ran into the corn field and escaped. They are living somewhere in Minnesota to-day. The white people were nearly all murdered. I could not bear to see the sickening sight, and so did not look out, but while the bloody work was being done an Irish woman named Hayden came running up to the house crying out for me to save her. I saw that she was being chased by a young Indian that had once worked for us, and I called to him to spare her, and he let her go. I heard that she escaped all right. Now, all this took place in less time than one can write about it.

When the killing was over the Indians came to the house and ordered us to get into one of the wagons and go with them back to the agency. This we did, my husband driving the team. The Indians drove the other team. Soon after we started an Indian gave me a colt to lead behind the wagon. About half way to the agency we saw the dead body of a man lying near the road.... When we got to the ferry the boat was in the middle of the stream, and standing upon it was a young white girl of about sixteen or seventeen years of age. The Indians called to her to bring the boat ashore, but she did not obey them. They were about to shoot her, when my husband told her they would kill her if she did not do as they ordered, and she brought the boat ashore. When it touched the bank a young Indian made this girl get on a horse behind him and he rode away with her, and I never heard what became of the poor creature. When I saw her being taken away I felt as badly as if she was being murdered before my eyes, for I imagined she would suffer a most horrible fate.

When we reached the agency there was a dreadful scene. Everything was in ruins, and dead bodies lay all about. The first body we saw was that of one of La Bathe's clerks. It lay by the road some distance from the buildings. The rest were nearer the buildings, Mr. Myrick's among them. We did not stay long here, but pushed on to Little Crow's camp. Soon other prisoners, many of them half-bloods like ourselves, were brought in. While we were in this camp we saw Capt. Marsh and his men coming from Fort Ridgely along the road towards the ferry. They could not see us, but we saw them, though at some distance. You know they were going to the agency, having heard that the Indians were rising. They stopped at our house and seemed to be getting water from the well. Poor fellows! Little did some of them think they were taking their last drink. They went on, and soon came to the ferry and fell into that bloody ambush where Capt. Marsh, Mr. Quinn and so many others were killed.[6]

While mayhem reigned supreme at the Lower Agency, all remained calm at the Upper Agency, 30 miles to the northwest. Indians were renowned for having news travel faster than whites, by flashing mirrors and other means, and the upper bands heard of the outbreak by 8 a.m. Not until about midday did the whites hear rumors, disbelieved by most. Trouble was brewing somewhere out there. But exactly where was it? The Big Woods?

Not realizing the trouble was at the Lower Agency, Dr. John Wakefield of the Upper Agency decided Fort Ridgely would be the safest place for his wife and two children. They set off in the family wagon, driven by Lower Agency employee George Gleeson, straight for the lion's den. Gleeson assured Sarah Wakefield that all was well, and Lower Dakotas would fight alongside the whites if there was any trouble. "Poor misguided man," Sarah recalled. "All this day these lower Indians had been committing these awful murders, and we, not knowing it, were going down into their country for safety."[7] Gleeson was shot and killed, but Sarah and the children were saved by Chaska, a farmer Indian. Many whites and mixed-bloods would be protected by Dakotas who had no desire for war. Chaska took the woman and children to Shakopee's camp, where, with difficulty, he continued to provide protection from harm and "a fate worse than death." Not all women would be so lucky.

Earlier, while the Upper Agency whites were skeptical of any outbreak, the well-informed local Indian leaders held a council. What should they do? Join the revolt or declare for peace with the whites? Hot words were exchanged between rival factions. Chief John Other Day was a Christian farmer who had assisted in the rescue of Abbie Gardner from Inkpaduta's band in 1857, and been part of the treaty delegation to Washington the following year. During his stay he had befriended a white woman, and once he was back in Minnesota, they married and had a child. Other Day was vehemently opposed to war with the whites. Little Paul, speaker for the Upper Dakotas, was of a like mind, as were Akepa, Simon Anawangmant and others. They warned their hostile kinsmen of the ruin that would follow. The whites had soldiers and cannon that would kill any who went to war. Yes, the opposing faction agreed. But now that white blood had been shed, the soldiers would shoot first and ask questions later. All Dakotas, friendly or otherwise, would suffer the white man's fury. Better to strike now before bluecoat reinforcements could arrive.[8]

Then more news came in. Troops had been cut down at Redwood Ferry. A great victory had been achieved. The white soldiers were not invincible. Strike now! Lean Bear, White Lodge and Blue Face were all for war. If Fort

Ridgely could be stormed, the Dakotas could take out the detested invaders all the way to Fort Snelling. Former hunting grounds would be restored.

The council broke up in disarray; different minds were bent on different courses. The local blacksmith was delighted when a flow of warriors appeared with a variety of weapons for sharpening and repair. Oblivious to events in the southeast, he believed what he was told: a big buffalo hunt was being planned. But then others said a foray against the Chippewas was about to take place. Whatever; all were good for business.

By twilight the whites finally realized the horrible truth. The rumors were true. John Other Day did the rounds and led over 60 people into the large brick agency warehouse for protection. Here a resolution was made to defend women and children to the last bullet, the last man. Other Day's own family were present, and that of the absent Agent Thomas Galbraith. Dr. Wakefield was also there. What had become of his wife and children, sent south into the killing zone? While defensive preparations were made, hostile warriors prowled about. But John Other Day and four relatives stood guard, and there was no assault.

As daybreak approached on the 19th, firing broke out and war whoops were heard as the stores in the lower valley were attacked. Those Indians menacing Other Day's party dashed off to reap their share of the spoils. A badly wounded storekeeper, Stewart Garvie, made his way in after being shot. Another survivor, Peter Patoile, despite a musket ball that had ripped right through his body, made his escape with an astonishing 13-day trek to the north. After hobbling about 120 miles, living off scraps of food in abandoned homes, he was found by settlers who took him to St. Cloud.

John Other Day gave orders to harness five wagons, and a little before dawn the nervous refugees departed their brick haven and moved towards the Minnesota River. Behind them, warriors soon stripped the warehouse of goods and provisions. Other Day managed his group safely across the river, and a separate party of about 30 people under the Reverend Riggs of the nearby Hazelwood Mission also crossed. While Other Day headed north, Riggs took the road southeast to Fort Ridgely; a hazardous choice through the heart of hostile territory. A photographer, Adrian Bell, was with the party, and on August 21 set up his camera to capture a unique image of the refugees as they stopped to eat. A young cow provided roast beef, and bread was baked over open fires.

The following day, another party under Thomas Williamson of the Yellow Medicine Mission, following their wagon tracks, caught up and joined them. Not believing the Indians would harm him, Williamson had tarried until learning that Amos Huggins, a teacher who had lived amongst the Dakotas since childhood, had been killed.[9] Along the way the horrific sight of dead bodies, burnt-out homes, and discarded plunder met their eyes. They

Refugees fleeing with the Rev. Riggs three days after the outbreak began. While stopped for a meal, they were photographed by Adrian Bell (Library of Congress).

arrived safely at Fort Ridgely on August 22 to learn just how lucky was their escape. The post itself had been under attack. "The God who had led us during these long days, would neither suffer us to perish in this prairie wilderness, nor be taken by savages," recalled Martha Riggs.[10]

Other Day's party, meanwhile, continued north, but danger still threatened as the revolt spread. Squads of Indians were on the rampage, killing whites in small settlements and isolated homesteads. As they marched, Other Day was chagrined to realize that some under his care had little trust in any Indian, including himself. His white wife, however, assured all of his good intentions, dampening such fears. They arrived in Cedar City to find it deserted, the terrified inhabitants having fled to the safety of an island in Cedar Lake. Here the refugees joined them to spend a wretched night under steadily falling rain. Next morning, Other Day's party moved on. The ailing Stewart Garvie, shot in the valley, was left in the care of the island refugees. Too badly wounded, he soon died.[11]

Other Day's survivors moved on to safe settlements, and Thomas Galbraith, having left his post, was delighted to hear his family was safe. "Led by the noble Other Day, they struck out on the prairie," he recalled, "literally placing their lives in this creature's hands and guided by him and him alone. After intense suffering and privation they reached Shakopee on August 22, Other Day never having left them for an instant; and this Other Day is a full-blooded Indian, and was not long since one of the wildest and fiercest of his race."[12] No doubt the noble Other Day was gratified with such praise, but whether or not he appreciated being referred to as a "creature" is open to question. Other Day's arrival in St. Paul caused great excitement. The town had been flooded with rumors and some refugees had already arrived with their own accounts.

John Nicolay, private secretary to President Lincoln, was in Minnesota as part of a delegation to treat with the Chippewas. The state's population, he observed, "was largely made up of foreign immigrants, German, French, Norwegians, and Swedes. They were unaccustomed to danger, and unused to arms."[13] All of which made them easy targets as the normally beautiful Minnesota Valley was turned into a place of bloody horror. A mass exodus of thousands took place while settlements and isolated homesteads were attacked, hundreds murdered in cold blood, and prisoners taken. The marauders took horses, oxen and cattle, burned buildings and haystacks. But Indians were not the only thieves. White looters moved in to plunder abandoned homes once the Dakotas had moved on.

Those settlers who formed large parties for protection were often poorly armed, and provided an easy target for mass killings along the trails. Thirteen German families, hearing of the outbreak, gathered in Flora township, Renville County, at the home of Paul Kitzman. Under cover of dark, they boarded 11 ox-drawn wagons and set out for Fort Ridgely, but were overtaken by a Dakota war party shortly after sunrise. Kitzman, however, knew one warrior and believed his story that the Chippewas were on the warpath, not his own tribe. The Dakotas would provide an escort to see them safely home. The convoy turned and headed back, but soon the supposed escort stopped the train and demanded money. Once the robbery was complete, they rode off, and the refugees continued on, seeing two dead bodies along the way. They headed for the Krieger house to use as a redoubt.

But 14 warriors rode up. With wild whoops, they opened fire. All except three of the men were killed, and the Indians called out that any women who went with them would be spared. One woman walked off with a warrior, only to be shot when she paused to wave back. The Indians opened fire again, killing seven women and two men. Frederick Krieger, now the only surviving male, also died as a general massacre took place. Not to waste powder, many children were killed by rifle butt and tomahawk. "Some soon rose up from the ground," Justina Krieger recalled, "with the blood streaming down their faces, when they were beaten again and killed. This was the most horrible scene I have ever yet witnessed." Justina was shot in the back but survived to be badly sliced along the abdomen while her clothes were cut off. She regained consciousness to see one Indian holding her young niece upside down while he hacked off her leg. "Oh God! Oh God!" the child cried.[14] She was

"I am happy to inform you that, in spite both of blandishments and threats, used in profusion by the agents of the government of the United States, the Indian nations within the confederacy have remained firm in their loyalty and steadfast in the observance of their treaty engagements with this government."

(The above Extract from JEFF DAVIS's last Message will serve to explain the News from Minnesota.)

Newspapers printed horrific accounts and images of the massacre, some claiming a Confederate plot, thus the "Agent C.S.A." on the whiskey jug (*Harper's Weekly*, September 7, 1862).

stripped and left to die. As the slaughter took place, some managed to make their escape into nearby woods. In all, 24 people were brutally murdered. The Indians rode off, and one white woman and ten children made their way into the Krieger house. The woman, herself badly wounded, could do little to care for the others. After sheltering there for two days, she departed to seek help, taking a baby and two older children. They had not gone far when they saw the Indians return, loot the house, and burn it to the ground with the seven remaining children inside.

Survivors, including some of the Krieger children, eventually made their way to Fort Ridgely to tell the horrific story. Justina Krieger, left for dead, wandered for 13 days eating berries and other plants before being rescued by troops.

The Indians were capricious in their actions, sometimes sparing lives. Susan Brown, of the Upper Agency Sisseton band, was married to former Indian Agent Joseph Brown. They lived in a fine stone house on the north side of the river. Her group of 26 refugees, heading for Fort Ridgely, was stopped by a large war party led by Cut Nose, one of the most vehement Indian leaders. Her life was spared when a warrior told how she had cared for him, saving his life, during freezing weather. Cut Nose, described as incredibly ugly, with "blackened face and long bushy hair like a Zulu's and a half nose (one nostril was missing)," insisted that the others must die. Susan, however, bravely stood in the wagon and, in their own tongue, told the warriors her Upper Dakota relatives would seek revenge if they killed the whites with her party.

Hesitating under the tongue-lashing, the braves let the white men, except two needed to drive wagons, flee for their lives. But, recalled Susan Brown's son, 16-year-old Sam: "The white women—Mrs. Wohler and the two Misses Ingalls—were then parceled out among the Indians and ordered to follow them." He added, "One beautiful young girl of about 17 years of age refused to alight from the wagon when ordered to do so. Cut Nose had told her he wanted her for his wife, and to get out of the wagon and follow him. She screamed and resisted, when he drew his knife and grabbed her by the hair and threatened to scalp her and frightened her so that she got out and he led her away. Presently the Indians came back with the women and ordered them all to get into one of the wagons."[15] Brown makes no comment on the state of the women, or what happened to them while absent.

Ordered to follow the Indians, they started for an unknown destination. Taken to Little Crow's house, surrounded with tepees, they came under the chief's protection. Realizing Mrs. Brown's family connections, he had no desire to antagonize the Upper Dakotas. If all went well, they too may well raise the tomahawk. Assuring Mrs. Brown of her safety, Little Crow "was anxious to get into conversation with her," recalled Sam Brown, and said that "his young men had started to massacre; that he at first opposed the movement with all his might, but when he saw he could not stop it he joined them in their madness against his better judgment, but now did not regret it and was never more in earnest in his life." Little Crow had grand plans for a concerted push by united Dakotas, Winnebagos and Chippewas and all would meet to "make a grand charge on Fort Snelling; that this was a stone fort and might take a day or two to batter the walls down."[16] Thus, Little Crow had convinced himself of an impossible dream.

Helen Carrothers (later Tarble) had moved with her husband James to Minnesota and borne two children, Althea, now 4, and Thomas, 2. She had befriended the local Indians, learned their language, and acquired the wisdom of the medicine man's skills with roots, herbs and barks in curing illness. Her husband was away working as a carpenter when the outbreak took place. At first she could not believe her Indian friends would do her any harm, but was finally convinced to flee. Overtaken by Indians, the party of 27 whites heard gunfire break out. "The dreadful truth flashed upon me," Helen recalled, "the Indians were killing us!"

A pillow slip was handed over by an ill woman in a wagon, Clarissa Henderson, and waved as a flag of truce, "but was instantly riddled with bullets and the same volley shot off Mr. Henderson's thumb." Most of the men and boys, including Stephen Henderson, saved themselves by flight, but others were not so fortunate. While Helen and her children looked on, others came under attack. "An Indian seized the older of the children, a sweet pretty little girl of about two and a half years, and beat her savagely over the head with a violin box, mashing her head horribly out of its natural shape. Then he took the poor little thing by her feet and swinging the body about dashed her against the wheel of the wagon, the blood and brains spattering over the dying mother.... Another red fiend caught up the nine-months old baby girl, and holding her by one foot, head downwards, deliberately hacked the body, limb from limb, with his tomahawk." A fire was lit and the ailing Clarissa Henderson was hauled from the wagon. The Indians "tossed bed and woman and the mangled portions of her children into the flames. O, the horror of this scene! The dense smoke of the feathers on the bed and the burning human flesh, the yells of the Indians, the shrieks of anguish of those who witnessed the horror, and the groans of the poor woman!"

A brave approached Helen. "Are you going to kill me?" she asked.

"No," he replied, "the medicine man says we must not kill you.... All the nice women we will not kill; they will be squaws for the Indian braves."

Helen, her children, and others were taken to Little Crow's village, where "the Indian warriors and their squaws were coming into camp from every direction, the squaws laden with plunder, the men with the bloody scalps of their butchered victims at their belts. A great many white women and girls were brought in as captives.... I soon began to fully realize what it meant to be a prisoner of the Indians, and to suspect the fate—far worse than death—which awaited me." They were given food, and Helen was told to dress in Indian garb.

Next morning, "serious trouble threatened me." Helen was told by an Indian woman that she had been claimed by four braves, which was causing a great fuss. The matter had been referred to Little Crow, but unable to find a solution, he had "ordered that I should be killed, for he would not have trouble among his best warriors on account of a white woman." Helen appealed to the Indian woman to help her and the children escape. Despite an initial refusal, the "squaw" appeared that night, and saying warriors were on their way to kill Helen, she led the three captives to a cornfield. Here Helen's Indian garb was replaced with a tatty white women's skirt taken from plundered goods.

The Indians quickly discovered the escape and went out in pursuit through a driving rain. "Just then the storm came on with a terrific volume of rain and hail and the wind blew with the force of a cyclone. To the fury of that storm I and my children owe our lives. It prevented the Indian pursuit until I reached the timber along the bluff on the south side of the river." Helen and her children made their arduous way, as best they could, on a perilous trek towards Fort Ridgely.[17]

5. A Dreadful Scene

As death and destruction had reigned at the Lower Agency on August 18, Milford township, on the eastern edge of the reservation between New Ulm and Fort Ridgely, also came under attack. Dakotas from nearby villages swooped on their neighbors, mainly Germans, who were oblivious to the threat. "Nippo!" (kill) was heard as the Indians made their way from one home to another. Men, women and children, including infants, died by knife, tomahawk and gun. "I knelt down but the Indian saw me and I can still hear the ting tingle as he tommyhawked me," recalled Franz Massopust, aged only four at the time. Lucky individuals managed to flee, but in another home one of Franz's relatives had her head cut off after being shot. The ghastly trophy was hung from a fishhook on a nail.[18] The Indians found whiskey, fueling their fury, and set up howls of vengeance as they moved through the town and into the adjacent fields.

Five wagons were seen approaching Milford along the New Ulm Road. A flag fluttered from the first vehicle, and a brass band played. The 25-man party were out on a recruiting drive for the Federal Army. Something was seen in the long grass, and Joe Messmer was found "lying on his face and apparently groaning in great agony." One arm and one ear had been hacked off. The wounded man was loaded aboard, and the two rear wagons turned back for New Ulm. Then Indians were seen to their front. Though unarmed, the men in the remaining three wagons decided that attack was the best form of defense. Whips were cracked and the horses dashed forward at full speed in the hope that the Indians would fall back. And they temptingly did. But as the wagons reached a bridge, a sudden blast of gunfire erupted from the undergrowth. The whites jumped out to shelter behind the vehicles as the drivers attempted to turn. One driver and two other men were killed. The first two wagons were abandoned as further gunfire wounded two more men. The survivors scrambled aboard the last vehicle and moved off rapidly back towards New Ulm. The triumphant Indians climbed aboard their captured trophies and drove them back into Milford through scattered bodies and burning homes. With over 40 killed, Milford had seen what would be the highest death rate of any single community.

At the same time, the wagon of trader Francis Patoile rattled along about 10 miles upriver from New Ulm. On board were two other men and three girls, Mary Anderson, Mattie Williams and 14-year-old Mary Schwandt. As they traveled, Miss Schwandt's family was attacked by Dakotas in their home. She later recalled that her married older sister, Karolina, saw her first Indians when the family arrived in Minnesota. Karolina "was much frightened by them. She cried and sobbed in their terror, and even hid herself in the wagon and would not look at them, so distressed was she. I have often wondered whether she did not have a premonition of the dreadful fate she was destined in their cruel hands."

Karolina was killed along with her husband and other family members. Her unborn child was cut from her body and nailed to a tree. The only survivor was her 10-year-old brother, August, who lived after being tomahawked. Left for dead, he managed to make his way from the scene of carnage to Fort Ridgely.

About 50 Indians approached Patoile's wagon. Most were mounted, but some drove vehicles loaded with plunder from looted homes. "They were nearly naked," Mary Schwandt recalled, "painted all over their bodies, and all of them seemed to be drunk, shouting and yelling and acting riotously in every way." The Indians halted the wagon. "As we jumped out Mr. Davis said, 'We are lost!'" The Indians opened fire, and Patoile, hit by four bullets, fell dead. The others ran towards cover, but the Indians fired again, killing the two men. "Mary Anderson was shot in the back," recalled Mary Schwandt, and "some shots passed through my dress, but I was not hit. Miss Williams, too, was not hurt." The girls were caught, Mary placed in one wagon and the other two in another. The critically wounded Mary Anderson would die a few days later.

The wagon carrying Mattie Williams and Mary Anderson headed off towards the Lower Agency, while the other carrying Mary Schwandt moved out across the prairie. They soon rendezvoused with Indian women who "set up a joyful and noisy chattering as we approached," recalled Mary, "and when we stopped they ran to the wagons and took out bread and other articles. We stopped for about an hour, and the Indians dressed their hair, fixing it up with ribbons."

The wagons journeyed to the house of Chief Wacouta, about half a mile from the agency. What followed was a "dreadful night" and "four following dreadful days." Mary hoped "all my memories of this period of my captivity may soon and forever pass away."[19] Wishing to "avoid the subject" she declined to give details in her 1894 memoir, but in 1864 her "Narrative" had appeared in *A History of the Great Massacre by the Sioux Indians in Minnesota*. In this she recalled, "They then took me out by force, to an unoccupied tepee, near the house, and perpetrated the most horrible and nameless outrages upon my person. These outrages were repeated at different times during my captivity." The book editors stated: "The details of this poor girl's awful treatment, in our possession, are too revolting for publication."[20] At the later trials, Joseph Godfrey, who fought with the Indians, testified she was abused "by seventeen of the wretches," wrote Court Recorder Isaac Heard.[21]

Mattie Williams received similar treatment. After interviewing her and other victims after the war, the Reverend Riggs wrote to his daughter, "Oh how glad that my girl was not among them. Poor Mattie Williams.... She grieves much over it. I am very sorry for her."[22] An Indian named Tazoo admitted having raped her, and would die on the gallows.

Margaret Cardinal testified that she had been raped. "I did bad towards her once," admitted Tehehdonecha, while denying a second assault, claiming another man was the culprit. Tehehdonecha would also hang.

George Spencer, protected by an Indian friend, survived to tell the tale of his captivity. While he admitted to being well treated himself, he claimed: "The female captives were, with very few exceptions, subjected to the most horrible treatment. In some cases, a woman would be taken out into the woods, and her person violated by six, seven, and as many as ten or twelve of these fiends."[23] Young women being "parceled out" from Sarah Brown's party, Cut Nose wanting one 17-year-old "for his wife," and Mary Schwandt's story indicate this may well have happened to some female prisoners. At least two women became pregnant as the result of rape. But evidence is lacking that rape occurred on the large scale implied by Spencer. He may well have been telling the infuriated white populace what they wanted to hear, which made good copy for newspapers happy to inflame emotions.

Mary Schwandt, 14 years old, taken captive on the first day of the outbreak, lived through six weeks of torment to tell her story after release (*The Story of Mary Schwandt*, 1894).

Some violated women, however, may have not admitted the fact, feeling shamed by stigma and the moralistic values of the time. Even in the present "enlightened" day, rape is claimed to be grossly unreported because of shame, stigma and trauma. Sarah Wakefield, a prisoner who ultimately defended the Dakotas, claimed she had fended off advances. She related the story of one Indian who "told of meeting a mother and three children, and after violating the oldest daughter, who was about fourteen years old, he beat them all to death with a club."[24] How many women met such a fate will never be known.

Flush with the early victory over Marsh, and unimpeded by the few troops at hand, the revolt gathered pace as more Indians, including "cut-hairs," donned breechclouts and war paint. On August 20, settlers at the Lake Shetek settlement, about 40 miles south of the Upper Agency, felt the Dakota wrath. Some whites managed to escape, but 34 settlers and eight local Dakotas under Old Pawn, professing friendship, took refuge in the home of John and Julia Wright. The men resolved to fight, and "the women would have fought well," recalled Lavina Eastlick, mother of five, "for we were determined to sell our lives as dearly as possible. My husband brought me a knife, and told me to use it, if it became necessary. It was not a small knife by any means. Had we stayed in the house, I certainly should have used it, had the Indians come in."

The hostiles appeared, but scattered when a volley was fired from the windows. Old Pawn offered to negotiate a free passage to safety, and went outside to parley. He returned "badly frightened," apparently. There were a great many Indians, he said, and the house was to burn. They should follow him out and take refuge in the woods. "The men hardly knew what to do," recalled Lavina. "Some wished to stay and some desired to go. Some started and some remained behind. I ran upstairs and caught my baby, then asleep, left my bonnet and my butcher knife on the bed, and was soon hurrying over the prairie with the others."[25]

The settlers set out for New Ulm, 65 miles away. Most were on foot, but the children and some women traveled in one wagon. "The Friendly Indians that were to fight for us, started with us," recalled Jefferson Duley. "They were in a bunch on our left as we left the Wright place, and the white men was on our right. We had gone but a short distance from the House, when the Friendly Indians, set up an awful Yell, and fired into the whites, Wounding several that were walking, the Men did not return the Fire, But thinking they wanted the horse and wagon, Had the women and children get out, and again started on the Road."[26]

But then horsemen were seen to their rear; the other Indians were now in pursuit. Henry Smith bolted, abandoning his wife, along with a bachelor named Rhodes, taking their precious guns with them. They made it New Ulm, thus saving their own skins while leaving the others to their fate. The hostiles "set up the war cry, and came riding down near us and fired into our crowd," recalled Jefferson Duley. His father, William, led the others to a dry slough, overgrown with long reeds. Some were wounded by Indian fire along the way. In the following fight, 15 white men, women and children died by gunshot and tomahawk. But they had the satisfaction of killing Lean Grizzly Bear, who had brazenly bared his chest and dared the fugitives to shoot. Ducking a split second too late, he died where he fell.

A peace parley was arranged. As the men spoke with the Indians, Lean Grizzly Bear's wife enraged wife took her revenge. Five-year-old Fred Eastlick was beaten to death, his head thumped against a rock. The thirst for vengeance

5. A Dreadful Scene

was still not satisfied, and four-year-old Belle Duly was tied to a tree and used for knife throwing practice, her mother forced to watch.[27]

Taken prisoner were three women and five children, some suffering bullet wounds. Jefferson Duley claimed his 1½-year-old sister was kept in a tent "next to my mother and [the Indians] would torture her every night and the Scream could be heard by my Mother, until this child was so weak that they killed her."[28] Laura Duley and Julia Wright were both raped, and fell pregnant before release.[29] Julia and her two children were later reunited with her husband, and she gave birth to a mixed-blood baby during 1863. When John Wright "saw the child was part Indian, he left her," wrote Harper Workman, a doctor who researched the affair. "He did not care to have a woman occupy his bed who would not die rather than submit to the treatment she did from the Indians."[30] Lavina Eastlick and two of her children were taken prisoner by Old Pawn. Her husband and three other children had been killed. Having assured Lavina of protection, Old Pawn shot her in the back, and left her for dead. Despite blood loss, hunger, and hardships, Lavina and some others including William Duley survived to reach civilization.[31] William Duley would take his revenge alongside a large gallows later the same year.

On the same day, August 20, the Scandinavian settlement of West Lake was hit. Most of the 13 killed died after attending a religious service in the home of Andreas Lundborg. Again, children as young as 10-month-old John Broburg were amongst the victims. The following day, the Dakotas struck the Norwegian Endreson family. Their isolated homestead was nestled amidst woods near Solomon Lake. Indians arrived professing friendship, and asked for milk. As the milk was poured, Lars Endreson was shot dead along with one son, and another was badly wounded. His wife Guri and their youngest daughter Anna hid in the cellar while their two older daughters, Gurid and Brita, were taken away as prisoners. The mother and young daughter set out on foot for Forest City, about 30 miles away. They discovered two badly wounded men in a cabin, and harnessing a wagon, Guri drove the small group of survivors to safety. To her delight and surprise, she was soon reunited with Gurid and Brita, who had managed to escape.[32]

Captive Sam Brown recalled how the "half-crazed warriors and their women and girls danced" around a pole from which dangled "the long red whiskers of a white man." Warriors would jump into the ring of the dance. "Each would boast of the exploits, relate his daring deeds. Then all would join in the demonic dance, with yells, whoops and songs and the beating of the tom-tom." One "hideous looking fellow [declared that] he had destroyed a whole family, for which he deserved much honor. That he went into a stable and shot a white man in the back and then beat his brains out with the but of his gun, then rushed into the house where he found the wife kneading bread and a babe in the cradle nearby. He grabbed the shrieking woman by the hair of the head and threw her violently against the wall, then took the babe, put it into the bread pan, and shoved it into the hot oven, then turned and shot the woman as she was trying to get up, then set fire to the house and hurried away and joined his comrades."[33] Later, after hearing Indian accounts of events yet to unfold, Brown would accuse American troops of their own atrocities.

But killing defenseless settlers was not the only Dakota scheme. Strongpoints like Fort Ridgely and New Ulm township must be removed if encroaching whites were to be swept from former Indian lands.

6

WE LAUGHED IN SPITE OF OUR DANGER

Townsfolk on the sidewalks of New Ulm looked around in surprise. A man galloped down the main street from the direction of Milford. "The Indians are coming," he shouted. "They've already killed the recruiting party."[1] But then two wagons raised dust as they clattered into town. Were they not part of the recruiting party?

The wagons came to a halt outside the doctor's office, and the mutilated Joe Messmer was taken inside. What had happened? What was going on? Then the last wagon rumbled into town carrying the ambush survivors.

Just a few drunken Indians out on a rampage, assumed Sheriff Charles Roos. But, just in case, he warned the local schoolmaster to send the children home. Roos gathered a party of armed men and they rode out to investigate. Over 40 dead and mutilated bodies at Milford revealed the horrific true story. It was Spirit Lake all over again. Indians appeared in the distance and opened fire. Roos' party returned to New Ulm with the bad news as an influx of horrified settlers came in. This was a major revolt. New Ulm itself could be under threat.

Founded by the German Land Company of Chicago in 1854 near the confluence of the Cottonwood and Minnesota Rivers, New Ulm was the largest town near the Dakota reservation, and it was difficult to defend. The town had a population of over 800, but few of the German inhabitants carried arms, having had no such need in the old country. The town was built mainly along the lower of two terraces above the Minnesota River, and a slough ran the length of the town between woods cresting the bluffs at the rear, and a higher, sparsely populated terrace. This depression provided a ready-made entry point for any attacking force.[2]

Roos appointed Jacob Nix, a general store owner, as *Platzkommandant* with the rank of major. He had served as a rebel captain during the 1848 German Revolution. Nix rode towards the Lower Agency and came back reporting that the Indians were "murdering everything" in sight. He rounded up about 90 men and formed companies armed with what rifles were available and the more numerous shotguns. In addition, reserves brandishing revolvers, hay forks and axes were organized.

During the night of the 18th, a steady stream of refugees moved into New Ulm, along with local residents who abandoned exposed dwellings on the outer fringes. Many were packed into the town's only three brick structures: the post office, the Flick building and the Erd building. But scores of others flocked into other buildings, soon overcrowded. In the prominent Dacotah House, "the women had to go downstairs, discard their hoop skirts and pile them in the back yard," recalled Gotleib Oswald. "We laughed in spite of our danger."[3]

Under Nix's direction, barricades went up, made from wagons and anything else that came to hand. Schoolteacher Rudolph Leonhart took his turn as a sentinel, a mere club his one weapon. At dawn he took leave to see how his family were faring inside Frank Erd's overcrowded variety store, only to find "the air so foul that only the need to see my family could have forced me to go any further." He led his family to the flat roof, and they were soon joined by Surveyor Brockmann with his telescope. From here he could scan the countryside and give warning should any hostiles approach. The defenders, meanwhile, marshaled what resources they had, and riders were dispatched to other settlements with calls for help. Gunpowder was abundant, but musket balls were another matter. Buckshot was melted down and poured into large caliber bullet molds.

Little Crow did not want to attack New Ulm—yet. On the morning of the 19th, he assembled about 300 warriors west of Fort Ridgely, a serious threat that should be taken out first, he argued. And had they attacked then, the sparsely garrisoned post would almost certainly have been overrun. But many of the young Dakota warriors had their own ideas. There would be no soldiers with artillery at New Ulm, they replied, and the township would provide far more plunder than a military post. Those bent on New Ulm rode southeast, leaving Little Crow with a force of about 125 men, not enough to attack the fort.[4] He tarried that day, waiting for the outcome of the New Ulm assault. The Dakotas had come to him for leadership, but now his advice was ignored, and his pride was hurt. Those warriors who followed his leadership were withheld from the attack on New Ulm.

A house divided against itself cannot stand, Abraham Lincoln had decreed.[5] And the same applied to Indian nations. The Redwood Ferry success had been achieved with unity, but the lack of discipline now signaled an even earlier demise for a cause that was doomed from the outset.

The First Battle of New Ulm

Men in New Ulm resolved to go out and bring vulnerable civilians in. On Tuesday morning, August 19, Sheriff Roos gave leave for a small expedition to set out: 10 men in three wagons and eight on horseback. As they carried some of the best guns in town, outspoken locals wanted them to stay, but they had no intention of sitting in New Ulm while families were exposed to scalping knives. William Carroll was appointed captain, and the party moved out towards Leavenworth township.

Settlers they encountered said they had seen Indians, and the rescue party soon found dead bodies from two different families at the home of Sebastian May. Despite having received tomahawk blows to the head, 3-year-old twins were found still alive, along with a 7-year-old girl, "crying piteously."[6] Moving on to Roeser's homestead, they found another toddler alive while his parents lay dead in their own blood. The four children were placed in a wagon and sent back to New Ulm. Further along the rescue party found Martin Bleum and family lying slain by the roadside. Margaret, the oldest daughter, had been "treated in a most shameful manner before killing," according to Luther Ives.[7]

Before long, the search party split up to cover more ground. Eleven men moved to one side of the Big Cottonwood River, while the remaining seven continued along the opposite bank. They were to reunite at the Tuttle homestead and return to New Ulm as one unit. The larger party, led by Carroll, soon lost sight of the others. Topping a rise, they saw distant buildings on fire; New Ulm was under attack. A disagreement broke out. Should they skirt round and enter town from the Mankato road or continue straight ahead? Accusations of cowardice were flung about. Carroll decided to go straight in, and, "if opposed, cut their way through."

The small band rode on, and soon two Indians carrying shotguns appeared to their front. Hinton, the leading man, drew his pistol and charged, the others following—straight into an ambush. A blaze of smoke and fire erupted from long grass, and five men including Carroll were cut down. The survivors in their wagon made a mad dash for New Ulm with warriors in hot pursuit. As the vehicle clattered into town, the loose reins tangled in the wheels, acting as a brake, and it came to a skidding halt right outside Dacotah House. "Had that happened in the open prairie," recalled Sam McAuliffe, "it would have meant the death of the entire party."

The second group of seven men recrossed the river and followed the same path taken by Carroll. Recalled Ralph Thomas:

> We came on about half an hour afterward, and, unconscious of any danger approached the fatal spot, when about one hundred and fifty savages sprang up out of the grass and fired on us, killing five horses and six men. My own horse was shot through the body, killing him instantly. My feet were out of the stirrups in a moment, and I sprang to the ground, striking on my hands and feet. I dropped my gun, jumped up, and ran. An Indian, close behind, discharged the contents of both barrels of a shot-gun at me. The charge tore up the ground at my feet, throwing dirt all around me as I ran. I made

my way into town on foot as fast as I could go. No other of our party survived; all the rest were killed.[8]

Yesterday, troops had received a bloody repulse at Redwood Ferry, and today, only seven of 18 well-armed civilians lived to tell of their encounter.

And New Ulm itself was under attack. Earlier that day, at 3 p.m., Surveyor Brockmann, on top of Erd's store, had given the alarm after seeing Indians approaching from the northwest. They separated near the cemetery and approached the town in two curving lines.

"Auf Eure Posten! Fertig zum Gefecht! [On your posts! Ready to fight!]" shouted Major Nix.[9] Men rushed to the barricades with what arms they had, a few rifles and some shotguns. Wagons had been overturned, forming barricades along three blocks of Minnesota Street from Center to Third North. Only the town center could be defended: the other structures were too spread out.

Bullets flew down the streets as the Indians opened fire. Despite orders for women and children to stay indoors, 13-year-old Emilie Paulie could not resist a quick look at her one chance in life to witness an Indian attack. She fell, killed instantly by a bullet to the head. And Jacob Nix suddenly found himself minus one finger, sliced off by a rifle ball. The Indians closed in with firebrands, and very soon smoke billowed from the brewery and houses on the edge of town. Scouting parties came back at the double and scrambled to fill gaps behind the barricades. As gunfire roared, the wagon carrying the survivors from Carroll's party came to its skidding halt outside the Dacotah House.

Volunteer relief parties, meanwhile, were riding from various settlements to aid in the town's defense. Nicollet County Sheriff Boardman with 16 men topped a rise and saw "a dense black cloud, against which, as a background, could be plainly seen the flash of guns, fired in either attack or defense, and burning stacks or buildings. The smoke and sparks were blown upon the town by the prevailing wind, its direction probably having determined the point of attack."[10] One man swam 50 yards to retrieve the Redstone Ferry. Boardman's party crossed the river and approached New Ulm from the lower end, not yet under attack.

They rode in unopposed, but Indians quickly swarmed across the road behind them. The new arrivals made an abortive mounted charge against the Indians, but then fell back amidst heavy fire behind the barricades. Future Minnesota Governor Horace Austin claimed Boardman, lacking confidence, resigned on the spot, and he took command of his party. What to do next? A quick conference was held with Roos and Nix. A force of 125 Frontier Guards were known to be on the way from St. Paul and Le Sueur, and Boardman was dispatched on a fast horse to hurry them along.

A lone horseman was seen galloping for town. His horse was hit and killed, but he ran for his life and came safely in. It was Ralph Thomas, the only man to ultimately survive the 7-man detachment from Carroll's party. One of the others, his hip broken, managed to drag himself in during the night, only to die shortly afterwards.

Late that afternoon, thunder rumbled as black clouds unleashed a torrent of rain—most discouraging to attacking Indians trying to keep their powder dry. And the Dakotas were virtually leaderless. No prominent chief had supported their push on New Ulm. The disillusioned warriors faded back into the hills along with the light.

To the glee of the beleaguered settlers, the 125 Frontier Guards arrived at about 10 o'clock that night. In command was Judge Charles Flandrau, the former Indian agent who had attacked Roaring Cloud's camp in 1857. Well respected throughout the state, he had helped many German settlers establish their claims around New Ulm. Riding with him were three doctors, Asa Daniels, Otis Ayer and William Mayo. Along with New Ulm's Dr. Carl Weschke, they set up hospitals in a spacious basement and just across the road in the Dacotah House. In addition to the 11 killed from Carroll's party, six settlers had died by gunfire and five were wounded. But the Indians were not through with New Ulm yet.

Flandrau set about reorganizing the town's defenses. Extra guards were placed on duty as more wagons, packing cases and barrels were hauled into place, and more volunteers arrived. The following morning, August 20, Flandrau was elected militia colonel in charge of the town's defense. Would the Indians renew their attack? Their numbers had not been overwhelming in yesterday's assault, but perhaps more warriors had arrived during the night.

Little Crow, however, had other plans. He rode about marshaling his forces to take Fort Ridgely. Built north of the Minnesota River between 1853 and 1855, Ridgely was a collection of stone and timber buildings around a 90-yard-wide parade ground. It had no protective stockade, and leafy ravines north, east and southwest provided excellent cover for a furtive enemy approach. The troops were quartered in a large, 2-story stone barracks on the north side of the parade ground; a one-story commissary building occupied the northwest corner; timber frame 2-story officers' quarters were on the west and east sides; and Captain Marsh's quarters, along with those of the post surgeon, occupied the southwest corner. Log civilian quarters were behind the barracks to the north. Horses were stabled over the New Ulm road to the south, leaving a large, tempting entry point for an attacking force. For safety from accidental explosion, the powder magazine stood 200 yards to the northwest. Such an exposed position revealed no concern that the post should ever come under attack. The sutler's and interpreter's homes, and other outbuildings such as a granary and warehouse, were also scattered around the perimeter.[11]

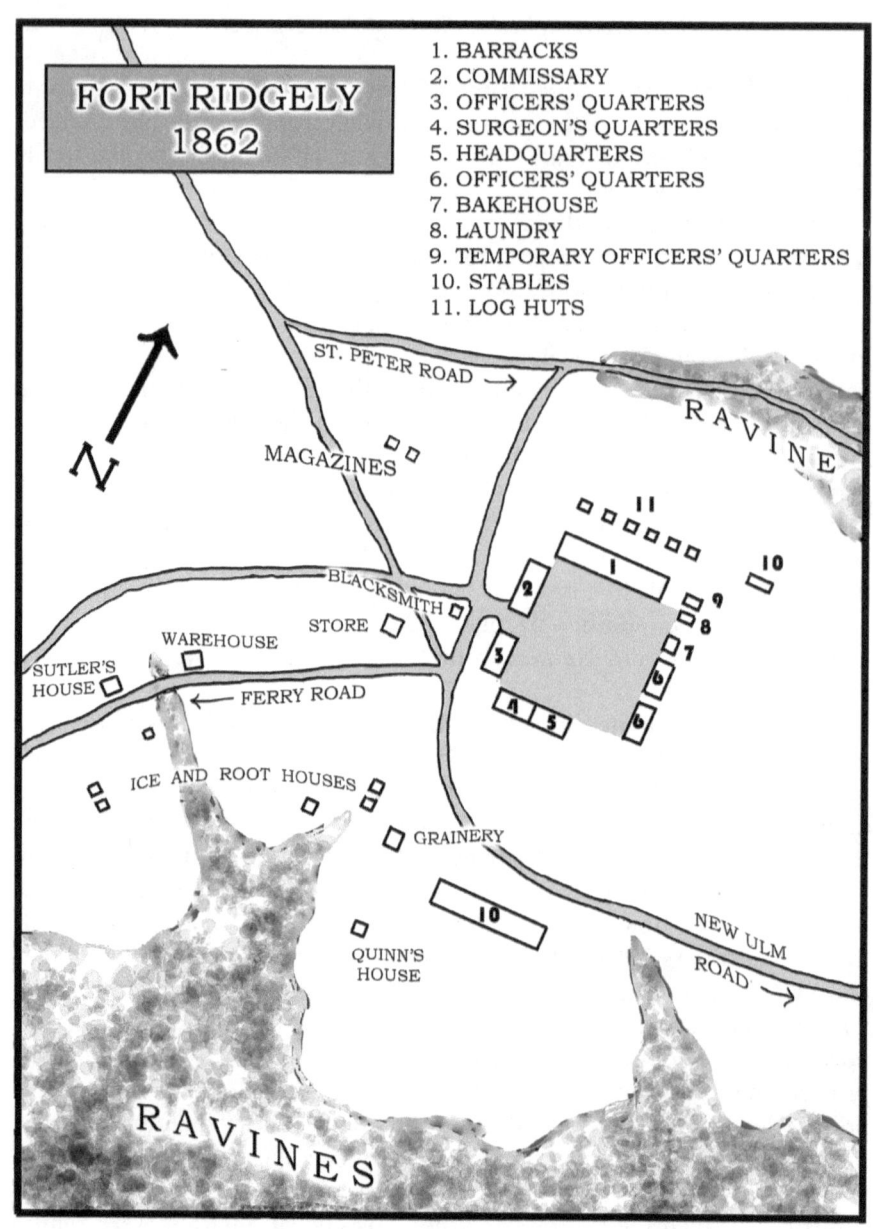

Fort Ridgely plan, 1862 (author's rendition).

The death of Captain Marsh at Redwood Ferry left the fort under the command of 19-year-old Lieutenant Thomas Gere, suffering from mumps. Post surgeon Dr. Alfred Muller had other patients under his care, and some soldiers were required as hospital orderlies. This left only 22 effectives to repel any Indian attack—but history has shown how well sick men can fight when about to lose their lives. Gere had joined the 5th Minnesota as a private the preceding January, but was soon promoted to sergeant. On the same day his older brother was promoted to major in the same regiment, Gere was commissioned as a 2nd lieutenant. With fighting rebs in mind, he was disappointed at being posted to Fort Ridgely, "away in the wilderness," where the average number of windy days was, he wrote, "eight and one half" per week. His parents arrived for a visit during June, and shortly afterwards Gere received a sword and sash as a gift from his men. "Fortune seems to smile continually on me," he wrote in his journal, "is she reserving her frowns for the future?" Gere would be awarded the Medal of Honor in 1864 after capturing a Confederate flag at Nashville.

But on the night of August 18, things looked grim. Marsh and half his command had been killed, and refugees were pouring in. Gere wrote to Fort Snelling: "Capt Marsh left this post at 10½ this morning to prevent Indian depredations at the Lower Agency. Some of the men have returned—from them I learnt that Capt Marsh is killed and only thirteen of his company remaining. The Indians are killing the settlers and plundering the country, send reinforcements without delay."[12]

It was, Gere recalled, "a tale whose import in view of the possible consequences to the frightened and well nigh unprotected mass of humanity then there, [was] sufficient to appall the stoutest heart."[13] Ironically, the $71,000 annuity payment had arrived at Fort Ridgely about midday. One day earlier, and the "stoutest heart" would not have been put through such a test.

Under cover of dark, Private William Sturgis made for Fort Snelling by horse and wagon, covering the 125 miles in 18 hours. At St. Peter, he encountered Indian Agent "Major" Galbraith and the Renville Rangers who, in short order, were on a forced march back to Fort Ridgely. No doubt Galbraith was already conjuring up excuses for having left his post. Following the war, the *St. Paul Daily Press* would publish an article, "A Question of Responsibility." During the tenure of "Mr. Agent," the paper said, "families perished from starvation, cold and hunger, and inhuman neglect, while Indian traders and officials were growing fat and insolent on the spoils pillaged from the Indian."

Galbraith wrote back: "I can prove that never at any time in their history have the Sioux of the Mississippi been better supplied with provisions, clothing, implements, seeds and aids to plant than during my administration."[14] But these were only supplied to farmer Indians, causing friction and jealousy. Galbraith insisted he had requested additional troops that had never been sent. But he had not recruited the Renville Rangers for home defense.

Secretary of the Interior John Palmer Usher, after traveling to Minnesota, would state, "His continued presence there might possibly have been the means of averting the terrible calamity which so succeeded his departure ... the fact that the Agent—the only officer of the Government to whom they looked for the payment of their anxiously expected annuities, and for counsel and guidance in trouble—had taken most of the employees and able-bodied men in the neighborhood, and left the Indian country, was not well calculated to remove from their minds the impression that they had been abandoned by the government." Galbraith, however, would be exonerated by two congressional investigations.

Following Marsh's order to return, Lieutenant Sheehan was on his way back to Ridgely when he received a message from Gere: "Force your march returning. Captain Marsh and most of his command were killed yesterday at the Lower Agency. Little Crow and about 600 Sioux warriors are now approaching the fort and will undoubtedly attack us. About 250 refugees have arrived here for protection. The Indians are killing men, women and children."

Spare muskets were supplied to civilians who took position as pickets beyond the fort's boundaries. One saw something move in the darkness. A shot shattered the night. "Indians!" he shouted. "The scene that followed defied description." Gere wrote, "There were men in terror breaking through the windows to get inside." But no Indians appeared. Gere recalled civilians from the picket line and replaced them with soldiers. "Each moment's flight," he recalled, "was watched by the little garrison with desperate resolve."[15]

The following morning, August 19, anxious eyes peered to the west. Indians could be seen, some in wagons, others on foot and horseback. An attack now with Gere's few soldiers and a handful of armed civilians would almost certainly prove fatal, a repeat of the frightful slaughter of men, women and children by Creek Indians at Fort Mims in 1813. But a wave of relief swept Ridgely when the Indians were seen to move off. As has been seen, the younger warriors, not heeding the advice of wiser heads like Little Crow, Big Eagle and Mankato, had decided to attack New Ulm instead.

To acclamations of joy, Sheehan arrived with the 50 men of Company C after an all-night march. No Indians were to be seen, giving his exhausted men a chance to down arms and catch much-needed rest. Being 1st lieutenant, Sheehan took command from a tired and still ailing Gere. Born in 1836, Timothy Sheehan had immigrated from Ireland at the age of 14, and before the war farmed near Albert Lea, Minnesota. Like Gere, he had risen from the ranks to become an officer, promoted to first lieutenant on March 9, 1862. Following the Dakota War, he would fight Confederates in various campaigns, rising to the rank of lieutenant colonel. Mustered out in 1865, he was appointed deputy U.S. marshal and took part in the Battle of Sugar Point against the Chippewas in 1898. While there were no Indian casualties, seven government men were killed, and among the 16 wounded was 62-year-old Timothy Sheehan.[16]

All eyes scanned the terrain around Fort Ridgely for any sign of attack, but none came. The action that day was taking place at New Ulm, 10 miles to the southeast, where buildings burned and bullets flew. As twilight came on, more shouts of joy were heard as the Renville Rangers marched into Fort Ridgely. Galbraith was with them, but command of the Rangers fell to their elected lieutenant, the very able James Gorman. Apparently they could get along without Galbraith's indispensible leadership after all. With them was Lieutenant Culver's squad of six men. Sheehan now had about 180 fighting men all up—50 Renville Rangers, 52 men of Company B, 50 men of Company C, and Sutler Randall had charge of about 25 civilians under arms.

Sergeant John Jones

Artillery Sergeant John Jones performed heroically during Fort Ridgely's defense, and would be promoted to captain as a result (author's collection).

had drilled members of Company B in the fine points of artillery fire. With the looming threat, he now formed crews to handle three guns. Jones and veteran artilleryman Dennis O'Shea took charge of a 6-pounder covering the fort's southwest corner. Sergeant James McGrew of Company B took charge of one 12-pounder mountain howitzer, and John Whipple, a civilian artillery veteran of the Mexican War, took charge of another. For the moment, Jones refrained from manning his three remaining guns. A loose cannon in the hands of amateurs could well do more harm than good, so more men were trained as back-up crews.

The First Battle of Fort Ridgely

Early that afternoon, August 20, the shout went up, "Indians!" All eyes peered to the west—exactly as Little Crow wished. The chief sat there on a black pony, just out of musket range, signaling for a parley. But no one dared make the first move. Then the Indians' true motives were revealed with a

3-volley blast from the northern ravine, the signal for a general assault. The whooping Indians broke from cover and dashed for the north and northeast perimeters. Lieutenant Sheehan, out on a scout with 20 men, made a dash for the fort. Riding a mule, the lieutenant found himself overtaken by fleet-footed infantrymen. The Dakotas "were in hot pursuit of us when we entered the fort," recalled Private Orlando McFall. The Indians occupied an old stable and took cover around log huts behind the stone barracks.

Sergeant Jones' wife, Maria, "in the family way," was in a hut a short distance to the west. Having already taken her three children to the barracks, Maria had returned to retrieve possessions when the Indians attacked. A warrior fired through the window but missed as she ducked behind an iron stove.

John Whipple's howitzer opened fire on the Indians from the northeast corner. At the same time, McGrew's gun was wheeled around at the northwest corner and aimed to the east. The combined fire of the two howitzers, along with musket fire, raked the Indian positions and drove warriors back into the northeastern ravine. With this respite, Mrs. Jones dashed from the hut to be reunited with her children in the barracks. But, traumatized, she gave birth to a stillborn child the following morning.

The Indians took fire from Jones' 6-pounder, along with musket fire from Company B and the Renville Rangers. "The reception they received when they got in range sent them flying down over the bank to the Minnesota bottom," Private McFall recalled, but Indian fire from the east "was sweeping the parade ground like a hail storm." The soldiers took refuge on the second story of the stone barracks, packed with civilians, "singing and praying and crying and screaming." Little Crow could hear this from a distance: "We were teasing the whites, shooting them through the windows of the fort and hearing them scream and cry like babies."[17] But in fact, few Indian bullets were hitting home. They could not see the defenders through the windows, according to Lightning Blanket, and they "were not sure we were killing any."

The soldiers "did not stop to shove the windows up but beat them out with the butts of our muskets," recalled McFall. "Pandemonium and hell now reigned."[18] Three men worked each of the 14 windows in the large barracks room. While two men stood on either side ramming powder and ball down their muzzleloaders, a third man stayed crouched on the floor. When handed a loaded gun, he "would peak over the window sill and let fly, sometimes at random and sometimes at a redskin." Ezmon Earle recalled that each time an Indian fired, "they uttered the war whoop" which was "blood curdling" and more frightening than the sound of bullets smashing into windows, doors and walls.

A shower of burning arrows arched through the sky. One flaming shaft "struck in the shingles of the officers' quarters and a blaze started to spread," recalled Joseph Coursolle. The mixed-blood corporal, known as "The Owl" to the Dakotas, was married to a white woman, and now fought with the troops. Ordered up a ladder to put the fire out, he worked hard amidst flying bullets. "Never did an axe swing faster than mine as I whacked out the fire." He landed with a thud after rolling off the roof rather than waste time using the ladder.[19] No principal buildings were destroyed by fire, but smoke billowed from outer cabins as flames took hold.

The siege settled down to long-range gunfire, and the fort's poor layout came into play. The powder magazines were some distance off on the open prairie, and the artillery ammunition was running low. A handful of volunteers made it there and back several times carrying shells. But, once safely stored behind the barracks' stone walls, they had to be moved across the exposed parade ground to the guns. Jones, standing on the barracks porch, ordered a pair of cowering German brothers to move the shells. "It is not for you to give civilians instructions," was the reply. Jones whipped his sword from its sheath and repeated the order—all to no avail. The worthy sergeant crouched down and commenced rolling shells across the parade ground himself. The brothers, now humiliated, moved from cover and helped roll shells to O'Shea's howitzer on the northwest corner.

Dusk came on. The assaults had failed; the fort was still intact. But the old, small stable outside the northeast corner was still in Indian hands. Sheehan ordered Whipple to remove the problem. Two shells landed on the stable, igniting the hay, and the whole lot went up in flames. Ranger George Dagenais, firing from the bakery, wounded one Indian attempting to flee. Dagenais and Joseph La Tour dashed out and, with war whoops, threw the suffering brave back into the flames. They dashed back: "I kill him one, I kill him one," yelled an exultant Dagenais.[20]

It had been a dispiriting day for Little Wolf. The plan had been to take the fort with the first mad rush. It was the first time he had been on the receiving end of artillery fire. And then there was his unruly warriors' failed assault against New Ulm the day before. The Indians withdrew to the Lower Agency for the night. About 400 braves had taken part. Lightning Blanket later complained: "If Little Crow had attacked when the signal volley was given, the soldiers who shot at us would have been killed."[21] Better coordination was required. The chiefs would need to think again.

Heavy rain fell during the night. The defenders saw no sign of hostiles, but a strange wailing noise was heard from the west. What was this? Some Indian ploy to unnerve the defenders before tomorrow's assault? A shell was sent flying towards the noise. A brief, explosive flash was seen amidst the night foliage, but the peculiar wailing continued. A squad was dispatched to investigate. They soon reappeared carrying a half-crazed white woman who had become lost in the woods while trying to find the fort.[22]

"No Indians appeared the next day," recalled Corporal Courselle, "and we worked feverishly at the defenses piling up stones, logs, bags of feed, hunks of sod—anything we could get our hands on that would stop lead and arrows." A detail went out to bring fresh water from Ridgely's usual source, a spring below the bluffs. The water tank had been destroyed, however, and the water poisoned. Sheehan immediately ordered a well dug on the parade ground, and a dozen willing hands went to work. "The well was completed about 2:30 a.m. on the morning of the 22nd," recalled Private McFall, "so they were failed in their purpose." An unused 12-pounder gun was hauled onto the parade ground to be kept in reserve. Sergeant Bishop, the young survivor from Marsh's command, was put in charge.[23] The last two unmanned cannons were also loaded and placed on standby. Every gun could well be needed in a last-ditch stand, and fresh gun crews were put through the paces of load and fire.

The Indians had been driven off with only two whites killed and seven wounded, but Sheehan was not pleased with the way all had performed. Joseph De Camp's civilian company was ordered to the parade ground, where the lieutenant "proceeded to make us a speech in which he called us all the mean names such as cowards and sneaks, etc. that he could think of," recalled Ezmon Earle. "I was surprised for I was not aware of sneaking, but I afterwards learned that many of them had deserted their posts and gone upstairs with the women and children."

"During the night, several people, remnants of once thriving families, arrived at the post in a most miserable condition," reported Sheehan, "some wounded—severely burned—having made their escape from their dwellings, which were fired by the Indians. The people in the immediate vicinity fled to the fort for protection, and were organized and armed, as far as practicable, to aid in the defense."[24]

All prayed for help to arrive. The following day dawned with no enemy in sight, but during the night, Little Crow had been reinforced. Four hundred Wahpeton and Sisseton Santee Dakotas from Big Stone Lake had arrived, doubling his force. "Early the next day," Lightning Blanket recalled, "we started with about 800 warriors.... We did not stop to eat this time, but each carried something to eat in his legging sash and ate it in the middle of the day, while fighting."[25]

White prisoner Sarah Wakefield recalled the procession: "The prairie that morning was alive with Indians, all in high spirits, and confident of taking Fort Ridgely. They were either overdressed *or not dressed at all;* their horses were covered with ribbons, bells, or feathers, all jingling, tinkling as we rode along, the Indians singing their war songs. It was a grand but savage sight to see so many great, powerful men mounted on their bedecked animals going to war. Many of the men were entirely naked with the exception of their breech cloth, their bodies painted and ridiculously ornamented."[26]

The Second Battle of Fort Ridgely

The plan of assault was the same as on the 20th, commencing with "three big shots from the north," recalled Lightning Blanket, "followed by a coordinated rush of men on the east, south and west all at the same time. Little Crow had given strict orders on account of the first failure." And perhaps, with 800 warriors, the same basic plan may have worked this time round. But relatively small events can sometimes destroy the best-laid plans of mice and men. As the warriors grouped for the attack, Eliphalet Richardson stumbled onto the scene. The settler had ridden from Glencoe in McCloud County to Fort Ridgely to get the latest news. This came in the form of three fatal shots from Indian muskets. "This the men on the south and west heard and took for the signal," recalled Lightning Blanket, "ran up to the top of the hill, and began shooting." But those on the north and east had heard no such signal; thus, once again, no simultaneous assault took place. "By the time the others had commenced, the big guns were fired at them [those attacking late from the south and west], who then ran back under the hill, by this time all [cannons] were shooting, most of all of us being hid."

"There were many more warriors in this attack than there were in the first battle," recalled Corporal Coursolle. "There seemed to be thousands. They were ten to our one and we knew we must stop them or every person in the fort would be killed—except the women. And we knew they would rather die than face the fate of prisoners."

Platoons commanded by sergeants had distinct sections of the perimeter to defend. Ezmon Earle was with De Camp's disgraced citizen company, now deployed along the log cabins to the immediate north. The Indians were able to get within 50 yards, concealed by the leafy northern ravine. Once firing broke out, De Camp walked along the line with his Sharp's breechloader in hand. "Boys, I am ordered to shoot the first man who leaves his post without orders," he bellowed, "and I'll do it, by God."

When the Indians launched their belated southern assault, Earle and three others were ordered away to help defend the south side of the H.Q. building. Here they were exposed to enemy fire "without even a spear of grass to hide behind. I could simply hug the ground and trust luck." Ordered back to rejoin his squad, now fighting on the eastern perimeter, he found himself no better off. His "only protection was in shooting so well that the Indians would not dare expose themselves long enough to take good aim." He found the Indians working their way in close, their heads camouflaged "with turbans of grass and wildflowers."

Earl realized one Indian was targeting him in particular, and exposed himself to shoot back, only to feel a vicious thud against his gunstock. In the heat of battle, he did not realize the same bullet had smashed the third finger of his right hand. Another defender, seeing the wound, pulled him down. "I was bleeding considerably and the bone was broken," Earle recalled, "yet it hadn't begun to pain me." But it soon did, badly. Dr. Muller dressed the wound with "a white powder" that relieved the pain considerably.

Now unable to hold a musket, the young man was put on observation duty by Sergeant Frank Blackmer with instructions to report enemy movements. But then Blackmer himself was shot in the face. The vicious wound was not fatal, but he joined the others under Muller's care with his teeth knocked out and his tongue nearly severed. The doctor was ably assisted by women who not only cared for the wounded, but also melted spent Indian balls into bullet molds, and shaved down oversize balls to fit the garrison's muskets. "There never was a nobler band of heroines lived than those women were," recalled Private McFall.

One wit suggested the Indians receive their $71,000 annuity in the form of a cannon blast, the gold coins making ideal grapeshot. The idea for the most expensive single artillery shot in American history did not gain ground.

With "demonic yells" the Indians took possession of the sutler's store to the west and the large main stable beyond the New Ulm Road to the south. From these perilously close positions they kept up a constant sniping fire. More Indians were soon seen moving from the north towards the southwestern ravines. McGrew, stationed with his gun on the northeast corner, reported the move to Sergeant Jones. The 24-pounder was moved to the fort's main entrance between the commissary building and officers' quarters, and a few shells were lobbed towards Indians gathering in the west. The hot fire from the sutler's store and stables, meanwhile, splintered "almost every linear foot of timber" along the top of the barricades protecting O'Shea's howitzer at the southwest corner.

The doctor's wife, Eliza Muller, had been an inspiration to the garrison, caring for the wounded, distributing food and drink. Now she threw her weight behind Jones' gun and helped push the hefty weapon into the surgeon's quarters. On his command, she pulled the rope opening the outer door, and the big gun boomed.[27] One shell exploded in part of the long stable, then the warriors took refuge in "a large mule barn," recalled Margaret Hern, who, despite orders to stay clear of windows, could not resist watching the action. Jones fired again, "blowing up the barn and setting the hay on fire. The air was full of legs, arms, and bodies which fell back into the flames."[28]

The Indians quickly fell back to the ravines. The big guns barked again and Ben Randall saw a shell hit his sutler's store, which went up in flames. Again the assailants scurried for the safety of the leafy ravines.

"We could hear the cannon from the Fort, and see the smoke from the burning buildings," recalled Sarah Wakefield, behind the Dakota lines, "and we could see the Indians as they fired, run down into the woods and reload, then rush backwards and forward. I expected every minute some one would return and in their rage destroy us, for they were nearly all drunk at this time."[29]

A mixed-blood Renville Ranger heard orders being yelled in the Dakota tongue. He told Jones to expect an all-out assault from a ravine spur only 150 yards from the southwest corner. Jones rapped out orders, and McGrew's 24-pounder was moved south, where it was loaded with a double dose of lethal canister. Nearby, O'Shea's howitzer held its southwest position, deployed behind a 100-foot-long barricade. Sergeant Bishop's reserve gun was moved to the southeast corner and angled to the right, straight at the ravine spur.

Jones addressed his gun crews. If Indians crossed the barricade, citizen soldiers were to retreat to the barracks to defend the women and children. "We are soldiers," he said to the enlisted men. It was their duty to "fire the gun until the Indians reach it, and then spike it with a file."

The Indians were seen gathering for the assault. "Little Crow didn't know how far our guns could carry," recalled Coursolle. "At the instant the Indians joined forces, all three cannons roared. The shells tore great holes in the ranks of the warriors and the crashing boom of the twenty-four pounder rumbled and echoed up and down the river bluffs."

"The gallant conduct of the men at the guns paralyzed them," reported Sheehan, "and compelled them to withdraw, after one of the most determined attacks ever made by Indians on a military post."[30]

"But for the cannon I think we would have taken the fort," recalled Big Eagle. "The soldiers fought us so bravely we thought there were many more of them than there were."[31]

Despite these losses, the Indians kept the garrison under sniper fire and, obscured by smoke from burning outer cabins, tried to move closer. "Indians with grass and flowers bound on their heads creep like snakes up to the fort," recalled Margaret Hern.

"During the day many small buildings were burned," Lightning Blanket observed, "and we tried to burn the big ones with fire arrows."[32] At 7:30 a flight of flaming shafts lit the sky. By now the roofs had dried out under the summer sun, but only one arrow actually caused a fire, and the Indians let out with "one of those blood freezing infernal yells that I imagine I can hear now as I write," recalled Private McFall. But 15 men with axes and hammers tackled the burning roof from inside the barracks attic. The burning debris was cut away, and the flames were soon quenched. Other intruding arrowheads were beaten outwards, and the flaming shafts slid away. As the Indian fire slackened, men went to work digging up sod and carrying it to the roof where, crouching low, they layered it over the flammable timber shingles, a ploy used by Indian fighters back east in much earlier days.

Twilight came on. Little Crow, wounded from a shell blast during the day, knew there was little point in continuing this battle. Even with 800 warriors, he had not been able to take the "Soldiers' House" as the Dakotas called Fort Ridgely. But he had certainly done much damage: "The buildings comprising the garrison proper are still up," reported Sheehan, "but they are very much wrecked. All of the out-buildings, except the guard-house and magazines, are entirely destroyed. Most of the mules and oxen belonging to the quartermaster's department were taken by the Indians, and we are left with a scanty supply of transportation."[33] The defenders, however, had suffered only one killed and eight wounded.[34] Accurate Dakota casualties are unknown. Lieutenant John Gorman and his Renville Rangers were praised by both Sheehan and Jones for their "veteran"-like conduct.

Even after this second assault on Fort Ridgely, more refugees arrived. This included Helen Carrothers and her two children, who had seen Clarissa Henderson burned alive. Since making good their escape, the trio had roamed for eight days in a pitiful and starving condition before approaching the fort in broad daylight in company with another male refugee. After spotting them through field glasses, soldiers came out to bring them in. "Two of the soldiers were sent back to the fort to procure me some clothing," recalled Helen. "The old skirt the squaw gave me in the cornfield and which I had used to bind my girl to my back was ragged when I first got it and was now nothing but strips. All the covering I had was the band of the skirt buttoned about my waist. But soon a soldier returned with a gray blanket, and in this I wrapped myself and soon made a joyous and triumphant entry into Fort Ridgely." The starving refugees were unwisely given "all we could eat," which caused immediate severe illness. Dr. Muller "despaired of the life of my little girl." He said they should have only been given "nothing but rice water at first and then small rations of simple but nourishing food." Three days later, little Althea was still gravely ill, and Muller told Sheehan that the illness, combined with exposure, meant "nothing could save her from death."

But Helen Carrothers had other ideas. Despite blistered, sore feet, "I insisted on getting up and going outside of the fort to search for the proper plants, herbs and roots which I knew the old medicine man would use in such a case." Dr. Muller, however, "pooh-poohed at my efforts." Both mother and daughter consumed the potion: "To his astonishment the next day the child was evidently much better, and in three days, though still weak, she was playing about the fort." In one week, both mother and daughter were in apparent good health, "although it took months to recover from the fearful mental strain which I had undergone."[35]

Following the second repulse from Fort Ridgely, Little Crow's thoughts returned to "the Place Where There is a Cottonwood Grove on the River," as the Dakotas called New Ulm. The defenders there had no cannon. But as the defeated Indians camped and cooked beef at Three Mile Creek, there was, once again, division about their best next move. Some wanted to renew the attack on the fort. Little Crow "was angry," recalled Thunder Blanket, "and said he would take the ones who wanted to go and capture New Ulm. He left the camp that night and started for New Ulm with part of the men, I should think about half of them, 400."[36]

In New Ulm, Colonel Flandrau continued his preparations for defense. He had about 300 men able to fight, but also over 1,000 nervous noncombatants: women, children and unarmed men. They were crowded into the buildings lining the barricaded area of the main street. Men from one company had left New Ulm and returned to protect their families in Blue Earth County. Rumors had circulated that the Winnebagos were also on the warpath.[37] But, in fact, only a handful had joined the Dakotas, the tribe as a whole remaining at peace.

The Second Battle of New Ulm

The booming of cannon from Fort Ridgely had been heard on August 22. Had the post fallen? Flandrau had no idea. "Saturday, the 23rd of August," he recalled, "opened bright and beautiful, and early in the morning we saw column after column of smoke rise in the direction of the fort, each smoke being nearer than the last."[38] The Indians were burning buildings and haystacks as they approached New Ulm. A lookout spotted warriors on the opposite (north) side of the river, the same side as Fort Ridgely. Flandrau dispatched Lieutenant William Huey with 75 men to reconnoiter and protect the ferry, two miles to the southwest. Indians on the north bank would have to cross at this point before doubling back for an assault on the town.

Not all were happy with Flandrau's decision. If concealed Indians approached along the south bank from the northwest, Huey's detachment would be riding in the wrong direction. They should stay in town, some insisted, and prepare for defense. Flandrau's order stood, however, and he later claimed the decision to cross the river to the north bank was Huey's "mistake." But others, like Frederick Fritsche, riding with Huey, said he was following orders, and Jacob Nix claimed: "One of the biggest mistakes was to order a company to cross the Minnesota River in order to fight the Indians."[39] Huey rode out and crossed the river, leaving about 20 men to guard the ferry.

As they rode north, they saw Indians in the distance set fire to a house, then a burst of gunfire was heard from New Ulm. The town was under attack. Huey turned back to find the ferry in enemy hands, the 20 guards having scurried back to safety. Gunfire was exchanged with Indians on the south bank, wounding three of Huey's men, one badly. With no way of recrossing the river, Huey ordered a withdrawal eastward to St. Peter. The fiasco thus removed 50 precious men from New Ulm's defense. This left Flandrau with about 250 men carrying a mixed bag of firearms to hold the town against an estimated 650 Dakotas.

As many feared, the Indians had struck New Ulm after approaching under cover along the south bank. Flandrau deployed his companies facing the sloping bluff to the westward, rear of the town. But many of his men were poorly armed with shotguns, only effective at close range. The Dakotas descended the slope, fanning to left and right till they covered the militia's entire front. Then: "Down came the Indians in the bright sunlight," Flandrau recalled, "galloping, running, yelling, and gesticulating in their most fiendish manner." The whites fired a few ineffectual volleys, and then "sudden panic seized our men in the trenches and those on horseback," recalled Captain Theodore Potter, "and together they made a wild rush for the center of the city, followed by the Indians yelling and whooping louder and fiercer than ever."[40] Potter had his horse shot from under him during the retreat, and a few others were killed and wounded. Some later claimed that an order to fall back had initiated the panic. Fleeing men passed the outlying homes, well spread out, and made for the barricades protecting the town center. The breastworks included wagons, grain sacks, farming equipment and anything else on hand. They were backed up by a final redoubt of wagons connected by timber planking, lined up on either side of the main street.

Flandrau felt the enemy may well have won the day if they had pressed the assault. But they slowed down. Perhaps the white retreat was a ploy to lure them into a trap?—a ruse often used by the Indians themselves. Instead of pressing on, they spread out through the outer structures. Most took possession of the southern end of the main street below the barricades, and began torching abandoned buildings they had no use for. "This delay of an hour on the part of the Indians was our salvation," recalled one defender, "but by noon they were burning houses in nearly all directions on the outskirts of town." Arrows as well as bullets rained in upon the barricades. Five-year-old Henry Gluth, out to see the action, was hit in the back of the neck by a feathered shaft. He survived to tell the story, the scar providing a good talking point for the rest of his life.

Some defenders, cut off, had taken refuge in outbuildings. Captain Saunders and 15 men occupied a partly built brick building on the town's northwest. It came under fire and Saunders was badly wounded. But by now the defenders behind the barricades had regrouped and rallied. Their women and children's lives were at stake as well as their own. A detachment of about 40 men set out to rescue Saunders' party. Under fire, the Indians fell back. Carrying the wounded commander, all made it back behind the barricades.

Rudolph Leonhart described the scene at noon: "Through the smoke of the burning houses I saw the almost naked Indians moving in a zigzag fashion to dodge the aim of our troops. It didn't require a vivid imagination to see them as devils wandering through the flames of hell." A mounted warrior draped in a red blanket charged in, rifle in hand. Leonhart, unarmed, wanted a gun to "stuff his mouth with lead." But the warriors sprung backwards in a somersault, hit by a sharpshooter alongside Leonhart. He saw some whites "hasten forward, capture the weapons and decorations of the fallen warrior and return triumphantly to camp." Other Indians dashed in and carried the body away. As buildings went up in flames, Leonhart felt the enraged Indians "didn't seem to realize that they hurt themselves more than us, as with every house that collapsed into ashes they destroyed a position from which they could have been able to launch an attack on us."[41]

At the same time, Indians were driven from a home a short distance outside the barricades. The man leading the assault, Daniel Shillock, was the only casualty, wounded in the leg. "We held several other outposts, being brick buildings, outside the barricades," recalled Flandrau, "which we loopholed and found very effective in holding the Indians aloof." Otto Barth, editor of the *New Ulm Pioneer*, had lingered during the first retreat to get in a good shot or two, but then realized mounted warriors had cut him off. He took refuge in the schoolhouse and opened fire with his shotgun—a bad mistake. The warriors set the building alight, and Barth decided to take his chances in the cellar rather than be driven out and shot down. He would be discovered the following day, still alive, but he died from extensive burns a few days later.[42]

"On the second plateau, there was an old Don Quixote windmill," recalled Flandrau, "with an immense tower and sail-arms about seventy-five feet long, which occupied a commanding position, and had been taken possession of by a company of about thirty men, who called themselves the Le Sueur Tigers, most of whom had rifles. They barricaded themselves with sacks of flour and wheat, loopholed the 4-story building and kept the savages at a respectful distance from the west side of town." Volunteers ran back and forth delivering ammunition to the defenders. "The wind Mill was a very safe place," recalled defender W.H. Hazzard, who recalled only 13 defenders commanded by Lieutenant George Stewart. The tall structure "located on a hill gave us a beautiful view of the country and Strong defense of the town."

Spent Indian rifle balls dug from mill flour sacks were found to be the "regulation Minie bullet." Some were brought back for Flandrau's inspection. "I confess I was astonished when I saw the bullets," he recalled, "for I knew the Indians had no such arms." This backed rumors that Missouri Confederates had stirred up the Indians and supplied them with weapons. But, upon reflection, Flandrau realized Captain Marsh's dead soldiers must have been the source. Despite accusations to be flung around by press and politicians, "I do not believe the Confederates had any hand in the revolt of these Indians."[43] No evidence of any Southern conspiracy was ever found.

The 2-story brick Forster Building, containing the post office, was just across the street from the main barricade. Defenders stuffed feather mattresses into the windows and fired through loopholes knocked through the walls. No doubt the safety of women and children sheltering in the basement gave extra drive to the spirited defense.

Amidst the gun smoke and din of musket fire, a lookout spotted what appeared to be a relief column under the Stars and Stripes approaching from the south. Flandrau's second-in-command, Captain William Dodd, felt these reinforcements could well need a helping hand. He suggested to Lieutenant John Meagher that they go out with volunteers to bring them in. Indians were firing from houses just a few blocks in that direction, Meagher pointed out. Such a venture was not worth the risk. Dodd, however, gave a "short, impassioned speech," and about 20 volunteers stepped forward.

The rash party dashed on foot from behind their protecting barricade, led by Dodd and Sergeant James Shoemaker, both riding horses. "The small volunteer force rushed forward with a cheer, hardly coming within the Indian lines before receiving a deadly volley," recalled Dr. Asa Daniels. Dodd was hit with five balls but still managed to turn his horse around. The animal, despite being shot, carried Dodd back towards his own lines. Shoemaker's horse was killed, while the sergeant himself escaped unscathed on foot. Two more men were mortally wounded as the volunteers scrambled back to safety. Dodd's horse collapsed as it reached Kiesling's blacksmith shop just outside the barricade. The bleeding captain was helped into the shop and placed on a bed, where he urged those in the lower story to leave him and join those firing from upstairs.

Coming under heavy fire, the building was soon abandoned, and Dodd was carried behind the barricade. "There was little that could be done," recalled Dr. Daniels, "as he was in dying condition, surviving only about one hour. He appreciated his condition, and met it courageously, giving me messages to his wife and Bishop Whipple, with the utmost coolness and consideration."[44] According to Daniels, the supposed reinforcements were actually Indians dressed in plundered white clothing, and Dodd had taken the bait. Fortunately for the volunteers, a more lethal repulse had been avoided because some warriors had fired too early.

As bullets flew, wounded men fell back from the barricade. Creszentia Schneider lived with her 15-year-old daughter near the town center, and her home became a hospital. Creszentia's towels, sheets, bedding and even her clothes were cut up to make bandages as she and others went to work.[45]

As the wind was driving from the south, the warriors were able to edge forward under cover of smoke blown from burning houses. "His [the enemy's] approach was constant," recalled Flandrau, "and about 2 o'clock a roaring conflagration was raging on both sides of the street, and the prospect looked discouraging."⁴⁶ A lookout perched on the Crone building saw a party of over 70 warriors gathering in a copse of trees in South German Park, about three blocks from the barricades.

"Judge," said Asa White, an old frontiersman, "if this goes on the Indians will bag us in about two hours."

"It looks that way. What remedy have you to suggest?"

"We must make for the cottonwood timber."

Flandrau shook his head. The cottonwood timber was 2½ miles away, and they had over 1000 noncombatants on hand. "White, they would slaughter us like sheep should we undertake such a movement. Our strongest hold is in this town, and if you will get together fifty volunteers, I will drive the Indians out of the lower town and the greatest danger will be passed."

Despite having received a buckshot wound to the face, Captain Potter stepped forward. He had been treated and given a "little stimulus" by Dr. Henry McMahon. How many volunteers joined the assault party is not known, but Potter claimed 100.

They "sallied out, cheering and yelling in a manner which would have done credit to the wildest Comanches." But the painted and feathered enemy were closer than they thought. Between 75 and 100 warriors, some mounted and others on foot, were in a depression only 1½ blocks from the barricades. Flandrau ordered two houses burned to make a clearing, the smoke helping conceal his movements. A white man rushed from one house, to be shot and wounded by Indian gunfire, and Flandrau, seizing the opportunity, ordered three men out to bring him in, thus distracting the Indians' attention. "Colonel Flandrau followed this feint by rushing with his whole party out of the smoke to the rear of the lot, taking the Indians there, as it were, in their rear and flank," recalled Chief-of-Staff Salmon Buell. At about 100 feet, both sides opened fire. "It was a bloody, close-range, desperate fight," recalled Potter. "A number on both sides were killed. Colonel Flandrau's clothes were in many places pierced by bullets, and his gunstock also."⁴⁷

The Indians turned and fled. The pursuit took place for over half a mile, the volunteers firing when they could, having to reload on the move. Once clear of the burning houses, Flandrau ordered a halt, and the men took cover behind a cluster of fallen saw logs. The Indians turned and fired back from tree trunks, rocks and ditches. Dr. Daniels noted that they "fought with the utmost boldness and ferocity, and with the utmost skill and caution from every hollow and grass patch, and from every house and hillock or log."⁴⁸ They returned "an incessant fire upon us whenever a head or hand showed itself above the logs," recalled Flandrau. But the Indian advance was checked, and Flandrau sent men back to burn every building, haystack, and fence that could provide cover for enemy marksmen between them and the barricades. Fresh flames broke out and smoke billowed into a sky already red from the setting sun. As twilight came on, the gunfire petered out, and the victorious volunteers made their way back between smoldering ruins that had once been fine houses. "The day was won," recalled Flandrau, "the Indians not daring to charge us over open country."[49]

Considering this close and frantic encounter, the white losses were light, with about four dead and several wounded. One noted fatality was Newell Houghton, considered by Flandrau "the best shot and deer hunter in all the Northwest."

Flames spread by the New Ulm men destroyed most structures outside the town center. But Turner Hall was still firmly in Indian hands. From that strongpoint the warriors "rained their bullets uninterruptedly towards the windmill," recalled Jacob Nix. But the Indians were soon driven out and Turner Hall also went up in flames.

"A new order greeted our ears," recalled W.H. Hazzard. "The commander of the post orders the Wind Mill burned that brought Sadness to our hearts it had been our strong defense during the day and we said to the Lieut—increase our numbers to 25 and we would hold the Mill and defend it at all Hazards.—Again the order came to burn the mill and we had to obey."[50] Hazzard climbed to the upper story and ignited piles of hay. The defenders abandoned their picturesque makeshift fortress and retreated to the brick post office, where the heroes found an "elegant supper" awaiting them. Leonhart watched the windmill and eventually saw "one of the most awesome events of my life," as the blazing "framework stripped of every cover now rose into the air like a gigantic chandelier." As the mill and other buildings burned, Jacob Nix recalled, "high towards the firmament whirled bursts of fire spreading afar their light, turning night into day. A spectacle so terrible and frightful, it is impossible to express in words, yet it is impressed so indelibly as a horrible memory on the memory of surviving eyewitnesses."

There was no guarantee the enemy were beaten. During the night, rifle pits were dug outside the barricades. Some wanted to abandon the town, regardless of what others did, and head for Mankato. Flandrau, however, refused such a move. Even if they were not killed trying to escape, a fight may result, and men would be forced to risk their lives with a rescue party. One man, however, slipped away during the night. He was discovered next morning "scalped, decapitated, and otherwise horribly mutilated."

"In the morning the attack was renewed," recalled Flandrau in his official report, "but not with much vigor, and subsided about noon."[51] According to Theodore Potter, a substantial number were involved, "beating Indian drums and other instruments, mingled with war whoops to lead them on to victory and slaughter." But they were scared off with a volley and the firing of cannon from each end of the barricade. How had this happened, since the defenders had no cannon? "Stovepipe mounted on wheels," according to Potter.⁵² Gunpowder was packed between blacksmiths' anvils and touched off to produce the boom and smoke.⁵³

During midmorning, Indians were seen moving quickly from the river bottoms to disappear over the bluffs. Then lookouts reported an armed force approaching from the direction of the lower ferry. "What could this mean?" mused Rudolph Leonhart. "Were they hatching some new tricks?" But an officer rode out and returned at the gallop with joyous news. The new arrivals were 150 well-armed men recruited from Nicollet and Sibley Counties under Captain Eugene St. Julien Cox. Riding with them were some of Lieutenant Huey's men, who had been cut off at the ferry the day before. Huey had run into Cox during his enforced trek to St. Peter, and some of his men rode back to New Ulm to find out what had become of their families.

Overcome with relief and pent-up emotions, men rushed out and "embraced one another even though they were strangers," recalled Leonhart. "Tears of joy rolled down many a bearded cheek and the expressions of joy were endless."

"We burned about one hundred and ninety buildings," recalled Flandrau, "many of them substantial and valuable structures. The whites lost some fourteen killed and fifty or sixty wounded." (Other sources place dead defenders at between 20 and 34.) Flandrau could not put a number on the Indian losses, but said they "found ten dead Indians in burned houses, and in a chaparral where they escaped the notice of their friends." Judging by the engagement overall, "their casualties must have equaled, if not exceeded ours."⁵⁴

What best to do now? With 150 extra guns for protection, it was deemed wise to evacuate New Ulm—or what was left of it. Of over 200 buildings, only about 30 remained. And these were packed with men, women and children living in what Flandrau considered hopelessly unhealthy conditions. But Dr. Daniels disagreed. He considered sanitary conditions reasonable, and Colonel Sibley was known to be on his way with a strong relief force. Best to stay put. If they moved out, a section of dense forest lay ahead where "had a few Indians attacked, a panic and massacre would have followed."⁵⁵ But food was a problem. Much had been lost in burned mills, and Cox's battalion meant 150 extra mouths to feed.

On Monday morning, August 25, "We made of a train of 153 wagons, which had largely composed our barricades," recalled Flandrau, "loaded them with women and children, and about eighty wounded men, and started. A more heart-rending procession was never witnessed in America"—witnessed by Charles Flandrau, that is. Despite the refugees' genuine hardship, no doubt Cherokees on the "Trail of Tears" in 1838 would see things differently. About 4,000 had died on their enforced trek to the west.

Mankato, about 30 miles away, was Flandrau's destination rather than St. Paul. This avoided having to cross the Minnesota River, a prime ambush point, with up to 2,000 people. About 15 miles down the track, at Crisp's farm, the wagons rolled on while Flandrau halted with a large force to act as a rear guard. But no Indians were seen, and the caravan arrived safely in Mankato that same evening. "Many have left or lost all," lamented Salmon Buell, "even their nearest and dearest ones ... lie buried without coffin, book or bell where they died, with naught to mark the spot." And the survivors "are going where? God knows—anywhere away from the Indians!"[56] Flandrau ordered the volunteers released from duty, and the settlers dispersed to various towns over the next few days.

7

WE SHALL NEED MORE GUNS

"The Sioux Indians upon our western frontier have risen in large bodies, attacked the settlements, and are murdering men, women and children. The rising appears concerted and extends from Fort Ripley to the southern boundary of the state." So opened the proclamation issued by Governor Alexander Ramsey, one of those who had profited while doing all in his power to diminish Indian lands. At the same time, August 21, the defenders at Fort Ridgely were building barricades following the first assault. The telegraph wire hummed the bad news to Washington, D.C. "Send the Third Regiment Minnesota Volunteers," ordered General-in-Chief Henry Halleck. Those troops had surrendered to Confederate forces at the First Battle of Murfreesboro in July, and been paroled for exchange with rebel prisoners. This excluded the Minnesota bluecoats from bearing arms against the South, but not from fighting Indians in their home state.[1] As yet, however, the exchange had not taken place.[2]

Ramsey called the Minnesota militia to action. They were to report with arms, horses and provisions to "the officer commanding the expedition now moving up the Minnesota River to the scene of hostilities."[3]

The officer commanding was former Minnesota governor Henry Hastings Sibley. Ramsey had received news of the revolt on August 19, and that same day appointed his old friend and political rival as militia colonel and expedition commander. Although the 51-year-old Sibley had no military experience, he accepted the role—but soon wished he had not. His troubles commenced straight away: "The arm, called the Austrian musket, furnished us, is a very poor affair. Many of them will not burst a cap," he complained to Ramsey. "Several thousand of the cartridges sent are utterly unfitted for the guns, and I have sent them back by boat.... We shall need more guns, more ammunition and more provisions."[4]

Sibley was no stranger to Minnesota and the Dakota tribe. He had arrived in 1834 as a partner in the American Fur Company and spent much time trading and living with the Indians. One he befriended was Little Crow. On one hunting foray, he was astonished at the chief's endurance, able to keep pace in bare feet with men on horseback over a few days' travel.[5]

Sibley fathered a child, Helen Hastings Sibley, in a de facto relationship with Red Blanket Woman, granddaughter of a Mdewakanton chief. At Mendota (later St. Peter), he built a 3-story limestone house that became a gathering place for all kinds of Minnesota frontiersmen. In 1843 he married Sarah Jane Steele, daughter of an old war hero, General James Steele, promoted "for gallant and meritorious service" during the War of 1812.[6] To his wife's discomfort, Sibley maintained a public relationship with Helen, who lived with a missionary family, until her death in 1859. Sibley, being a trader himself, profited handsomely from his Indian dealings, deducting money from their annuity payments, and over time became a rich and influential man.[7] As a former member of Congress, he had championed Indian rights, and argued that Indians be paid more for their lands—thus giving traders like himself access to more Indian funds.[8]

Governor Alexander Ramsey, instrumental in acquiring Dakota lands, was astonished when failure to meet treaty obligations led to a bloody revolt (Library of Congress).

Having helped sow the seeds of revolt, Sibley was now charged with crushing his former Dakota associates using a force of green militia and Union army recruits.

He set out on August 20 from Fort Snelling with 90 men, four companies of the hastily formed 6th Minnesota Regiment. Hundreds more were to follow once some semblance of order had been achieved. Sibley arrived at Belle Plaine on August 21. Joined by more volunteers, he now led 225 men. "Have just arrived after many vexatious days," he wrote his wife, "for a greener set of men were never got together, and of course I have to attend to most of the work." At this stage Sibley warned his wife not to "believe the thousand extravagant reports you hear ... people are absolutely crazy with excitement and credit every absurdity. Things are bad enough no doubt in the upper country, but I have no idea that the savages will withstand the attack of an organized force."

After dark, having tramped along "execrable roads," Sibley arrived in St. Peter with his exhausted command. Here he heard more stories of mayhem, and Jack Frazer, an old hunting companion, delivered a letter from Lieutenant Sheehan describing the first Ridgely attack. Now Sibley saw the full implications. Perhaps those stories of mayhem were not so absurd after all? He paused in St. Peter and wrote to Ramsey requesting "Springfield muskets and ammunition," which he understood the U.S. quartermaster was reluctant to issue before the regiments were fully organized, adding "I would respectfully suggest that if red tape is to be the way in this emergency, that you cut it with the bayonets of a corporal's guard." The remaining six companies of the 6th Minnesota arrived along with various militia units, and Sibley, "run to death with work," attempted to whip his growing force into shape.

Henry Hastings Sibley, with no formal military training, was given command of troops to suppress the revolt. He found the task grueling (author's collection).

Unable to wash, change clothes or shave, he lived in "a miserable dirty house which I will be glad to leave tomorrow for a tent," he wrote his wife. He was anxious to crush the Indians, and "my preparations are nearly complete to begin my work upon them with fire and sword, and my heart is hardened against them beyond any touch of mercy."

On August 26, the day following the arrival of the New Ulm refugees at Mankato, Sibley moved from St. Paul against the "fiends" and "devils in human shape." At Fort Ridgely the following day, "a cry was heard from the lookout stationed on the roof of the high barracks building that horsemen were approaching," recalled Helen Carrothers. "The warning sent a thrill of anxiety through all hearts, as we did not know whether the horsemen were friends or foes." But the new arrivals turned out to be Sibley's advance guard of 150 men. Colonel Samuel McPhail "rode into the fort and was greeted with the wild hurrahs of its inmates."[9]

Sibley arrived with the main force on the 28th, anxious to set out after Little Crow, believed to be entrenching his village 17 miles away. He wrote his wife, "I am waiting only for cartridges to follow and attack them wherever they may be found." And on the 30th, "I sent down here in wagons to St. Paul between three and four hundred white women and children who escaped into the Fort. They are penniless, and many of them almost naked, and God knows what is to become of them. They are objects of public charity. If you could only hear one tithe of the stories told by these poor people, you would be horrified." One of those sent to St. Paul was Helen Carrothers, now reunited with her husband James, who had arrived with Sibley's force.

Incoming troops saw the truth of massacre stories. "I went out in a northwesterly direction, 20 miles," Captain Leonard Aldrich wrote his brother. "I found everything turned upside down, and not a house escaped the ravages of the miserable savages." He found bodies "mangled in every conceivable way. Little children nailed up to doors of houses by their feet and thus left to die with their heads hanging downwards." Serving with Aldrich was George Doud, who went through New Ulm. "The town is now one complete reck," his diary recorded. Amidst grim images of mutilated bodies, he saw "one girl about twelve years old was found scalped and all her garments was torn off from her. She was fastened by the side of a house by driving nails through her feet. her head was downward."[10]

Sibley, meanwhile, awaiting supplies, found himself under attack, but not from Indians. Newspapers, politicians and settlers demanded to know what was going on. Why was he not marching on the murderous hordes? And what was being done to rescue the scores of prisoners in Indian hands?

About 650 warriors had taken part in the second New Ulm assault, but this was far from the total Dakota force. Many others were still on the prowl, attacking isolated homes and settlements in Brown and Nicollet Counties. Despite a mass exodus, however, many settlers had stayed behind, determined to defend their homes, livelihoods and possessions. Fortifications arose as men went to work with ax, saw, hammer and shovel. These were often simple "last stand" timber stockades about 10 feet high by 100 square, with loopholes to deliver gunfire.

But some individuals seized the opportunity to display their military engineering skills. Madelia saw an "artistic fortification" arise, built by Captain Cox. This was an octagonal 2-story structure surrounded by a moat six feet deep with extra rifle pits at strategic points. At Maine Prairie, farmers built a sturdy 2-story fort with double timber walls. In St. Joseph, three substantial blockhouses went up with walls one foot thick. St. Cloud saw three redoubts spring up with "Fort Holes." The redoubts were circular, bulletproof, 45-foot wide towers perforated with loopholes. A citizen-built fort at Sauk Centre would later become a substantial post occupied by the military, and

Forest City and Hutchinson saw strong stockades arise. "Our temporary home within the stockade consisted of a covering of poplar poles with hay, and blankets spread over brush to form a place to sleep," recalled Mary Lamson, a young child in the Hutchinson stockade. "So many families had fled to Hutchinson in haste without bringing food with them that the supply was short and I can remember crying myself to sleep because of hunger and dread of Indians."[11] Mary's father Nathan and her brother Chauncey would make history during a hunting foray in the Big Woods the following year.

Charles Flandrau, now formally commissioned as militia colonel, established fortifications along a defense line from New Ulm to the Iowa border. Built of logs or earth, they were typically square with corner bastions to allow enfilading fire. Houses were enclosed to protect noncombatants. In Little Falls, the Morris County courthouse was fortified to provide shelter for women and children during the night. The men camped outside, providing sentries, and armed parties tended fields during the day.[12]

On August 30, Sibley, under pressure for action, wrote his wife from Fort Ridgely, "Tomorrow we shall move forward slowly, so as to permit my re-enforcements, with ammunition and other supplies, to overtake my command. Little Crow and his followers have retreated, and I fear we shall have a long and weary chase before we can overtake them."

The Reverend Riggs, chaplain with the expedition, had no confidence in Sibley's mounted men. "Many of them were poor riders, and they were all poorly armed. They were without military organization and drill, and were felt to be an element of weakness rather than strength." Upon hearing a few shots fired, "The drum beat the 'long roll,' and the men that formed this 'string-bean cavalry' as they were called, crawled under the wagons. The next morning many of them had a clairvoyant communication with their families at home, and learned that their wives were sick."[13]

Sibley wrote his wife: "Unfortunately, the horsemen not being regularly enlisted, have to the number of two or three hundred skedaddled in view of dangerous service, leaving me with only twenty five or thirty of that description of force. If I had a few hundreds of trained cavalry, I could bring the whole matter to a speedy conclusion; as it is, the Indians instead of fighting as they now threaten, may escape from the infantry and lead us a weary chase in the wide prairie."

But no chase would be necessary. Despite being repulsed at New Ulm and Fort Ridgely, the Dakotas were ready for further combat, and a large force was about to head Sibley's way.

A sizable "peace party," however, headed by Christian convert Paul Mazakutemani, speaker of Upper Dakotas, was in the making. Tensions rose between the factions, and they camped some distance from Little Crow. On August 28, Mazakutemani give a lengthy speech:

> I want to speak now to you of what is in my own heart. Give me all these white captives. I will deliver them up to friends. You [Lower] Dakotas are numerous—you can afford to give these captives to me, and I will go with them to the white people. Then, if you want to fight, when you see the white soldiers coming to fight, fight with them, but don't fight with women and children. Or stop fighting. The Americans are a great people. They have much lead, powder, guns and provisions. Stop fighting, and now gather up all the captives and give them to me. No one who ever fights with the white people ever becomes rich, or remains two days in one place, but is always fleeing or starving.[14]

Little Crow listened. Mixed-blood relatives of the Upper Dakotas, taken captive, would be released, he decreed, and their property returned—but the other prisoners would stay to share in the hardships his people were about to endure. He was "leader of those who made war on the whites; that as long as he was alive no white man should touch him; that if he was taken alive, he would be made a show of before the whites; and that if he was ever touched by a white man it would be after he was dead."[15]

On September 1, Little Crow divided his remaining force. With 110 braves, he crossed the Minnesota River, and headed northeast to raid settlements around the Big Woods area. At the same time, Chief Gray Bird led about 350 braves along the southern bank towards Fort Ridgely. They drove empty wagons to pick up supplies from Little Crow's old village. Once loaded, the plan was to cross the river, rejoin Little Crow, and assault settlements to the north.

"I intended to march today," Sibley wrote on August 31, "but we had a fearful rain storm last night which lasted for several hours, saturating every thing in the camp, and it will take the whole day to dry." One thing that could be done meanwhile was to bury the dead. Bodies, exposed to the elements and animals, were scattered far and wide. Scouts sent out detected no hostiles, and on August 31 a burial party set out. Who actually commanded this expedition is open to dispute. After the event, Sibley stated it was commanded by former Dakota Indian Agent Joseph Brown. But, despite holding the honorary rank of major, Brown was not a trained soldier. Marching with Brown were Captain Hiram Grant, commanding Company A of the 6th Minnesota Infantry, and Captain Joseph Anderson, commanding 50 "Mounted Rangers."

Grant later claimed that he, in fact, was in charge, as instructed by Colonel William Crooks, commander of the 6th Infantry, and he was to "consult" Major Brown if "circumstances should arise where I wanted advice." Seventeen wagons came along, with ammunition, provisions, tents and other supplies. A work detail of teamsters, soldiers, and settlers looking for relatives brought the total to about 170 men, including Thomas Galbraith and Surgeon Jared Daniels.

Birch Coulee

Leaving Fort Ridgely at about 10 a.m., the command moved along the road towards the Redwood Ferry. Bodies were soon seen in the grass and alongside burned-out cabins. At least 16 victims were buried along the way. The bodies must have been in a deplorable state, ravaged by summer sun, birds and wild animals for over two weeks, but Dr. Daniels claimed that he could see none had been scalped or mutilated by human hand. The command set up camp that evening near the mouth of Birch Coulee Creek. Next morning, Brown crossed the Minnesota River with Anderson and his mounted men while Grant and the infantry stayed on the north side. Brown's party buried several corpses around the Lower Agency, including that of Andrew Myrick, identified by his brother, Nathan. An examination of Little Crow's former village showed no recent signs of habitation, and it was assumed by Brown, Galbraith and scout Jack Frazer that the enemy must be further north—a bad mistake, as it turned out.

Grant's infantry, meanwhile, buried the dead soldiers of Captain Marsh's command at Redwood Ferry. They continued towards Beaver Creek, burying "whole families" along the way, and soon Grant saw what he thought was an Indian "drop in the grass." He sent a squad of 20 men forward, who found "a woman who, thirteen days before, had seen her husband and three children killed." This was Justina Krieger, a survivor of the Kitzman party, who had been shot, gashed, stripped and left for dead. "When she came to her senses and realized the loss of her family, her brain gave away, and she wandered unconscious for twelve days, subsisting, probably on roots and water," recalled Grant. "Discovering her condition, I rode forward with a soldier's blanket and wrapped it around her, carried her to one of the wagons and made her a grass bed. Other soldiers kindly gave her their only blanket. Dr. Daniels dressed her wounds and made her as comfortable as possible."[16]

During the course of the day, the two detachments buried 54 people. As the sun fell in the western sky, they reunited at the "encampment selected by Captain Grant," Brown was careful to point out in his report. Again it was near Birch Coulee, and exposed to ravines and cover for the enemy on all sides. Grant stated this was because it was "the nearest place to get water." The original intention had been to return to base that evening, but the burials had taken time, and Fort Ridgely was about 17 miles away. The camp was set up "in the usual way," reported Brown, "on the smooth prairie, some two hundred yards from the timber of Birch Coolie, with the wagons parked around the camp, and the team horses fastened to the wagons. The horses belonging to the mounted men were fastened to a stout picket-rope, between the tents and wagons, around the south half of the camp—Captain Anderson's tents being behind his horses, and Captain Grant's tents being inside the wagons, which formed the north half of the camp."[17]

The camp settled down for the night with a ring of 10 three-man picket posts 30 yards out. Shortly before daybreak, "Private William Hart discovered what he thought was a dog or wolf crawling between his post and the camp," recalled Grant. "He fired, and it proved to be an Indian." An instant later an ear-splitting volley crashed out from the woods. Dozens of horses on the outer picket rope went down, thrashing and screaming. The Indians emerged, reloading while making a cautious advance.

"The firing, for probably a minute, was entirely on the part of the Indians," reported Brown, "during which time many of our men were either killed or wounded." Private Hart made it back to the camp, but his fellow picket, Richard Gibbons, fell mortally wounded. "At this moment," recalled Ranger James Egan, "the Indians could have killed the entire force if they had charged upon us. It was a perfect surprise."[18] Rudely awakened men scrambled from beneath wagons and tents. They returned fire, but 30 soldiers were hit in the first few minutes.

While Anderson's company took cover behind the wagons, Grant's party "commenced firing; but they, for some minutes, continued to expose themselves imprudently," reported Brown, "and in consequence were very much cut to pieces." Common sense prevailed and the men took shelter behind dead horses and wagons, the Indian bullets finding fewer targets. The troops began to return a disciplined fire, and the Dakotas were obliged to fall back, but a "shower of bullets continually fell upon us from all sides," recalled Egan. "The nature of the ground was such that with the coolie or ravine on one side, where was a heavy growth of timber, and the rest an open prairie with little hillocks here and there, just beyond our camp, the Indians could pour a fire upon us from every direction and themselves be protected."

"Already 22 of our men were dead or mortally wounded," recalled Grant. "Sixty more had received serious or slight wounds. One-half of our whole force was killed or wounded. Eighty-five horses were dead, leaving only two alive."

"Several of the men went crazy," recalled Egan, "and jumping out to give a full view met instant death." One man "did not shoot once, but kept crying out, 'Oh my God, my God!' George Turnbull, first lieutenant, pulled a revolver on him, cocked it, and said if he did not stop he would blow his brains out. He stopped."

Eager hands used the command's three spades and one pick, along with numerous bayonets, sabers, pocket knives and tin pans, to dig rifle pits. Despite the hard ground, 200 yards were completed with the loss of only one man killed and two wounded. "By noon," recalled Grant, "we had ourselves pretty well entrenched, using our dead soldiers and horses to help our breastworks." But ammunition was running low. "I was one of the men ordered to get it," recalled Joseph Coursolle. "We hunched along on our backs behind the shelter of the dead horses until we were directly under the wagon. Then we quickly raised our feet and tipped the wagon over. One of the men got a bullet through his leg but we got the ammunition! We slid the boxes along the ground, each man helping himself and pushing the boxes on to the next man in line." But the beleaguered troops were in for a shock. "All the bullets were for larger bore rifles." They had been supplied with 62-caliber balls for 58-caliber barrels. "With our knives we whittled lead from the minie balls," recalled Coursolle. "If the Sioux had charged then our goose would have been cooked. You bet we made every bullet count after that."[19]

The gunfire continued, and men sweltered as the sun rose in a hot summer sky. Would relief arrive? Had the sound of battle been heard at distant Fort Ridgely? The answer came at about 3 p.m. with the sound of a cannon boom. A shout of joy went up—but the Indians were not beaten yet. About half began withdrawing to prepare a savage surprise for the advancing troops. Indian leaders shouted their instructions, understood by mixed-bloods in the soldier camp. The Dakotas hoped to surround the small relief force and wipe it out. "This caused some uneasiness," reported Brown, "because we feared the troops would attempt to cross Birch Coolie about dark."

The relief force of 50 Mounted Rangers and three companies of infantry, with two cannon, about 240 men, was commanded by Colonel Sam McPhail. He sent two mounted scouts forward, but they "had their horses shot under them, and the scouts chased close to my column by the Indians. By this time the enemy had almost completely surrounded my command." The big guns boomed and the enemy "retired to a more respectful distance." But McPhail, not knowing Brown's exact location, ordered his command into a defensive corral and, as the sun set, sent Lieutenant Sheehan back for more men.

"It was a night of black despair. There seemed no hope," recalled Ranger Egan. "We expected to be starved to death, as anyone bold enough to raise up to put an arm into any wagon containing supplies was instantly shot. Our ammunition was almost exhausted, and each man laid his drawn saber near him and examined his musket, resolved not to fire again until the final moment came, when a fire would do some execution…. The agony we suffered, expecting every moment to be rushed upon, through that long, long night is indescribable."

"On September 3d the daylight and sunrise were most beautiful," recalled Grant—especially as they had survived a harrowing night. A warrior appeared on horseback and advanced with a white flag. Interpreter Corporal James Auge advanced and exchanged words. They had been reinforced during the night, claimed the Indian. The Dakotas now had as many warriors "as the leaves on the trees"—the troops would be wiped out. But if the "half-breeds" and others with Indian blood marched out now, they would be spared. During the night, a mixed-blood named Peter Boyer had deserted to the Indians, taking his musket with him.[20] Perhaps others would do the same. About 10 mixed-blood soldiers clustered about Auge and muttered amongst themselves. "We are going to stay with you, captain," they told Grant. The troops would be ready and waiting for any attack with two loaded guns per man, the Indian was told. And, furthermore, he had best waste no time in departing. A truce with such an offensive offer could not be respected. "He turned his horse and rode slowly towards the meadow," recalled Grant. "I then gave the order to fire. About twenty shots were fired at him. We killed his horse, but he got off safely." Captain Grant, it would appear, had little respect for a white flag.

The men tensed, waiting for the promised assault. "While almost holding our breath, expecting every moment to hear the war-whoop, we discovered a large, powerful Indian come up out of the woods, yelling at the top of his voice." Corporal Auge listened and interpreted the warrior's words. A soldier column three miles long was coming, he said. Upon receiving word, Sibley had marched with his remaining troops, eight companies of infantry, and joined McPhail's command a little after midnight.[21]

"Suddenly the boom of a cannon is again heard," recalled Egan, "and again and nearer and clearer, until its roar, usually terrible, sounded as the sweetest harmony of heaven." The Indians began moving off in confusion, "but we did not move from our holes until General [Colonel] Sibley, with a few officers, came right up to us, and then and not till then, did we feel we were saved."

"I was the first man to enter the doomed camp after driving off the savages," Sibley wrote his wife, "and as the survivors emerged from their holes they had dug in the ground in and around the tents, a more delighted set of mortals I never saw. There lay 91 horses shot dead, and a very few hobbling about wounded. The killed and wounded men were lying around, and as warm weather hastened decomposition, the odor was sickening."[22] Thirteen men were already dead and 47 others severely wounded, four mortally. The dead included Stephen Henderson, the man who had previously escaped before the Indians burned his wife and two dead children.

The men had scarcely eaten for 30 hours and the wounded were in a bad way, groaning and crying for water. Justina Krieger had lain in a wagon on the front line peppered with musket balls, but again she survived. Every tent in the camp was now unfit for service, one riddled with 140 bullet holes.

The wounded were placed in wagons, and the column headed back to Fort Ridgely. They arrived at about 8 that evening, and stories were swapped and yarns told. The following morning, Grant handed his written report to his "commanding officer" (whether Crooks or Sibley is unclear), to be "coolly

7. We Shall Need More Guns 91

informed that I should make my report to Maj. Joseph R. Brown, who was in command of the expedition." Grant was dumbfounded. Had he not been in command? "No order had been given me by Major Brown," he claimed, "not an intimation that he considered himself in command. To say that I was angry, when told to make my report to him, would only express half of what I felt." The infuriated Grant tore his report to shreds. "All officers, soldiers and citizens obeyed my orders," he insisted. "I had the full charge."[23]

"Having received no report from Captain Grant," Brown reported, "I am unable to give the names of the killed and wounded of his company.... Probably the desire of Captain Grant's company to charge upon the Indians led to their exposure, consequently so many deaths and wounds."

But who was really in charge? It has been claimed that Grant was the man, Brown's nomination only coming after the fiasco, a ploy by Sibley to claim it was a civilian expedition, not military, therefore the casualties no fault of his.[24] But Brown's report to Sibley stated, "In compliance with your order, I left the encampment...." Still, Brown reported that it was Grant who selected the dubious campsite. Colonel McPhail's report referred to "Captain Grant's command." Ranger James Egan referred to "Maj. Joe Brown" being in command, and Captain Anderson's report was made out to Brown, "Commanding Expedition."[25]

But why would anyone want the "distinction" of being in command? Any command was better than none, apparently. "The battle of Birch Coolie," wrote the *St. Paul Daily Express*, "although it speaks well for the bravery of our troops, yet displays an utter lack of skill, care or attention with regard to the situation of the encampment by the commanding officer." And, furthermore, "Within half a mile, or less, a camp could have been selected on high ground with open approaches on all sides.... The excuse rendered for establishing the camp at the point selected, was that it was convenient to wood and water; yet when the attack was made the party was as effectively cut off from both, as if none had been within a day's journey."[26]

While the Birch Coulee fight took place, Little Crow, over 40 miles to the north, had seen combat too. At Acton, in the yard of the murdered Robinson Jones, camped 20 new recruits of the 9th Minnesota Infantry, backed up by 45 "citizen soldiers." The inexperienced Captain Richard Strout, in command, had orders to protect Meeker County civilians. At around 3 a.m., three men rode into the slumbering, unguarded camp. Captain Whitcomb, stationed at Forest City, had skirmished with Indians the preceding day, they warned, and the same hostiles may still be about.[27]

Strout broke camp next morning, September 3, and set out for Forest City with the three couriers acting as guides. Two miles out, despite no breeze, long grass was seen to waver some distance to their front. Stroud ordered a halt and deployed the supply wagons behind his men. They had not continued far before the dreaded war whoop was heard and Indians rose from the grass. Amidst a blast of gunfire, two soldiers were killed and many others wounded. The embattled, inexperienced whites found themselves outnumbered as the warriors spread out on all sides. Placing four squads on each side of the wagons, Strout moved forward and gained the high ground of Kelley's Bluff. "I had never fired a gun before the battle," recalled citizen soldier A.H. Rose, "but they showed me how to load, and I pointed my gun at the Indians and pulled the trigger."

Low on ammunition, Strout ordered Lieutenant William Clark to lead a bayonet charge. The thrusting steel line broke through the Indian line, and a running fight followed as the troops were pushed south towards Hutchinson rather than Forest City. Wounded soldiers jumped into the wagons and threw out provisions and supplies. Falling for the ploy, the Indians stopped to collect booty, giving the troops a chance to widen the gap. After a 2-hour flight over eight miles, Strout's command made it into the safety of the Hutchinson stockade. Three men had been killed, about 23 wounded, of whom three later died. Two wagons and their supplies were also lost, along with nine horses.[28]

During the night, Little Crow was joined by 20 Upper Dakota warriors, and the following day Hutchinson came under attack. "I can recall seeing the Cross family, the mother and two little children, who had been murdered within a few hundred yards of the stockade," recalled young Mary Lamson. "In some way I eluded my father and went over to see them. They had not been scalped, simply chopped with an ax and I never forgot that awful sight."[29] A few buildings went up in flames, but the Indians had no success against the stockade. At the same time, in Forest City, muskets fired from behind a just-completed stockade saw other Indians driven off.

8

I Have a Great Many Prisoners, Women and Children

Three days after the evacuation of New Ulm, far bigger events took place back east. The graybacks of Robert E. Lee and the bluecoats of Major General John Pope came face to face near Bull Run Creek, the scene of the Union defeat the previous year. They slogged it out over three days, and again the rebels won. The retreat on Washington this time was a far less chaotic affair, but Abraham Lincoln "felt almost ready to hang himself," his cabinet was informed.[1]

Not all in the Union camp were unhappy with Pope's defeat. Personal rivalries sometimes cast a longer shadow than the ultimate common cause. Union General George McClellan had withheld the support of his troops. But Pope had won few friends amidst his own men due to his pomposity and reference to earlier victories he had achieved in the west. There, he said, the enemy had never seen the back of his troops. "It can with truth be said of him that he had not a friend in his command from the smallest drummer boy to the highest general officer," wrote General Alpheus Williams to his daughter. "All hated him."

Following his humiliating defeat, John Pope had to go. But where to send him? On September 4, as settlers in Hutchinson and Forest City repelled Little Crow's warriors, an embittered Pope arrived at the White House. He laid before Lincoln seven pages of grievances about McClellan's activities, or lack thereof, in regard to Bull Run. Lincoln sympathized, but the troops had no confidence in Pope, while they adored George McClellan.

On September 6, 1862, the Department of the Northwest was created to deal with the Dakota outbreak. That same day, Pope received a letter from Secretary of War Edwin Stanton: "The Indian hostilities that have recently broken forth and are now prevailing in that department require the attention of some military officer of high rank, in whose ability and vigor the Government has confidence, and you have therefore been selected for this important command." Pope was instructed to set up headquarters in St. Paul and "take such prompt and vigorous measures as shall quell the hostilities and afford peace, security, and protection to the people against Indian hostilities."[2]

So Pope could no longer be trusted to fight Confederates—a slight if ever there was one. He was now demoted to crushing a pack of mere backwoods savages—in his view at least. The unhappy general packed his bags and traveled west by the iron horse.

Colonel Sibley, meanwhile, came under more fire from his own side. Birch Coulee had done nothing for his reputation. Sheriff Roos, feeling himself a veteran following New Ulm, wrote to the newspapers, "Send a young ernest man instead of Col. Sibley to take Command, and he will do more with the present force than Col. Sibley with 10 or 15,000 men, he is in my mind a coward and a rascal." Future Minnesota governor Horace Austin, a veteran of the New Ulm fight, deplored Sibley's being in charge "while murder, rapine and plunder surround his imbecility [which] staggers us all."[3] Fiery newspaper proprietor Jane Swisshelm wrote a suggestion that "some *live* man be put in command of the force against the Sioux," while Sibley be detached with "100 men or there about to have in his undertaker's corpse."

Perhaps crushing Little Crow was going to be hard work. Perhaps there would be no glory in this expedition. The very day Sibley brought back the dead from Birch Coulee, September 4, he wrote to Governor Ramsey that he had "learned, with much pain," of the dissatisfaction with his "fitting the

General John Pope, beaten by the Confederates, was sent west to take overall command of the Indian campaign. He decreed they be treated as "maniacs or wild beasts" (Library of Congress).

8. I Have a Great Many Prisoners, Women and Children   95

expedition for field service," and offered to "place my commission at your disposal."[4] That same night he penned a letter to his wife, "Well, let them come and fight these Indians themselves, and they will [have] something to do besides grumbling." And the next day, "The responsibilities of my position are so great that I am deprived of necessary rest. I can hardly sleep at all.... It is hard indeed, while we are fighting and doing our best, to have a set of ninnies and poltroons abusing us at home."[5]

But expedition chaplain Stephen Riggs wrote to Governor Ramsey: "At present the Indians have all the advantages in this war. Their passing with certainty from place to place on horseback, their mode of shooting and fleeing, their perfect knowledge of the country, its ravines and hiding places, their bushwhacking and ambushing, all give them a decided advantage in fighting with our troops. The lesson we have learned at Birch Coulee will not, I trust, soon be forgotten.... I am satisfied that Colonel Sibley has acted wisely in not advancing until he is well prepared for offense and defense. The safety of his command requires it."[6]

Ramsey and Adjutant General Oscar Malros knew only too well Sibley's difficulties. It was they who received his demands for arms, ammunition and supplies. They, in turn, bombarded the War Department for help. On September 6, as General Pope received his new assignment, Ramsey wired Abraham Lincoln: "Those Indian outrages continue. I asked Secretary of War Edwin Stanton to authorize the State Quartermaster to purchase, say, 500 horses. He refuses.... This is not our war; it is a national war.... Answer me at once. More than 500 whites have been murdered by the Indians."[7]

When leaving Birch Coulee, Sibley had left a note on a split stake stuck in the ground. "If Little Crow has any proposition to make, let him send a half-breed to me, and he shall be protected in and out of camp." No doubt the dead and wounded lying about influenced Sibley to think smoke from the peace pipe rather than the gun may well be the best way forward. On September 7, he received a response that was the result of much heated debate between the Dakota peace and war factions. Literate mixed-blood Antoine Campbell, commonly known as Joe, had been captured with his family and acted as a scribe for Little Crow. Two mixed-bloods took the letter to Fort Ridgely in a mule-drawn buggy under a flag of truce:

Dear Sir,

For what reason we have commenced this war, I will tell you. It is on account of Major Galbraith. We made a treaty with the government, and beg for what we do get and then can't get it till our children are dying with hunger. It is the traders who commenced it. Mr. A.J. Myrick told the Indians they could eat grass or dirt. Then Mr. Forbes told the Lower Sioux that they were not men. Then Roberts was working with his friends to defraud us of our moneys. If the young braves have pushed the white men, I have done this myself. So I want you to let Governor Ramsey know this. I have a great many prisoners, women and children, It ain't all our fault. The Winnebagos were in the engagement, and two of them was killed. I want you to give me an answer by the bearer all at present.

Yours truly,
Friend Little Crow[8]

From the couriers, Sibley learned of the rift between the war and peace factions. Influential Upper Dakotas wanted the prisoners released. Pleased with this turn of events, Sibley replied:

Little Crow:

You have murdered many of our people without sufficient cause. Return me the prisoners, under a flag of truce, and I will talk with you then like a man. I have sent your message to Governor Ramsey.

H.H. Sibley
Colonel Commanding
Military Expedition[9]

Sibley also penned what he termed an "open letter" to "those half-breeds and Sioux Indians whom have not been Concerned in the Murders and Outrages upon White Settlers." He promised them protection if they separated from the "guilty people" and showed a white flag upon the approach of his troops.[10] On September 17, he wrote his wife that the peace faction wanted to "play good Indian," but they must separate from the "unclean thing" or share the same fate.

Little Crow well realized one way for the peace party to placate Sibley would be to hand over not only the prisoners, but Little Crow to boot. To finish his days in a hangman's noose was what he most dreaded. To enter the spirit world of his ancestors as a forlorn disgrace was no way for a warrior chief to end his days. To die honorably in battle was another matter. What to do now? He could flee westwards, out onto the broad Dakota plains. But winter was still some time off, and Sibley's troops could follow. Once the icy snows and winds arrived, however, such pursuit would be impossible for the clumsy whites who relied on wagons loaded with supplies. The way the war was going, he would have to run sooner or later—but not yet. There was still time to reverse his fortunes with another fight.

Sibley, despite earlier feelings, wrote his wife on September 7, "It would not do for me under these present circumstances peremptorily to resign my commission, for the safety of the State would be jeopardized if one less experienced in Indian wiles and modes of warfare than I am should be assigned to the command of the only force which stands between the central portion of the State and desolation." But he was still not going to march from Fort Ridgely "without a sufficient supply of ammunition and rations."

In the Indian camps, the debate continued. Wabasha's son-in-law, Rdainyanka, delivered an impassioned speech to the uncertain: "I am for continuing the war, and am opposed to the delivery of the prisoners. I have no confidence that the whites will stand by any agreement they make if we give them up. Ever since we treated with them their agents have robbed and cheated us.... We may regret what has happened, but the matter has gone too far to be remedied. We have got to die. Let us, then, kill as many of the whites as possible, and let the prisoners die with us."

On September 10, Sibley wrote his wife, "If I should make an advance movement, two or three hundred white women and children might be murdered in cold blood. I must use what craft I possess to get these poor creatures out of the possession of the red devils, and then pursue the latter with fire and sword."

Despite living in fear, the prisoner Sarah Wakefield had mixed feelings: "Had they not been cheated unmercifully, and not their money had been delayed; no troops were left to protect the frontier and their Agent, their 'father,' had left them without money, food or clothing, and gone off to the war. I often said to the Indians if they had left innocent people alone, and robbed us all they never would have been blamed. But they knew no justice but in dealing out death for their wrongs."[11]

On September 11, Sibley saw the arrival of 50,000 musket cartridges, and over the next few days, wagons creaked into Fort Ridgely loaded with provisions and clothing. And then 270 men of the 3rd Minnesota Regiment marched in, Civil War veterans who had been paroled by the rebels following their commander's surrender at Murfreesboro the previous July. Their former officers, however, were still guests of the Confederacy, like it or not. The 3rd's new commanding officer was Major Abraham Welch, a veteran who had been wounded at First Bull Run.

Three days later, September 16, General John Pope booked in at the International Hotel, St. Paul. Edwin Stanton's assurance that this posting required an "officer of high rank, in whose ability and vigor" the government depended, had not placated his injured pride. But Pope was no stranger to the Minnesota frontier. Twelve years earlier, Captain Pope of the Topographical Engineers had delivered his 20,000-word "Report of an Exploration of the Territory of Minnesota." He praised the Minnesota River Valley and surrounding prairie lands. "I can only attribute to ignorance of its great value the apathy and indifference manifested by the government in failing to yet extinguish the title of the Indians, and to throw up to the industry of the American people a country so well adapted to their genius and their enterprize." And, as the Indians were "as yet entirely ignorant of the great value of their lands," no time should be wasted in their acquisition.[12]

General-in-Chief Henry Halleck and Major General John Pope had something in common: both were intensely disliked by those who worked with them. But Halleck, described by one reporter as a "cold, calculating owl,"[13] was considered an organizational genius. Known as "Old Brains," he had authored military texts including *Elements of Military Art and Science*, most influential in the Civil War when it came.

Pope arrived in St. Paul on September 16 and wasted no time in conferring with Governor Ramsey and other flustered officials. At 5:30 that evening he shot off a telegram to Halleck:

> From all indications and information we are likely to have a general Indian war all along the frontier, unless immediate steps are taken to put a stop to it. I have requested the Governors of Iowa and Wisconsin not to send any troops from their States [to fight the South] without advising me about it, and have requested the Governor of Wisconsin to send forward three or four regiments now ready for service. You have no idea of the terrible destruction already done and the panic everywhere in Wisconsin and Minnesota. Unless very prompt steps are taken these States will be half depopulated before winter begins. Already populations [settlements] have been totally abandoned with everything in them. Crops are all left standing, and the whole population fleeing to the river.

General-in-Chief Henry Halleck, described as a "cold, calculating owl," was more concerned with suppressing rebels down South than Indians out West (Library of Congress).

Wisconsin was, in fact, in no danger of being depopulated, but Pope wanted their troops to hunt Indians rather than rebels. He also claimed that the Chippewas "have already begun to rob and murder, and need immediate attention."[14] Despite minor troubles, the Chippewas were, in fact, at peace with the whites, and would remain so.

8. I Have a Great Many Prisoners, Women and Children 99

Fort Abercrombie

But the Dakotas had also been active far north of Sibley's troops. Before Pope's arrival, Ramsey had been obliged to send a relief force to Fort Abercrombie, established 140 miles north of the Upper Agency in 1857 on the Red River, just inside Dakota Territory. The post was now garrisoned by Company D of the 5th Minnesota Regiment under 31-year-old Captain John Vander Horck. It was their job to protect steamboat traffic and wagon trains traveling to the rich Montana goldfields. But, like Fort Ridgely, the post lacked a stockade, and foliage along the riverbank provided cover for an attacking force. It did, however, have a battery of three 12-pound mountain howitzers.

When news arrived of the Indian outbreak on August 23, Van Horck dispatched runners to alert local settlers, and at least 80 people came in for protection. He also sent orders for a wagon train, recently passed through, to return, and dispatched a request to St. Paul for ammunition and more men.

The garrison went to work, hastily constructing earth and log breastworks, and a company was formed from civilian volunteers. Van Horck dispatched Lieutenant John Groetch with a squad to reconnoiter as far as Breckenridge, a hamlet about 15 miles to the south. No enemy warriors were seen, but they found several mutilated bodies in a deserted hotel. Shortly after their departure, Indians put the hotel to the torch. Next day the patrol returned to find a wounded woman by the riverbank. She told of seeing her son killed and grandson taken captive, and she was taken back to the safety of the fort.[15]

All remained quiet for several days, but on August 30, Indians drove off cattle grazing within a mile of the post. The garrison was put on alert, and during the dark morning hours of September 3, Vander Horck set out with an orderly to inspect the outer picket posts. A jumpy sentry opened fire, wounding Vander Horck in the arm. At dawn, as he received medical attention, Dakota warriors struck the stables at the south end of the fort in an apparent attempt to secure horses. With the captain wounded, Lieutenant Groetch took charge. The howitzers proved their worth, along with a determined fight by the armed citizen company under Captain T.D. Smith. The Indians fell back amidst a cloud of gun smoke after a 2-hour fight, leaving hay bales in flames. Only two whites were wounded, one fatally, and two Indians were found dead, their other casualties carried off.

Taking a breath, the defenders were appalled to learn they had only 350 rounds of .69-calibre musket balls left. Once again the troops had been supplied with incorrect ammunition. But the women went to work taking .69-calibre balls from the artillery canister shot and replacing them with scrap iron fragments. On September 4 and 5, gunfire was exchanged at long range, Indian snipers in treetops making life perilous for the defenders behind their improvised breastworks. At dawn on September 6, the Indians attacked again and managed to infiltrate the stables, only to be driven off by a determined countercharge. Two Indians found inside the stables were shot, and one was finished off with a bayonet thrust.[16]

Then the warriors charged from north, south and west, those flanks not protected by the Red River. This was the most determined attack, and two Indians were killed within thirty feet of a rough breastwork protecting the commissary building. Inside, terrified women and children cowered as bullets flew. Musket fire and the booming big guns broke the Indian lines, and again they were driven back to cover along the river bank. Mixed-blood interpreter Joseph Demarias later learned that high casualties in this attack forced the Indians to abandon any more thought of frontal assault.

Van Horck, having received no word of a relief force, dispatched two more couriers on September 21 with an escort of 20 men. Once clear of the Indian lines, the couriers went their own way while the escort turned back, riding straight into an ambush. Two men were killed before the escort reached the fort, in what turned out to be a waste of life. Two days later, the relief force dispatched by Ramsey arrived, comprising 450 men and one field gun under Captain Emil Bruerger. Despite the reinforcements, the Indians struck a water-carrying party on the morning of September 26, but were driven off; several Indians were killed, and one white teamster fatally wounded. A howitzer was brought into action, and the cavalry pursued as the Indians fled. Their campsite was discovered loaded with plundered booty, and once anything of value had been removed, the camp was set ablaze. "Now and then some Indians will make their appearance, but they have not dared to make another attack," reported Bruerger on September 29. The siege of Fort Abercrombie had drawn to a close.[17] The following day, about 60 civilian men, women and children were escorted to St. Cloud, arriving five days later.

The defenders estimated the Indian force at several hundred, the real numbers not known. The Upper Dakotas later denied having taken part, but some defenders said they recognized a Sisseton chief, Sweet Corn, as being involved. White losses for the siege were five killed and five wounded. Indian casualties are not known.

Shortcomings in Abercrombie's defenses were apparent, and plans drawn up to remedy the problem. Surrounding undergrowth and trees were cut back, and a stockade on all flanks except the river went up, along with three blockhouses.

"I learn that General Pope has been designated to command of the new Department of the Northwest," wrote Sibley on September 13. "I shall soon ask to be relieved of my present command." But Pope wrote to Sibley: "I am rejoiced to find you in command of the expedition against the Sioux, and to assure you that I will push forward everything to your assistance as fast as possible." Pope went on to detail his planned deployment of several thousand men to "put a final stop to Indian depredations by exterminating or ruining all the Indians engaged in the late outbreak." He urged Sibley to move "as rapidly as possible" against the Indian farms to destroy their crops. Conspicuous by its absence, however, was any mention of the prisoners in Indian hands, or how to avoid their murder. Pope wanted the revolt crushed as rapidly as possible, "as I expect to be but a short time among you." The general had a proper war waiting back east. Surely he would be recalled, and soon. Little did Pope realize that a command out west would be his lot till after the South was crushed.

Sibley replied, thanking Pope for his "kind manner in which you refer to me as commander of this expedition." He detailed his wants and needs, and the problems involved, but then gave Pope a reminder: "I am anxious for the safety of the many white women and children held captive by the Indians, but it is difficult to know how they can be secured." And, as regards Pope's "admirable" grand plans, "I only fear they will partially fail by reason of the lateness of the season and the difficulty of organizing expeditions on a large scale with new troops before the cold weather sets in to prevent military operations in a prairie country." And Halleck wired Pope that troops can be mustered "only in conformity to law and regulations.... It is not believed that you will require a very large infantry force against the Indians, as their numbers cannot be very great."[18]

Pope fumed. He had been instructed to "employ whatever force may be necessary" to suppress the revolt, and make "whatever requisitions may be needed for that purpose."[19] His attempts to make requisitions, however, did not please Halleck, who stated they were "beyond all our expectations, and involve an immense expenditure of money. Moreover, they cannot be filled without taking supplies from troops now in the field. The organization of a large force for an Indian campaign is not approved by the war department because it is not deemed necessary." Pope, according to his adjutant, reacted "like a bear with a sore head," and imagined himself to be the "most talented general in the world and the one most wronged."[20]

"You do not seem to be aware of the extent of the Indian outbreaks," Pope replied. "The Sioux, 2,600 strong, are assembled at the Upper Sioux Agency, ready to give battle to Colonel Sibley ... they have murdered the settlers along the frontier of Dakota and nearly depopulated the territory. In Nebraska the same.... The Chippewas and Winnebagos are on the verge of outbreak and the whole of the Indian tribes as far as the mountains are in motion."[21]

All of which would have delighted Little Crow, if only it were true.

9

They Will Never Get My Live Body

Sibley garnered ammunition and supplies as the officers, many green themselves, attempted to train unruly recruits amidst the battered buildings of Fort Ridgely, now under repair. Following two days of delaying rain, "tomorrow we shall cross to the south side of the Minnesota River," Sibley wrote his wife, "and go in search of my *friend* [!] Little Crow, with whom I have kept up a correspondence and now 'have a crow to pick.'"[1]

On the afternoon of September 19, Sibley marched at the head of 1,619 men. Riding with them was John Other Day and other Indians acting as scouts. "At last we left," recalled Fort Ridgely veteran Corporal Joe Coursolle. "Our company was in the lead and the column stretched back through the woods further than I could see. I was glad we had the cannons with us. The big guns scared the daylights out of the Sioux." Having to cross the river by boat, the column covered only two miles the first day. When the first troops touched the southern bank, they were confronted by a disheveled, demented German who, thinking they were Indians, attempted to commit suicide by cutting his own throat with a blunt knife. He was disarmed and sent back to the fort.

The troops set up camp and moved on the following day, but Sibley had decided on a somewhat defensive search for his "friend" Little Crow. "We moved like snails," lamented Coursolle, "I could have crawled on my stomach and made faster time. Again we cursed Sibley. He was so slow! Every day we started the march in the middle of the forenoon, halted for a noon meal, camped at four o'clock, dug rifle pits and built barricades. Why waste such precious time! We would never catch the Indians dawdling like this."[2]

The column set up camp, complete with rifle pits, not far from the remains of the Lower Agency. Some soldiers searched houses once occupied by "cut-hairs" to return with souvenirs like Indian trinkets, beads and buffalo robes. They also discovered the body of Philander Prescott. The 60-year-old interpreter had lived amongst the Dakotas for 45 years and married into the tribe. On the morning of the outbreak, Little Crow had advised him to go home and stay there, but Prescott, alarmed, had set out for Fort Ridgely despite his wife's advice to stay close to her and their mixed-blood children. Prescott was overtaken by Medicine Bottle's band. "My wife and children are among you, of your own blood. I have never done you any harm, and been a true friend in all your troubles. Why should you wish to kill me?" But all to no avail. The old interpreter was shot down where he stood.[3]

The troops laid Prescott to rest, and the following day mounted Indian scouts appeared on the bluffs. A note was found attached to a wooden fence in their line of march that urged the soldiers on; the Indians were waiting for them.[4] Little Crow was playing at psychological warfare, hoping to damage the morale of Sibley's troops. Soon their scalps would be in dangling Dakota lodges. But, in fact, Little Crow was unwittingly playing right into Sibley's hands. The colonel had only 25 mounted men, and the elusive Indians could have simply stayed out of the plodding infantry's way.

In addition, tempers between the peace and war factions still flared. Little Crow's men had knocked over tepees in the friendly camp, and guns had been drawn. Friendlies had shouted they too were prepared to die in battle— but fighting fellow Dakotas rather than whites. Despite being outnumbered five to 1 by those in the hostile camp, they still managed to get extra captives into the safety of their lodges as some warriors defected from Little Crow's cause. But how safe was that? Sarah Wakefield, under the protection of her Indian friend Chaska, recalled him saying, "You stay where you are; don't go up to the friendly camp; don't talk to any half-breeds or white women; if you do, you will be killed." Little Crow was preparing for battle, and Chaska's cousin told her "that Little Crow intended to destroy the friendly camp as soon as he returned; therefore Chaska's anxiety to have me stay where I was."[5]

As the troops advanced, they saw grim evidence of the Indians' fury. "I have seen a great many things since I left home," wrote Charles Watson of the 6th Minnesota. "I have seen some awful sights, men with their heads cut off and their skulls all mashed to pieces."[6]

Wood Lake

With Sibley's approach, Little Crow prepared for the coming fight. "As soon as the tepees were set the squaws and Indians commenced running bullets," recalled captive Urania White. "They had bar lead, bullet molds, and a ladle to melt lead in. They also had a large amount of powder which they had plundered, so they were well prepared to make some defense. They gave us to understand that they expected to have a battle in a short time with the white soldiers."

Some in the friendly camp felt their best move would be present Little Crow to Sibley along with captives already in hand. Paul Mazakutemani, however, felt this would be a bad move. Other captives still held by the hostiles could be killed in retribution.

As the column moved cautiously forward on September 22, the remains of George Gleeson were found. After assuring Sarah Wakefield she had nothing to fear, Gleeson had driven to his own death and the captivity of Sarah and her children. Gleeson received a quick burial as the troops moved on.

That evening found the troops encamped alongside what they thought was Wood Lake, but was actually Lone Tree Lake. But the name Wood Lake would stick. Scouts had seen no signs of Indians close by, but the usual breastworks were thrown up and pickets placed outside to thwart a surprise attack. Little Crow knew exactly where Sibley was and how the camp was laid out: in triangular fashion with the Sixth Minnesota Infantry on one flank, and the Third and Seventh on the other two. After the Fort Ridgely and New Ulm failures, Little Crow knew this was his last chance to reverse the fortunes of war. "Little Crow's camp crier went around saying that the Soldier's Lodge had decreed that every man in camp must go at once to Yellow Medicine and meet the troops," recalled Sam Brown. And any man who captured an American flag, Sibley's scalp, or other whites on a wanted list, "would receive as a present from the tribe all the wampum beads in camp and be showered with the honors within the gifts of the people, and be thereafter looked up to as the hero and chief warrior of the tribe."[7] Sam's father, Joseph Brown, was on that wanted list.

All warriors of fighting age were cajoled to take part in the coming fight, including those in the friendly camp. Despite the rift with the Upper Dakotas, many of their warriors fell into line. They were warriors, after all, and if Little Crow thrashed the whites, they would look like cowards for having not taken part. A mixed-blood in the Indian camp, Gabriel Renville, recalled: "Little Crow's plan was to quietly advance under cover of the darkness until the guards fired, and then rush in, and as soon as the troops rose up, to halt, fire one volley, charge forward and massacre them."[8] But Renville stood and advised them against such an attack, and his cousin, Solomon Two Stars, agreed. Not only was it cowardly, he told the warriors, but advanced pickets would give the alarm too early for Little Crow's plan to work, so that "they would be driven back before they could get near the camp." He said the Teton Sioux of the plains made daylight attacks, getting close in to the enemy before making "a sudden rush upon them, and then they could handle them very easily." He elaborated on how and where this could be achieved.[9] "I think this was a good plan of battle," recalled Big Eagle. "Our concealed men would not have been discovered. The grass was tall and the place by the road and the ravine were good hiding places. We had learned that Sibley was not particular about sending out scouts and examining the country before he passed it.... The whites were unconscious. We could hear them laughing and singing."[10]

Little Crow gave Solomon Two Stars' plan the nod. Perhaps his own strategy was a little too much like Birch Coulee. Although they had given the whites a severe bruising, the enemy camp had not been overrun. His old friend Sibley was no fool, he knew. Once forewarned, he may well be prepared, or even be inviting such an attack. The chiefs agreed to go with the plan.

"There were 738 Indians on the battle ground at Wood Lake," recalled Sam Brown. "Two trusty warriors were stationed on the road," and "as each brave passed he handed to the warriors a stick ... found to number 738."[11] The optimistic Indians took wagons along. Following the coming victory, abandoned weapons, provisions, blankets and ammunition would provide a bounty of loot.

Under cover of darkness, the warriors spread out to prearranged hiding places and began the long wait. Soon the Minnesota Valley would be back in Dakota hands for months, if not years. Perhaps the Confederacy would win the war, and the defeated bluecoats would never return. Pope, the new white commander, had been thrashed at Bull Run, a good omen for a Dakota triumph now. A victory by Little Crow would see the chief vindicated. Those who had deserted his cause and turned "friendly" would come back in droves, their prisoners with them. Little Crow would succeed where great chiefs like Tecumseh and Pontiac in earlier days back east had ultimately failed.

A dim light shimmered in the eastern sky. The troops would march soon—straight into Little Crow's trap. But the sun got higher. The troops did not move. Once again Sibley felt no need to hasten ahead. Perhaps, lacking cavalry, he felt they were never going to catch their prey in any case.

The monotonous military diet of meat and hardtack was enough the drive a man to break ranks. And on the morning of September 23, it did just that. Some men of the 3rd Minnesota set out with wagons to harvest abundant Indian potato crops near the ruins of the Upper Agency. Being Civil War veterans who had "seen the elephant," they were held in high esteem, and quite possibly thought themselves above rules and regulations. They "had lost a great deal of their former high discipline and were quite unruly," recalled Sergeant Ezra Champlin, one of their own. The officers who had surrendered them to the Confederates had been cashiered for cowardice. But they had new officers now, including their veteran commander, Major Abraham Welch.

Conspicuous by its absence from Sibley's report was any mention of the wayward foragers inadvertently doing a scout, quite possibly saving his scalp. They "came on right over the prairie," recalled Big Eagle, "right where part of our line was. Some of the wagons were not in the road, and if they had kept straight on would have driven right over our men as they lay in the grass."[12]

Half a mile out, the barking of a soldier's dog in the advance gave the game away.[13] The soldiers were astonished to see a line of warriors rise from the long grass to their front. In the next instant a cloud of gun smoke erupted and musket balls flew. Most missed, but one soldier received a mortal leg wound leg. Others grasped their rifles, jumped from the wagons and returned fire. "Little Crow saw it and felt very badly," recalled Big Eagle. Once again, things were not going to plan.

Back at Sibley's camp, all eyes turned towards the shooting. "All who want to fight, fall in," ordered Major Welch. The men scrambled for their guns and the 3rd Minnesota fell into line. On Welch's order, about 270 soldiers, aligned in companies, moved at the "double quick for the scene of action," and were soon hotly engaged. The Dakotas, being hit at the extreme front of their proposed ambush line, with relatively few warriors on hand, were soon pushed back several hundred yards. But other warriors ran towards the shooting. "The savages formed a semi-circle to our front," recalled Sergeant Champlin, "and to right and left, moving about with great activity, howling like demons, firing and retreating. Their quick movements seemed to multiply their number."

The 3rd Minnesota surged forward, driving the Indians over the undulating prairie towards the Minnesota River. For Champlin, it brought to mind "Tennyson's Charge of the Light Brigade, with Indians to right of us, Indians to left of us, Indians in front of us, whooping and yelling." But then a mounted staff officer galloped up to Welch through the smoke. "Get back to camp the best way you can," he shouted. Then a bugle sounded a discordant call. What was that? Was it the retreat? All of which "created much confusion," recalled Champlin. The skirmishers on the front line about-faced and ran in on the reserves. Chaos reigned supreme, each man for himself. They fell back down a slope towards a creek, "and here was pandemonium itself, with Indians to right of us, Indians to left of us, Indians behind us, charging and yelling."[14] Sergeant Bowler attempted to rally the men: "Remember Murfreesboro fight boys, remember Murfreesboro." There would be no defeat this time around.

Major Welch valiantly did all he could to restore order. They scrambled across the creek to be reinforced by the Renville Rangers under Lieutenant Gorman, ordered out by Sibley. Here, on higher ground, the combined force made a stand. But then: "I'm shot boys!" Welch called out. Champlin rushed forward and grabbed Welch as he fell, his leg bone shattered by a ball. "Take me in," the major said. With another man, Champlin started carrying the wounded officer back to camp, a quarter of a mile away. They were quickly overtaken by men on the run. "Go back and fight, you white-livered cowards," Welch yelled, "go back and fight or I'll shoot you." Once back in camp, Champlin told Welch he would leave him behind a wagon for protection. "No," he said, pointing to a low bluff. "Take me up on the hill where I can see the fight." He was left on the hill, "with his face to the foe."[15] Welch survived Wood Lake only to be wounded at Vicksburg and die in a Nashville hospital in February of 1864.

Champlin returned to the fray to witness Lieutenant Olin of the 3rd lead about 50 men on a wild bayonet charge. The surprised Indians scarcely had time to scatter, and the fight almost became hand-to-hand.

Lieutenant Colonel William Marshall, meanwhile, on Sibley's orders, led his five companies of the 7th Regiment to the north side of the camp in support of the 6-pounder gun commanded by Captain Hendricks. While Company H manned the rifle pits dug for the camp's defense, the other four companies advanced towards a ravine occupied by the enemy. Taking their time, the soldiers moved forward, crawling through long grass, loading and firing as they went. The 6-pounder, meanwhile, pounded the ravine. Reinforced by Captain Grant's company of the 6th, Marshall gave the order to charge. The troops leapt to their feet, bayonets to the fore. They dashed into the ravine and the Indians scattered, chased by the jubilant troops.[16]

Other warriors, meanwhile, had dashed through long grass and behind hillocks to the south to assault the rear of the camp. But a hot fire was delivered by troops under Major Robert McLaren. The men held their line as they rammed powder and ball home, then fired again. "The Battle raged for about two hours," reported Sibley, "the 6-pounder and mountain howitzer being used with great effect, when the Indians, repulsed at all points with great loss, retired with precipitation."[17]

"Commonly the roar of a cannon is a dreadful sound in the ears of women," recalled Nancy Huggan, "but to us captives in the Indian camp the sound of Gen. Sibleys guns was as sweet as the chimes of wedding bells to the bride." And Urania White remembered, "While the battle was raging, the squaws went out with one-horse wagons to take out ammunition to the warriors and bring in the dead and wounded Indians. Once when they returned one squaw was giving vent to her feelings by chanting, or singing 'Yah! Ho! Ho!' On making inquiry I was told that her husband had been killed."

"The Indians that got into the fight did well," recalled Big Eagle, "but hundreds of our men did not get into it and did not fire a shot. They were out too far."[18] Sibley gauged the number of Indians involved at 300. But Sergeant Champlin had other ideas: "Little Crow brought his whole force to bear, as it was a vital point, his main camp being but a few miles beyond; 800 was the estimate made at the time and it is probably not far from right." According to captive Sam Brown, a despondent Little Crow lamented: "Seven hundred picked warriors whipped by the cowardly whites."[19]

Prominent war chief Mankato "was killed by a cannon ball that was so nearly spent that he was not afraid of it," recalled Big Eagle, "and it struck him in the back, as he lay on the ground, and killed him."[20] According to mixed-blood George Quinn, fighting with the Dakotas, an old warrior called Walks On Iron "went out from the Indian side with a white flag, but a cannon ball took off his leg and he died. He had taken no part against the whites."[21]

By about 9 a.m. the battle smoke cleared and the prairie fell silent. No living Indians were to be seen. Sibley had won the day. Some time later, a Joe Campbell appeared bearing a flag of truce. He carried a message from Upper Dakota Wahpetons who had taken part in the fight. They were not strong enough to fight the troops, they said. They wanted peace, and permission to carry away their dead and wounded. "When you bring up the prisoners and deliver them to me under the flag of truce I will be ready to talk of peace," Sibley wrote back. "The bodies of the dead Indians that have been killed will be buried like white people and the wounded will be attended to as our own; but none will be given until the prisoners are brought in."[22]

While Sibley awaited a response, he penned a battle report to Governor Ramsey. Campbell claimed "30 killed and a large number wounded" on the Indian side, while Sibley wrote his own loss at four killed and between 35 and 40 wounded, three of whom later died. "I am very much in want of bread rations, 6-pounder ammunition, and shells for the howitzer; and unless soon supplied will be obliged to fall back which, under the present circumstances would be a calamity as it would afford time for the escape of the Indians with their captives." He hoped that a large cavalry force was on its way, for if he had been "provided with 500" horsemen, he "could have killed the greater portion of the Indians and brought the campaign to a successful close." Unknown to Sibley, he had achieved just that, thanks to Little Crow's determination for front-on combat rather than guerrilla warfare or flight. But Sibley was chagrined to learn that his men had scalped dead Indians. "The bodies of the dead," he wrote in general orders, "even of a savage enemy, shall not be subjected to indignities by civilized and Christian men."[23]

That night Sibley had his troops stay put. Next day he wrote to friendly chiefs in the village of Red Iron. "I have not come to make war on those who are innocent, but upon the guilty. I have waited here one day, and intended to wait still another day to hear from the friendly Half-breeds and Indians, because I feared that if I advanced my troops before you could make your arrangements the war party would murder the prisoners."

Not realizing Sibley's concerns, not all appreciated his go-slow policy. Joseph Coursolle had two daughters as Indian prisoners. "Hurry! Hurry! I shouted. Then Sibley ordered a dress parade! For two hours we maneuvered and then passed in review. I would have been court-martialed if Sibley could have heard what I called him under my breath! And instead of going to the rescue we camped again that night!"[24]

Little Crow, meanwhile, had fled. Following the defeat, his friend Wabasha, opposed to the war from the start, suggested that the prisoners be released. This would curb the white man's wrath. Who knows what fate would befall the Dakota tribe now? To execute the prisoners would merely bring more violent reprisals.[25]

But, during the battle, with the hostile warriors absent, friendlies had brought most prisoners to their village, now about 100 lodges. They may have to defend themselves once the braves returned. "We immediately set to work digging holes in the center of the lodges," recalled Sam Brown, "big enough for the women and children to get into, and ditches outside and around for the men."[26]

This angered Little Crow when he returned from the defeat. The captives "seek to defy us, and dug trenches while we were away," he said. "They must die." By this time, however, many former hostiles had turned friendly. They moved with their captives to the friendly camp and "vowed they would stay by us," recalled Brown. "We simply laughed at Little Crow's bombastic talk."

Little Crow had no choice but to back down. There would be more casualties if the factions came to blows, and deaths among the captives. This would make it all the worse for Indians who chose to surrender rather than follow him into exile. And the chief himself had relatives in the friendly camp. He gave orders for his family and followers to prepare for departure. They would have to trek some considerable distance to keep out of the white man's avenging hands.

Although Joe Campbell had been secretly aiding the peace party, he felt obliged to answer a summons from Little Crow—with eight friendlies as an escort. Little Crow held council in a tent pitched on a knoll—ironic, perhaps, that as it was the canvas tent of a white man, not a tepee. "The tent belonged to Beausejour, a French Canadian," recalled Campbell's daughter Cecilia. "He had been practicing curcys [circus] acts before the outbreak. The lower corner of the door was carried up and fastened back so the end of the tent was open. Little Crow sat just inside to the right of the open door. They spread a robe or blanket in the center for father to sit on. The warriors were all dressed and painted, standing outside next to their chief, all leaning on their guns." Campbell was relieved to receive a warm welcome. Little Crow, knowing that Joe had no intention of joining him in flight, asked if there was anything he could do for him in the meantime. No, Campbell replied, but he did think things would go better for those who stayed if Little Crow surrendered with them. "The long merchant Sibley would like to put the rope around my neck," Little Crow replied, "but he won't get the chance."

"I don't think they will hang anybody," said Campbell, "they never did before."

But Little Crow knew far better than Joe Campbell of the mass slaughter of settlers. "No, Cousin," he said, "anything else but to give myself up to hang by the neck like a woman. If they would shoot me like a man I would, but otherwise they will never get my live body."

Campbell asked if Little Crow would release those prisoners still in hostile hands.

"Yes," he replied, "you shall have them."

Most remaining prisoners were released to the friendly camp. But Little Crow's power had been broken, and some warriors refused the order. They would hold on to their prisoners for several months longer. About 46 additional captives, however, were delighted to be delivered into relative safety. "Let them alone," Little Crow told his warriors. "Too many women and children have been killed already. If you had killed only men, we could make peace now." But Little Crow had known women and children would die as warriors went on the attack. Such was the way with Indian warfare, even between the tribes.

And perhaps he was not so opposed as he claimed. "One day I was sitting quietly and shrinkingly by a tepee when he came in a full chief's costume looking very grand," recalled the much-abused Mary Schwandt.

> Suddenly he jerked his tomahawk from his belt and sprang towards me with the weapon uplifted as though he meant to cleave my head in two … but I looked at him, without any fear or care about my fate, and gazed quietly into his face…. He brandished his tomahawk over me a few times, then laughed, put it back in his belt and walked away, still laughing…. He was a great chief, and some people say he had many noble traits of character, but I have another opinion of any man, civilized or otherwise, who will take for a subject of sport a poor, weak, defenseless, broken-hearted girl, a prisoner in his hands, who feels as though she could never smile again.[27]

The morning following the defeat, Little Crow and his remaining followers made final preparations to flee. Those going with him well knew what deeds they had performed, and to be identified by survivors would negate any assurances offered by Sibley. How long would the vengeful arm of the whites be able to reach? One hundred warriors or more, many with families, chose to follow Little Crow, and others fell in with other leaders, including Shakopee, a prime mover of the revolt. The four Rice Creek Indians who started the whole sorry affair at Acton rode with the followers of war chief Red Middle Voice.

Before departure, Little Crow delivered one final speech: "I am ashamed to call myself a Dakota," he said. "Seven hundred of our best warriors were whipped yesterday by the whites. Now we had all better run away and scatter out over the plains like buffalos and wolves. To be sure, the whites had wagon guns and better arms than we, and there were many more of them. But that is no reason why we should not have whipped them, for we are brave Dakotas and whites are cowardly women. I cannot account for the disgraceful defeat. It must be the work of traitors in our midst."[28]

That day, September 24, Joe Campbell rode into Sibley's camp and handed Sibley a letter from Paul Mazakutemani of the friendly camp. It read:

> The enemy are holding a council this morning, and wanted us to join them. They are rebels. We prefer our own councils and writing our own letters. The captives have been coming to us for safety until we have the greatest number, and so we are in danger of a battle from them immediately. Now, dear sir, please come right away without delay, or we may all fall victim, for fight we must soon. The enemy are not large in numbers, but you well know they are cruel savages. All the Indians, with the exception of these, are friendly, and we were prepared for defending ourselves, we should conquer; and if you don't hasten, our women and all the captives will suffer.[29]

But again Sibley did not move. Instead he penned a reply: "I repeat what I have already stated to you, that I have not come to make war upon those who are innocent but upon the guilty. I have waited here one day, and intend to wait still another day, to hear from the friendly half-breeds and Indians, because I feared that if I advanced my troops before you could make your arrangements, the war party would murder the prisoners. Now that I learn from Joseph Campbell that most of the captives are in safety in your camp, I shall move tomorrow, so that you may expect to see me very soon. Have a white flag displayed so my men will not fire upon you."[30]

Little Crow, meanwhile, led his followers across the Minnesota River. They crested a bluff on the northern bank. He looked around. "We shall never go back there," he said. He knew the fertile valley that had been home to the Dakotas for generations had now been forfeited in a carnage of bloodshed and mayhem. Now he was a hated man, he knew, not only by the whites but many of his own people. No doubt he looked back with anguish on his rash decision to make war, against all common sense, simply because someone had called him a coward. His own vanity had helped bring on this catastrophe for the Dakota people. Real courage would have been to oppose the mob.

The cold winter winds about to be unleashed seemed a fitting end to the great Dakota rebellion. The James and Missouri Rivers would freeze over, but the spring thaw would see steamers carrying white soldiers to pursue Little Crow.

But he still held out hopes for an alliance with friends further west. The Dakota Nation was made up of seven major tribes, speaking three different dialects of the same language. Apart from the four Minnesota Santee tribes, there were the Yanktonais and Yanktons, and the Lakotas (or Tetons). The Lakotas were made up of seven subtribes: Brule, Oglala, Sans Arc, Hunkpapa,

Miniconjou, Blackfeet, and Two Kettle. Perhaps they would join Little Crow in a renewed push against the whites.

Failing that, there was always Rupert's Land, which would become part of the Dominion of Canada in 1868. The vast territory had been governed by the Hudson's Bay Company under royal charter from the British government since 1670. Perhaps weapons and supplies to continue the war could be supplied there. Or even a sanctuary where Yankee rule did not prevail.[31]

10

Maniacs or Wild Beasts

The captives' spirits soared when Joe Campbell returned to camp with the good news: liberation was at hand. Many warriors exchanged their captives' Indian garb for plundered white clothing to placate resentment amongst the troops. "About this time some squaws brought me a dress belonging to Mrs. Dr. Humphries," recalled Sarah Wakefield. "How strange are God's ways! How little did I think when I assisted her in making this dress of my ever wearing it, and at such a place and under such circumstances. Now she was dead, and I, where was I? In a camp of Indians not knowing but I should, at last, be murdered by them, for I had many miles to travel before reaching civilization."[1]

Indians who had defended Sarah and her children asked her to write a letter of support to show the victors when they arrived. This included Chaska. His mother cried when Sarah said goodbye. "You are going back," she said. You will "have good warm houses and plenty to eat, and we will starve on the plains this winter." To her, Little Crow was a "bad man who has caused us so much trouble." Sarah took her children to the village center, where a large American flag fluttered in the breeze.

"How we looked for Sibley all the next day," recalled Sarah, "but he did not come; all that night we watched also, but no sign of him yet. Where can he be? He was only twenty-five miles away. At last we concluded that he was afraid. The Indians began to get uneasy, and said Little Crow will be back and kill us, if Sibley does not soon come."[2]

Chaska told Sarah it would be far safer for him to flee. Was Sibley regrouping for an all-out assault? But the colonel had promised to shake hands with the friendlies, Sarah reminded him. There would be no punishment for the innocent. But Chaska felt uneasy. Perhaps some inner voice foretold dark, future events. He finally agreed to stay, but told her, "If I am killed, I will blame it all on you."

The night passed, and then the next day. Still no Sibley. The second night a Dakota scout reported that he was puzzled. Sibley had only covered eight miles that day. Despite the chiefs having assured Sibley that the road was safe, he had set up camp once more and dug entrenchments. In the friendlies' camp, all wondered with great anxiety what was going to happen. If Little Crow got wind of this, he may well return and slaughter them all.

That night, "twenty or thirty Indians came in with a young white girl of sixteen or seventeen," recalled Nancy Huggan. "She was nearly heartbroken, and quite in despair. When the half-breed men saw her they determined to rescue her, and we women encouraged them. Joe Laframboise and nine other mixed bloods went boldly up and took the girl from her brutal captors. The Indians threatened to shoot her if she was taken from them; but Joe was very brave, and said: We are going to have her if we have to fight for her; and if you harm her it will be the worse for you. Remember, we are not your prisoners any more."[3]

The following day, August 26, at last, "No grander sight ever met the eyes of anybody than when the troops marched up with bayonets glistening in the bright noonday sun and colors flying, drums beating, and fifes playing," recalled Sam Brown. "I shall never forget it while I live. We could hardly realize our deliverance had come."[4] They halted about 500 yards from the large cluster of tepees Sibley had named "Camp Release." Overwhelming joy swept through the captives. Some wept while others laughed hysterically—better late than never.

The Indians were most anxious to prove that they were all of the friendly camp—despite what they may have perpetrated before Wood Lake. They jumped about as though they too had been saved, waving scraps of white cloth. "White rags were fastened to the top of tepee poles," Brown recalled, "to wagon wheels, cart wheels, to sticks and poles stuck in the ground, and every conceivable object, and in some grotesque manner and ludicrous way. One Indian who was boiling over with loyalty and love for the white man threw a white blanket on his white horse and tied a bit of cloth to its tail, and then, that no possible doubt might be raised in his case he wrapped the American flag around his body and mounted his horse and sat upon him in full view of the troops as they passed by, looking more like a circus clown than a 'friendly' Indian."[5]

At two o'clock, two companies of infantry tramped towards the tepee village. The troops halted outside the perimeter while Sibley and other officers marched to a central clearing. Once assembled, the chiefs listened as Sibley repeated the contents of his letter; only those guilty of crimes would be punished. He demanded the immediate release of all prisoners.

The chiefs readily agreed. But first, as it was with all councils, they had a few words to say. They condemned those who had committed atrocities and gave assurances of their own innocence. They would not dare shake Sibley's hand, they said, if their own was stained with blood. One by one they came forward and shook hands with Sibley and those around him.

Friendly party spokesman Paul Mazakutemani had personal words for Sibley: "I have grown up like a child of yours. With what is yours, you have caused me to grow; and now I take your hand as a child takes the hand of his father. My hand is not bad. With a clean hand I take your hand. I know whence this blessing cometh. I have regarded all white people as my friends, and from this I understand this blessing has come. This is good work we do today, whereof I am glad. Yes, before the great God, I am glad."[6]

Also glad were the prisoners. "They were bought into the circle to the number of between a hundred and a hundred and fifty," Sibley wrote his wife, "and a pitiable sight they represented. The poor creatures cried for joy at their deliverance from the loathsome bondage in which they had been kept for weeks, suffering meantime nameless outrages at the hands of their brutal captors. Most of them were young, and there were a score or more of fine, lady-like appearance, not withstanding the ragged clothes they wore. They all clustered close around our little group, as if they feared that attempts would be made to keep them in custody." He wrote of Mrs. Adams, "whose six months old child was killed when she was captured, who is exceedingly pretty, and has a complexion as white as snow. She says she was let alone and protected by a really friendly Indian, who treated her like a sister."

According to Sibley, the one white male captive to survive, George Spencer, praised him for not marching to the camp "the night after the battle. A plan was formed, had you done so, to murder the captives, then scatter to the prairies."[7] But Sarah Wakefield took a different view: "I can never give Sibley any credit for releasing the prisoners," she recalled, "or capturing Indians, for do you, my readers, consider it a capture when men willingly wait two days and nights for their captors to march twenty-five miles? It was a wonderful affair! Glory, honor and renown, ought to be written on their brows. God influenced those Indians to remain with us, and to God and the Indians I give my thanks."[8]

"A few of the more attractive had been offered the alternative of becoming temporary wives of select warriors, and so, helpless and powerless, yet escaped the promiscuous attentions of a horde of savages bent on brutal insult revolting to conceive, and impossible to be described," wrote Sibley. "Officers and men, affected even to tears by the scene, denuded themselves of their entire underclothing, blankets, coats, and whatever they could give, or could be converted into raiment for these heart-broken and abused victims of savage lust and rage."

Despite the joy of deliverance, for some there was a less happy side. Bonds of friendship and emotion had been forged with Indians who had provided protection. Chaska's mother tore her shawl in two and gave half to Sarah, before they hugged each other in tears. In all, 107 white and 162 mixed-blood prisoners were released.

"I remember how angry the soldiers were with the Indians who surrendered there," recalled Mary Schwandt, "and how eager they were to be turned loose upon the vile and bloody wretches." Chaska trembled. "You are a good woman," he told Sarah, "You must talk to your white people or they will kill me. You know I am a good man and did not shoot Mr. Gleeson, and I saved your life. If I had been a bad man I would have gone with those bad chiefs." Sarah assured him that all would be well. She approached Sibley and told him how she and her children had been protected. The colonel praised Chaska and shook his hand.

But many Indians now professing friendship had not always been so. Retribution would follow—and mistakes would be made.

Mary Schwandt was sad to say farewell to 23-year-old Snana, called Maggie by the whites. She had traded a pony in exchange for Mary. Snana's oldest daughter had died recently, and Mary, she felt, could help fill the void in her heart. Mary remembered Snana as "one of the handsomest Indian women" she ever saw. Snana could speak, read and write English fluently, and was "one of the best." Snana and her husband Good Thunder had previously converted to Christianity and heard of captives being murdered in retribution for braves killed in battle. When threatened by young braves one night, Mary recalled, "Maggie sprang up as swiftly as a tigress defending her young, and almost as fierce, and ordered them out."[9] As the hostiles were preparing to flee Camp Release, Snana later recalled that they "dug a hole inside my tent and put some poles across, and then spread my blankets over and sat on top of them, as if nothing unusual had happened. But who do you suppose were inside the hole? My dear captive girl, Mary Schwandt, and my own two little children." Sibley's arrival meant being parted from the "dear child" she had saved. "My heart ached again," Snana recalled, when it came time to say a tearful farewell. "From that day I never saw her or knew where she was for thirty-four years." In 1894, Snana learned that Mary was living in St. Paul, the wife of William Schmidt. The two women were cheerfully reunited, and Snana recalled, "It was just as if I went to visit my own child."[10]

"No sooner had the white captives been brought over to our camp," recalled the Reverend Riggs, "than, from various sources, we began to hear of Indian men who had maltreated these white women, or in some way had been engaged in the massacres on the border. On the morrow, Gen. Sibley requested me to act as the medium of communication between these women and himself."[11] Riggs' enquiry resulted in the apprehension of several "friendlies" in Camp Release. Sibley planned a military commission to place all the accused on trial, but this was to remain under wraps for the moment. He wanted to round up as many alleged offenders as possible before they could escape.

Mixed-bloods went out saying those who surrendered would be treated as prisoners of war, and Sibley sent two detachments up the banks of the Minnesota River. They had orders to bring in all Indians they could find by force, if necessary. "Unless these people arrive very soon," Sibley wrote, "will go in search of them with my troops and treat them as enemies."[12]

The number of Indians grew as small parties were either rounded up or came in under a flag of truce—better to surrender than starve in the open. Why had they fled? Possibly because of guilt, and they were isolated in a separate village from Camp Release. Eventually Sibley had about 2,000 Indians under his charge.

Sibley received letters demanding retribution, and newspapers howled for revenge. "They must be exterminated," said one editorial, "and now is a good time to commence doing it." And General Pope gave his enthusiastic endorsement: "The horrible massacres of women and children and the outrageous abuse of female prisoners, still alive, call for punishment beyond human power to inflict," he wrote Sibley. "It is my purpose to utterly exterminate the Sioux if I have the power to do so and even if it requires a campaign lasting the whole of next year. Destroy everything belonging to them and force them out to the plains, unless, as I suggest, you can capture them. They are to be treated as maniacs or wild beasts, and by no means as people with whom treaties or compromises can be made."[13]

A wave of unease swept through the Indians as rumors arrived. The whites were out for their blood—guilty or not. Following her release, Sarah Wakefield returned to Camp Release to retrieve her belongings, and here she found Chaska, "very pale and frightened." The whites were rounding up the warriors, he told her, and he felt certain he would be arrested and killed. Sarah now urged her friend to flee. "No," Chaska replied. "I am not a coward. I am not afraid to die. All I care about is my poor old mother. She will be left alone." Sarah said she would care for his mother, but Chaska put no faith in her words.

Sarah was soon appalled to hear of Chaska's arrest. That evening she approached a group of officers, "laughing and talking" in camp. Captain Grant remarked that some captives will hang "before to-morrow night." Sarah asked if this included the man who had protected her. "Yes," replied Grant, "he will swing with the rest." Sarah, aghast, blurted out, "Capt. Grant, if you hang that man, I will shoot you." No doubt Grant's reaction told her she had made a bad mistake. She attempted to make light of the situation. "But you must first teach me to shoot, for I am afraid of a gun, unloaded even." Sarah blamed her "violent, impulsive disposition" for the remark, and likened it to threatening naughty children, "Do be quiet, or I'll whip you to death." Hot words not really meant, a "rude way of expressing myself."[14]

Colonel Sibley had previously written to his wife that a woman "had become so infatuated with the red skin who had taken her for his wife,

Following the Indian surrender at Camp Release, a search for guilty parties got underway. A boy identifies the man he believed killed his mother (*Harper's Weekly*, December 20, 1862).

although her white husband was still living at some point below, and had been in search of her, she declared that were it not for her children, she would not leave her dusky paramour." News of her threat spread like wildfire, and in Sibley's following letter, the woman "threatens that if *her* Indian, who is amongst those who have been seized should be hung, she will shoot those of us who have been instrumental in bringing him to the scaffold, and then go back away with the Indians. A pretty species of a white woman she is, truly."[15]

There were no hangings the following day, but judicial heads with the gallows in mind were plotting behind the scenes. Sibley selected five officers, including Captain Grant, to sit on the military commission. They would judge Indians accused of various crimes.

But while most saw the revolt purely as Indian barbarism, some deep thinkers acknowledged another side of the coin. The *Mankato Semi-Weekly Record*, while still calling for extermination to keep its sales on track, stated: "When the whole matter has been thoroughly and fairly investigated, the main cause of the outbreak will be the fraudulent conduct of Indian officials.... The Department at Washington is not wholly blameless for the murder of our frontier settlers, for time and again the frauds of Indian officials have been made known there, to all of which a deaf ear was turned." The editorial stated that "a thieving agent, leagued with equally dishonest traders," prevented sufficient annuity payments to prevent the Indians "from starvation and they are turned loose to supply the deficiency by stealing from white settlers. The bulk of their goods go to fill the coffers of those in whose care they are entrusted."[16]

Despite this, the same paper had no time for the Reverend Williamson, who stated he could find no evidence of cruelties beyond legitimate acts of war. "He might have heard of outrages such as only a Sioux Indian could perpetrate. A number of instances have occurred where females have been brutally ravished after death. We have it upon good authority that two children were found in Brown County with their feet tied together and strung across a fence. Also one instance where a body was nailed to a wall. In the face of such facts, we fear the doctor will not make much headway in manufacturing sympathy for his Indian wards."

Sibley had refrained from making mass arrests to prevent word spreading. But the time had come, he felt, to bring more culprits to justice. The guards were reinforced at the second camp; where those who came in late were held. Eighty-one warriors were rounded up and led away, their ankles in chains.

Food was a growing problem, and 1,250 Indians, men, women and children, were sent with 150 soldiers to the Upper Agency to gather potatoes and corn to feed both Indians and troops. "The large number of cattle, horses, wagons carriages and buggies" recalled Sam Brown, "made the train a long one."

By October 15 the number of prisoners in chains had risen to 101, and Sibley noted that 236 men at the Upper Agency "will be secured in the same way today." He felt that "some of them are probably innocent, but by far the greater part will be found guilty of murder, rape, etc. As they will all be sent under guard to Fort Snelling, in obedience of orders, my command will be deprived of the gratification of strangling the guilty ones." Sibley gave Thomas Galbraith the responsibility of arresting his former charges. Sam Brown, enrolled as an interpreter, informed the Indians that all men must assemble for a roll call and count in order to receive their annuity payment. "This ruse worked like a charm," recalled Brown. When called up, the men were channeled into a building where they were disarmed and clapped in leg irons. Forty-six men considered above suspicion remained free, along with "three or four who had 'smelled a mice' and ran away during the night," recalled Brown. "In this way we succeeded in arresting and safely detained in custody 234 of Little Crow's fiercest warriors. And since the Indian men outnumbered the soldiers two to one and were fully and well armed, I think that in this case, 'the end justified the means.'"[17]

Regarding the proposed trials, "I see the press is very much concerned lest I prove too tender-hearted" Sibley wrote his wife. "I shall do full justice, but no more. I do not propose to murder any man, even a savage, who is shown to be innocent of the 'great transgression,' or to permit the massacre of women and children." But was that true? Was Sibley, the wily politician, writing what he wished future generations to believe? He excused himself from sitting on the commission. And the "full justice" meted out would be open to question. "Instead of taking individuals for trial," recalled the Reverend Riggs, "against whom some specific charge could be brought, the plan was adopted to subject all grown men, with a few exceptions, to an investigation of the commission, trusting that the innocent could make their innocence appear." In other words, they were presumed *guilty*—unless the accused could prove otherwise. Under 1862 military law, a defendant did not necessarily have a right to a defense counsel, as in a civil court. It was the Judge Advocate's job not only to prosecute, but also to defend the accused's rights, as defined by law.[18]

On October 7, Pope wired General Halleck that he had placed a reward of $500 on Little Crow's head, "so as to make him an outlaw among the Indians. Nearly the whole of his band have deserted him and come in begging for mercy." Five hundred dollars seems a paltry sum for a man held responsible for so much slaughter and carnage. Confederate guerrilla leader John Mosby would have $5000 placed on his head after fighting what many considered an honorable war.[19]

11

FIVE MINUTES WOULD DISPOSE OF A CASE

There is no substitute for success, and Sibley's critics cringed after Wood Lake. On September 29, Halleck wired Pope, "Colonel Henry Hastings Sibley is made brigadier general for his judicious fight at Yellow Medicine. He should be kept in command of that column and every possible assistance sent to him." Lincoln's promotion transferred Sibley from a state militia colonel to the rank of a U.S. brigadier general of volunteers, subject to the president of the United States.[1]

Just one day earlier, the trials had commenced. First up was Joseph Godfrey, 27, a mixed-blood former slave of black and French-Canadian parents. Married to a Dakota woman, he had lived with the Indians for about five years before hostilities commenced. Mary Woodbury, Mattie Williams and David Fairibault all testified that he claimed to have killed seven whites. "The black wretch Godfrey had been with the Indians murdering and plundering," recalled Mary Schwandt, "and about his waist were strung quite a number of watches."[2] Godfrey claimed that he had been forced to join the war party under pain of death. His claims of killing settlers had been false, made to impress the Indians. Although he admitted having fought against troops, he denied having killed anyone when raiding settlements. His one act of violence, he claimed, was to strike a man with the blunt edge of a hatchet in view of other Indians to create a false impression.

"He had such an honest look and spoke with such a truthful tone," recalled Court Recorder Isaac Heard. "His voice was one of the softest I ever listened to." Godfrey was found guilty, and Sibley wanted him to hang, but in this solitary instance the commission differed.[3] He had agreed to testify against others, and later on, President Lincoln would commute his sentence to 10 years behind bars. Since he was the first tried, the commission took two days to hear Godfrey's case. But, recalled Isaac Heard: "The trials were elaborately conducted until the commission became acquainted with the details of the different outrages and battles, and then ... five minutes would dispose of a case." Forty men could be tried in a single day.

In at least two thirds of the cases the prisoners admitted that they fired, but in most instances insisted that it was only two or three shots, and that no one was killed; about as valid an excuse as one of them offered who was possessed of an irresistible impulse to accumulate property, that a horse which he took was only a very little one, and that a pair of oxen which he captured was for his wife, who wanted a pair. In regard to the third who did not admit that they fired, their reasons for *not* doing so were remarkable, and assumed a different shape every day. One day all the elderly men, who were in the vigor of manly strength, said their hair was too gray to go into battle; and the young men, aged from eighteen to twenty-five, insisted that they were too young, and their hearts too weak to face fire.... Several of the worst characters, who had been in all the battles, after they had confessed the whole thing, wound up by saying that they were members of the Church! ... One young chap, aged about nineteen, said he always used to attend divine worship at Little Crow's village below St. Paul, and that he never did a bad thing in his life except to run after a chicken at Mendota a long time ago, and that he didn't catch it. The evidence disclosed the fact that this pious youth had been an active participant in some of the worst massacres at Beaver Creek.[4]

If one account is to be believed, Colonel Crooks, head of the commission, could hardly be called impartial. Sixty years later, Thomas Watts, a soldier, recalled: "Cut Nose, through the interpreter, was asked a question, and he began babbling away in his native tongue until all were out of patience, then he was asked to answer the question 'yes' or 'no.' He commenced the same incoherent babble again, when Colonel Crooks said to Mr. Riggs, (who was interpreting) 'Tell him to shut his mouth or I will split his head open with my sword.' Crooks was second in command of the expedition and I write to show that the private soldier was not the only one that harbored a grudge against the reds."[5]

Perhaps Crooks' inappropriate threat to "split his head" was influenced by some of the testimony: "Cut-nose, while two others held the horses, leaped into a wagon that contained eleven, mostly children, and deliberately, in cold blood, tomahawked them all—cleft open the head of each, while the others, stupefied with horror, powerless with fright, as they heard the heavy dull blows crash and tear through flesh and bones, awaited their turn. Taking an infant from its mother's arms, before her eyes, with a bolt from one of the wagons they riveted it through its body to the fence and left it there to die, writhing in agony."[6] It comes as little surprise that Cut Nose was amongst those sentenced to hang.

Sarah Wakefield's friend Chaska came before the bench charged with having taken part in the murder of George Gleeson. Despite her testimony that it was another warrior, Hapa, who had killed Gleeson, and Chaska had protected her, he was sentenced to hang, thus fulfilling his fears that he would receive no justice in Sibley's hands. But Chaska himself testified that he and Hapa had aimed guns at Gleeson to make sure he was dead. Chaska said he only wished to put Gleeson out of his misery if still alive. "Chaska raised his gun, but it snapped fire," recalled Sarah. "I don't believe his gun was loaded at all. That was what convicted him." She claimed, "Through misrepresentation it made it appear that Chaska had intended to kill him.... I was angry, for it seemed to me that they considered my testimony of no account; for if they had believed what I said, he would have been acquitted." Sarah's threat to shoot Captain Grant would not have helped. "But I soon discovered that the commission was not acting according to justice, but by favor; and I was terribly enraged against them. The more angry I got, the more I talked, making matters worse for Chaska as well as myself." Stories of Sarah and Chaska being lovers were "horrid, abominable reports," she wrote, but "God will see me righted—if not here, I hope in Heaven."[7]

"My boy, my boy, they will kill him," cried Chaska's mother. "Why didn't you save him? He saved your life many times. You have forgotten the Indians now your white friends have come." Sarah assured her she was doing all she could, and went to visit Chaska. She found him chained by the legs to 20 other prisoners. An attempt to shake hands was refused. She had told "falsehoods" to the soldiers, Chaska claimed. He reminded Sarah of the many kindnesses he had shown her, and she burst into tears, noted with disapproval by the guards. Her attempts to save him had lost her all her friends, she said, and it was wrong for him to blame her. "I at last convinced him that I was not to blame for his imprisonment, and I said I would like to shake hands and bid him goodbye in friendship. He shook hands with me, and that is all that passed between us. I never saw him again, for I left very soon for my home."[8]

The "trials," such as they were, rolled on. In all, 392 Indians faced Sibley's Commission, but most guilty warriors had fled and not returned. Someone, however, must pay the price. Having fought at Fort Ridgely, New Ulm, Birch Coulee and Wood Lake was enough to be condemned to death. For the Indians, these had been fair fights, the result of starvation and broken treaty obligations. By late October, over 100 Indians had been found guilty and sentenced to hang.

But there were legalities to be observed and considered. Sibley, unsure of his judicial position, passed the responsibly to John Pope. On October 10, Pope wired General Halleck: "The Sioux war is at an end. All of the bands engaged in the late outrages, except five men, have been captured. It will be necessary to execute many of them. The settlers can all return.... The example of hanging many of the perpetrators of the late outrages is necessary and will have a crushing effect."[9]

Pope's assertion that only five offenders remained on the run made no sense. Little Crow, with over 100 warriors, was still on the loose in Dakota Territory, along with other bands. Pope's ardent inclinations did not go down well with Lincoln's cabinet back east. On October 14, Navy Secretary Gideon Welles wrote in his diary, "I was disgusted with the tone and opinions of the dispatch. It was not the production of a good man or a great one. The Indian outrages, I doubt not, have been great—what may have been the provocations we have not been told." Welles also perceived a larger agenda: the removal of all Indian tribes, guilty or not. "The Winnebagos have good land which white men want and mean to have."

On October 17, Pope informed Sibley, "The President directs that no executions be made without his sanction."[10]

On October 20, Governor Ramsey pressured Lincoln to expel all Dakotas from Minnesota. The outbreak had been a "sudden and terrible blow," and the whites had learned "to disregard this perfidious and cruel race with a degree of mistrust and apprehension which they will not tolerate their presence of their neighborhood in any numbers or in any condition." The Sioux were "assassins" and ravishers of "wives and sisters and daughters." Therefore, "the Sioux of Minnesota have forfeited all claims for the protection of the government." But Lincoln wanted to hear from less partial voices. He had already dispatched Assistant Secretary of the Interior John P. Usher to Minnesota to assess the situation.[11]

Sibley, meanwhile, had a variety of problems on hand. "I find the greatest difficulty in keeping the men from the Indian women when the camps are close together," Sibley wrote his wife. "I have a strong line of sentinels entirely around my camp to keep every officer and soldier from going out without my permission; but some way or other, a few of the soldiers manage to get among the *gals*."

Food was another problem. Indians, troops and stock alike would all starve once winter set in, leaving Camp Release isolated by snow and ice. He gave orders for everyone to move to the Lower Agency, closer to civilization and easier to supply. On October 23, the tents came down and the prisoners were loaded into wagons. Before noon, a long column of men and stock moved southeast.

Patrols, meanwhile, had been dispatched to find food and bury victims. There was no shortage of bodies; the dead were found in singles, families, and groups. Cabins had been plundered with the contents smashed and strewn about.

With time, there seemed little hope that any survivors would be found, but nine weeks after the outbreak began, "two soldiers came to the door, and gently pushed it open," recalled 28-year-old Justina Boelter. "As they looked cautiously in, I crawled up to meet them, under the impression they were Indians come to kill me." Almost blind from starvation, Justina had survived after grubbing for potatoes and turnips in the fields. A 5-year-old daughter had already died of starvation. Her husband and neighbors had been killed, and now she and her 3-year-old daughter were on the brink of death. "I crawled up to them and took one of them by the hand, and prayed them not to kill me. Looking up I saw the tears running down the face of the man I had by the hand, and also the other one who stood by."[12]

11. Five Minutes Would Dispose of a Case

A chicken was found at a neighbor's house, a fire lit, and the two survivors were soon sipping chicken soup. "The food gave relief to the stomach, but caused the limbs to cramp and become feeble," Justina recalled. They were placed in a wagon, provided with warm coats, and taken to Sibley's camp, where a slow and painful recovery began. Justina and her child were the last victims to be found alive.[13]

A log-built kitchen at the Lower Agency provided a crude venue as the trials went on. Former owner Francois LaBathe had been amongst the slain. Summary justice continued, and over the next 10 days the remaining 272 accused were tried. Some cases took less than 10 minutes, the prisoners being brought up in groups of six or 8, chained at the ankles. Some were condemned simply because they could produce no witness to vouch for their innocence. The sentences handed down were not read out, causing bewilderment on the part of the accused. Some prisoners assumed that the commission had found all guilty and they were to be executed at the one time. Others thought that, as they had not been taken to the gallows or separated from the other prisoners, they had been found not guilty. The result was confusion, anxiety and fear.

Pastor John Williamson wrote to his mission board:

> 400 have been tried in less time than is generally taken in our courts with the trial of a single murderer. Again in very many of the cases a man's own testimony is the only evidence against him. He is first prejudiced guilty of any charge any of the Court choose to prefer against him and then if he denied he is cross examined with all the ingenuity of a modern lawyer to see if he cannot be detected in some error of statement. Then they are not allowed any counsel. They are scarcely allowed a word a word of explanation themselves, and knowing nothing of the manner of conducting trials if a mistake occurs they are unable to correct it. And often not understanding the English language in which the trial is conducted, they very imperfectly understand the evidence upon which they are convicted.[14]

On November 5, after the trial of 392 accused, the proceedings were wound up. Of these, 16 had received jail sentences and 304 had been condemned to hang. Sibley reviewed the results and approved all sentences except one. John Other Day, the savior of over 60 whites, had appealed to have his brother's sentence commuted to prison rather than the rope. Sibley conveniently felt the evidence was inconclusive and granted the request.[15]

On November 7, the impatient Pope sent by expensive telegraph a complete list of the 303 condemned men to Abraham Lincoln. When news got out, the *New York Times* suggested the massive bill of $400 be deducted from Pope's salary. Three days later, Lincoln replied to Pope, requesting the trial records of each man—to be sent by mail. Lincoln wanted to see for himself who had been convicted, and exactly of what. Rape and murder, or fighting in pitched battles such as Fort Ridgely and Wood Lake? The cantankerous Pope replied, by mail, "The only distinction between the culprits is as to which of them murdered most people or violated young girls. All of them are guilty in more or less degree." Lincoln, an experienced lawyer, was no remote easterner with little knowledge of Indian wars. As a young captain of militia, he had seen scalped and mutilated bodies of white settlers and soldiers during the Black Hawk War of 1832. The Dakotas had supported U.S. troops in that war, and he wished to see justice prevail.[16] Life and death decisions could not be left in the hands of the pugnacious General Pope.

Pope issued orders for the condemned to be taken downriver to Mankato, while those deemed innocent, along with 1,700 women and children, were to be taken by wagon overland to Fort Snelling. Here they would remain till the Office of Indian Affairs decided their fate. Lieutenant Colonel Marshall was given charge of the Fort Snelling expedition, and wrote to the *St. Paul Daily Press*: "I would risk my life for the protection of these helpless beings, and would feel everlastingly disgraced if any evil befell them while in my charge. Through the PRESS, I want the settlers in the valley, on the route we pass, to know that they are not the *guilty Indians* (some 300 of whom are to be executed at South Bend) but *friendly Indians, women and children.*"

President Abraham Lincoln, determined to see justice done, resisted calls for the hanging of over 300 men (Library of Congress).

On November 6, Marshall's long, bustling train of Dakotas and troops crossed at the ferry site where Captain Marsh's command had been overwhelmed. Thomas Galbraith traveled with them, along with missionaries John Williamson and Samuel Hinman. What was to become of these Dakotas? Their fate had yet to be decided by politicians back east.

Two days later, the second party, those found guilty, were loaded into a variety of vehicles at the Lower Agency. "We were bound securely," recalled one man, "and on our journey resembled a load of animals on their way to market."[17] At dawn, Sibley marched with an escort of two infantry regiments,

11. Five Minutes Would Dispose of a Case

On the outskirts of New Ulm, Indian captives in transit were set upon by enraged citizens. Troops had trouble driving them back (*Harper's New Monthly Magazine*, June 1863).

followed by supply wagons and artillery. Dakota women serving as cooks or laundresses followed on foot. That night they camped near the farm of John Massopust, whose father, two sisters and 6-year-old cousin had been killed on August 18. The following day, a Sunday, the column headed southeast towards what remained of New Ulm. There the residents were hard at work rebuilding the town and burying bodies as they were found amongst the ashes.

On the outskirts, Sibley was confronted by two men. One, 21-year-old Frederick Brandt, was dressed in a military uniform and claimed to be a major in the state militia. He handed Sibley a letter stating that to move prisoners through New Ulm was an insult to the residents who were "just today burying the dead." He advised Sibley to take a different route, but at the same time demanded that those prisoners who had attacked New Ulm be handed over. Needless to say, Sibley did not surrender any prisoners, but did think it prudent to take a different road a little to the south of town. Suspecting trouble, he deployed one company of 80 soldiers, armed and ready, on each side of the column.

As they marched along bluffs overlooking the town, they came upon a furious mob of men, women and even children blocking the road. They carried "all conceivable weapons," including clubs, knives, stones, pitchforks, guns and brickbats. "The first I knew," recalled one soldier, "one very large German woman slipped through in front of me, and hit one of the Indians on the head with a large stone. Well, he fell backwards out of the wagon, he being shackled to another Indian that held him, so he was dragged about five rods."[18] The Indians were showered with missiles until Sibley, rifle in hand, led a bayonet charge to disburse the crowd. "The presence of the women and children alone," recalled Sibley, "saved the male actors in this attack from being punished as they deserved from the fire of my forces." One soldier and 15 Indians were seriously wounded during the clash, and the troops took Frederick Brandt prisoner, along with 40 others.

The column arrived outside Mankato that night, and work commenced on Camp Lincoln, a compound to hold the condemned Indians. Brandt and his compatriots were released to make their way back home. Sibley sent a letter to Ramsey detailing the events and asking for the supposed militia officer Brandt to be investigated.

Colonel Marshall's 1,700 friendlies and noncombatants, meanwhile, despite his plea for calm, had problems of their own. On November 10, the slow-moving, four-mile-long column approached Henderson township, at which point they would turn northwards towards Fort Snelling. Henderson and St. Paul had received a huge influx of devastated refugees, and the residents were in no mood to tolerate Indians, innocent or otherwise. "Men, women and children, armed with guns, knives, clubs, and stones, rushed upon the Indians as the train was passing by and, before the soldiers could interfere and stop them, succeeded in pulling many of the old men and women, and even children, from the wagon by the hair of the head and beating them," recalled Sam Brown, "and otherwise inflicting injury upon the helpless and miserable creatures." One nursing baby was snatched from its mother's breast by a white woman and dashed violently to the ground. The aggressor was dragged away by the soldiers, who "restored the papoose to its mother—limp and almost dead." Brown's Indian uncle, Charles Crawford, almost fell victim to the mob when "one of the citizens with blood in his eyes and half crazed with drink rushed up with a gun," but Marshall, "the bold charger of the plains," galloped up and "struck down the gun with his sabre and got Crawford out of the way, thus saving a life at the risk of his own."[19]

The column passed the mob and township before setting up camp on a prairie flat some distance up the river. Marshall dispatched scouting parties to disburse any following civilians bent on further trouble. The battered baby's life ebbed away, and the body was "quietly laid away in the crotch of a tree." Sam Brown described the ceremony as "perhaps the last of its kind within the limits of Minnesota; that is, the last Sioux Indian 'buried' according to one of the oldest and most cherished customs of the tribe."

The afternoon of November 13 saw the weary troops and Indians arrive on a rise just to the south of Fort Snelling. Here cold winds sweeping through the camp made for a miserable night. Next day, the more sheltered bottomlands alongside the confluence of the Minnesota and Mississippi Rivers provided more tolerable camping conditions.

Looking down from the walls of Fort Snelling, 100 feet above, one soldier, Thomas Rice, later recalled: "There was something about it so weird, strange and unnatural it seemed more like a dream than reality. The many and oddly constructed tepees, some made of reeds and rushes, others of skins of animals, etc. The many camp fires, smoke from which hung over the camp like a pall. The barking of dogs, of which there seemed to be a goodly number. The shrill voices of the squaws as they performed their various duties. All of this combined to make a strange scene."[20]

Visitors from St. Paul and further afield came to gawk, thrusting unwelcome faces into tepees. Cameras were set up, and photos posted all over the United States. In St. Paul, meanwhile, a patron of the Opera House could view "The Panorama of the Indian Massacre of 1862 and the Black Hills." This, according to promoters, was "The Great Moral Exhibition of the Age." The customer viewed a screen 12 feet wide by six feet high with rollers on each side. To melodramatic music, the panorama of events in 36 images painted on 222 feet of canvas was cranked across in front of an awe-struck crowd. A gesticulating narrator explained the images of murder and mayhem: "Tumultuous horrors rent the midnight air, until the sad catalogue reached the fearful number of two thousand human victims from the gray haired sire to the helpless infant of a day, who lay mangled and dead on the bloody field. The dead were left to bury the dead, for the dead reigned there alone."[21] The show was a great success, soon touring Minnesota, Wisconsin and Iowa.

Dime novels and popular histories also cashed in. *Dakota War Whoop or Indian Massacres and War in Minnesota of 1862–1863* by Harriet Bishop was one fine example, virtually a dime novel masquerading as history. The St. Paul educator and reformer had previously denounced Inkpaduta as "the vilest wretch un-hung."

At Fort Snelling, construction of a timber enclosure began, but on November 19 the *St. Paul Pioneer Express* reported the killing of "an Indian squaw." The writer felt that "there will be many such incidents" if Abraham Lincoln did not consent to the hanging of those deemed guilty. This led to a fusillade of conflicting articles, and the demand for an investigation. The *St. Paul Daily Union* published a letter stating: "The truth of the matter appears to be, that the squaws have been in the habit of gathering wood for their campfires and one of them, thus engaged, having wandered some little distance from the encampment, was seized by a number of soldiers and brutally outraged." Such crimes, once proven by court-martial, were punishable by death, but effectively policing the vast village was virtually an impossible task.[22]

A deterrent to unwanted white intruders arrived in the form of measles. The Indians blamed it on crackers handed out to the children, as they were the worst affected. The Dakotas, having little immunity, saw the death rate climb, and about 160 died that first winter.

The ultimate fate of the friendlies rested with the Department of the Interior and the Commissioner of Indian Affairs, while the fate of those at Camp Lincoln, deemed guilty, rested with the Great White Father, Abraham Lincoln. The Dakotas in both places waited, anxious and depressed, for the electric telegraph to bring news from the east.

On December 1, Abraham Lincoln delivered his second annual message to Congress. Regarding Indian Affairs, he observed:

> In the month of August last the Sioux Indians in Minnesota attacked the settlements in their vicinity with extreme ferocity, killing indiscriminately men, women, and children. This attack was wholly unexpected, and therefore no means of defense had been provided. It is estimated that not less than 800 persons were killed by the Indians, and a large amount of property was destroyed.... The people of that State manifest much anxiety for the removal of the tribes beyond the limits of the State as a guaranty against future hostilities. The Commissioner of Indian Affairs will furnish full details. I submit for your especial consideration whether our Indian system shall not be remodeled. Many wise and good men have impressed me with the belief that this can be profitably done.

Two days after the president's address, Camp Lincoln commander Colonel Stephen Miller heard that trouble was in the wind. Men from various settlements were arriving in Mankato, and the town's taverns were in popular demand. An attack was being planned on the Camp Lincoln prison stockade, went the rumors, they weren't waiting for any presidential decision; a mass lynching was required. Knowing he could well be facing up to 1000 armed drunks, Miller sent out a call for reinforcements. The following night, after a long, hard ride, cavalry arrived. Miller now had 500 men, but many of them also loathed the Indians. How many would be prepared to open fire on this particular mob? Any soldier disobeying would be shot, he assured them. Shortly before 11 p.m., the troops, a short distance to the north, were deployed around the road from Mankato. The soldiers waited in the dark, and soon the tramp of many feet came down the road. Colonel Miller rode out alone. "Who comes here?" he called out.

"We have come to take the Indians and kill them."

"Well," said the colonel, "you will do nothing of the kind."

The mob looked around to see blue-clad horsemen emerge on all sides. The civilians leading the mob were placed under arrest and the remainder told to go home. Next morning, Miller freed the leaders after they had provided oaths of good behavior. But upon departure they claimed that 2000 men were going to descend from New Ulm, led by Frederick Brandt. They would finish the job. Perhaps, however, news of Miller's warm reception had a cooling effect on vengeful passions, as the promised threat never materialized.[23]

In a dispatch, Sibley exaggerated the situation, claiming the garrison had been "assaulted by about 200 citizens with intent to murder the Indians." Settlers wished to see Dakota bodies swinging in the breeze, and they were

11. Five Minutes Would Dispose of a Case   131

Indian prisoners at Camp Lincoln await news of their fate. At one point, troops had to go out and turn back a threatening mob (*Leslie's Illustrated Newspaper*, January 31, 1863).

incensed that Lincoln was taking his time about giving the nod. The longer it took, the more it seemed these murderous savages may escape just retribution. On December 6, Sibley wrote to headquarters at St. Paul, "Colonel Miller informs me that large numbers of citizens are assembling, and he fears a serious collision. I have authorized him to declare martial law, if necessary, and call to his assistance all the troops within his reach. He thinks it will take 1000 true men to protect the prisoners against all organized popular outbreaks.... Please telegraph the facts to the president, and ask instructions. Any hour may witness a sad conflict, if it has not already occurred."

And two days later:

> Dispatches and private letters just received indicate a fearful collision between the United States forces and the citizens. Combinations, embracing thousands of men in all parts of the state, are said to forming, and in a few days our troops, with the Indian prisoners, will be literally besieged. I shall concentrate all the men I can at Mankato. But should the president pardon the Indians, there will be a determined effort to get them in possession, which will be resented, and may cost the lives of thousands of our citizens. Ask the president to keep secret his decision, whatever it may be, until I have prepared myself as best I can. God knows how much excitement is increasing and extending.[24]

Did Sibley really believe his own words, "thousands of men in all parts of the state"? He seemed to have taken a page from Pope's book: the way to get support was to inflate the situation beyond all reason. And his request that Lincoln keep secret his decision "whatever it may be" made no sense. A presidential decree that all would hang would surely defuse tensions.

Governor Ramsey issued a proclamation calling on all to desist from "barbarous violence amongst our own citizens." Justice will be done, he said. "Our people, indeed, have had just reason to complain of the tardiness of executive action in the premises, but they ought to find some reason for forbearance in the absorbing cases which weigh upon the president." Ramsey urged patience, but noted that should Lincoln "decline to punish them," then the State Legislature would take independent action.[25]

Lincoln received a written demand from St. Paul citizens not only for the executions to take place, but also that the Dakota tribe be banished from the state. "The blood of hundreds of our murdered fellow citizens cries from the ground for vengeance. 'Vengeance is mine, I will repay, saith the Lord,' and the authorities of the United States are, we believe, the chosen instrument to execute that vengeance.... The Indian's nature can be no more trusted than the wolf's. Tame him, cultivate him, strive to Christianize him, as you will, and the sight of blood will call out the savage, wolfish, devilish instincts of the race."[26]

A.J. Van Horhes of the *Stillwater Messenger* had arrived at Fort Ridgely along with the late annuity payment. Rumors circulated that Lincoln may pardon the condemned, and he published a lengthy editorial which included:

> In the name of a thousand murdered victims on our frontier—in the name of scores of violated women and a thousand desolated farms, and hundreds of burned dwellings—in the name of rivers of scalding tears, and of suffering and anguish which can never be written up—in the name of an outraged people whose vengeance can only be satiated by the blood of their destroyers—in the name of Christianity and common humanity, we warn you PRESIDENT LINCOLN and you, SECRETARY STANTON, never issue such an edict in the face of the people! ... We tell you plainly and soberly ten thousand men can be found who will dedicate their hopes, their fortunes, and if need be their lives, to the extermination of that race. The war against the rebellion will pale in the presence of the war against the savages. 'NO PEACE!—DEATH TO THE BARBARIANS!' is the sentiment of our people.

But even the caustic Van Horhes was outdone by a member of the "gentle" sex. Jane Swisshelm had the unusual distinction, for the time, of being a woman who ran her own newspaper, the *St. Cloud Democrat*. The Pennsylvanian abolitionist dumped white slave owners and marauding Indians into the same pot. "The Indian and the Slaveholder have been the aristocrats of American society," she wrote. "They have been fostered and fed and kept in idleness like a den of rattlesnakes and cage of pet panthers until grown strong and insolent they have simultaneously broken loose to sting and tear at those who have fed and fondled them." As regards Lincoln's reviewing the trial records:

It rests upon the people who do not expect to make money by the Red Fiends to arm themselves and see to it that every Sioux found on our soil gets a permanent homestead 6 ft. by 2. Shoot the hyenas and ask no odds of any man. But we do not know a Minnesotan who is not sworn to this. Exterminate the wild beasts, and make peace with the devil and all his host sooner than with these red-jawed tigers whose fangs are dripping with the blood of the innocent! Get ready and as soon as these convicted murderers are turned loose, shoot them and be sure they are shot dead, *dead,* DEAD! If they have any souls the Lord can have mercy on them if he pleases! But that is His business. Ours is to kill the lazy vermin and make sure of killing them.[27]

Sergeant Champlin had likened Major Welch's advance at the Battle of Wood Lake to Tennyson's "The Charge of the Light Brigade." In early December the *Mankato Record* saw other parallels:

The Charge of the Hemp Brigade.

Hemp to the throat of them,
Hemp to the neck of them,
Hemp under the ears of them
    Twisting and choking;
Stormed at with shout and yell,
Grandly they'll hang and well,
Until the jaws of Death,
Until the mouth of Hell
    Takes the three hundred.

Theirs not to make reply,
Theirs not to reason why,
Theirs but to hang and die.
Into the valley of Death
    Send the three hundred.

Hemp on the throat of them,
Hemp round the neck of them,

Hemp under the chin of them
    Twisting and choking,
Stormed at with shout and yell,
Where wives and children fell;
They that had killed so well,
Come to the jaws of Death,
Come to the mouth of Hell,
All that is left of them,
    Left of three hundred.

When can their mem'ry fade?
O! the sad deaths they made!
    All the states mourned,
Weep for the deaths they made;
But give to the Hemp Brigade,
    The Devilish three hundred![28]

But there were also earnest appeals for mercy. Indian Commissioner William Dole was not happy with the idea of a mass hanging. "The execution of this sentence would partake more of the character of revenge than of punishment. It must not be forgotten that these savages, still red with the blood of our slaughtered kinsmen, have voluntarily surrendered as prisoners, and that we shall never be justified in judging them by our standard of morals. They are savages, far beneath us in either moral or intellectual culture."[29]

Others pointed out that over 300 men dangling in a mass execution would be a black image the United States would carry through future generations, a stain on the history of the country. One of the most outspoken Indian defenders was the forceful Bishop Henry Whipple, related to General Halleck. He wrote to Governor Ramsey: "We leave them without any government—then after nurturing every mad passion, standing unconcerned to witness Indian wars with each other, looking on their deeds of blood, and permitting every evil influence to degrade them, we turn them over to be robbed and plundered and at last we wonder we have reaped what we have sowed." Whipple visited Lincoln in the White House and delivered his own eloquent account of events leading to the outbreak. This included broken treaty promises, starvation, and the late annuity payment. The president was impressed. "He came here the other day," Lincoln told an acquaintance, "and talked with me about the rascality of this Indian business, until I felt it down to my boots."

The trial records were in the hands of two young lawyers, Frances Ruggles and George Whiting. They had been tasked with examining the proceedings and presenting a summary to Lincoln. Of those tried, they found solid evidence proving only two cases of rape. Obviously far more had occurred, but proving it was another matter. Most guilty parties were still on the loose. During the war, Lincoln reviewed over 1600 court-martial proceedings and exasperated army officers by saving lives whenever possible. "If a man had more than one life, I think a little hanging might not hurt this one," he said, "but after he is dead, we cannot bring him back no matter how sorry we may be."

On December 6, having considered the evidence, Lincoln personally wrote an order for the execution of only 39 of the 303 condemned. He provided a list of names along with their individual numbers. Those destined for the gallows were considered guilty of murder, and violation of female captives. Other Indians condemned for fighting in battles were reprieved. They were, however, to be held "subject to further orders, taking care that they neither escape or are subject to any unlawful violence." The execution day was set for Friday, December 26, 1862.[30]

It comes as little surprise that many were not happy with Lincoln's decision; a voter backlash at the next election was promised. But he responded, "I could not afford to hang men for votes." Despite grumblings, hanging 39 was better than the total pardon many had feared. There was no popular rising by the settlers of Minnesota. But Jane Swisshelm was not impressed. The following February she delivered an address in Washington stating "that if justice is not done," Minnesota whites "will go to shooting Indians whenever these government pets get out from under Uncle Sam's wing. Our people will hunt them, shoot them, set traps for them, put out poisoned bait for them—kill them by every means we use to exterminate panthers."[31]

Lincoln had provided a list of the condemned, but carrying out a precise identification of those proved challenging. More than one of the condemned had the same or similar names. There were three Washechoons, for example, and four Chaskays. But then each had been numbered, and the numbers were included on Lincoln's list. Correct records regarding the numbers, however, if ever kept by the commission, seemed to get lost somewhere in the system. Joseph Brown was selected to examine the Indians and identify the guilty parties on Lincoln's list. He admitted he was not positive with each identification—but in this case someone must hang, whatever doubts there may be.

On December 22, Brown led a squad of soldiers into the log stockade housing the 303 prisoners. Without saying why, he read out 39 names, and each man was instructed to step forward. But when he read out "Chas-kay-don," meaning "first born, if a male," Chaska, Sarah Wakefield's friend and protector, stepped forward. He had no idea that he had just placed a noose around his own neck, thus fulfilling his own fears. The intended man was a certain Chaskaydon who had been convicted for the murder and dissection of a pregnant women.

The 39 condemned found themselves separated from the other inmates and shown into a stone building alongside the stockade. As they moved, flanking soldiers enjoyed informing them of their fate. Chains were rattled out and each man, paired with another, was secured to the floor. Later the same day, Colonel Miller and the Reverend Riggs arrived. Miller spoke, with Riggs translating. "The commanding officer at this place has called to speak to you on a very serious subject this afternoon. Your Great Father in Washington, after carefully reading what the witnesses have testified in your several trials, has come to the conclusion that you have been guilty of wantonly and wickedly murdering his white children; and for this reason, he has directed that you each may be hanged by the neck until you are dead, on next Friday, and that order will be carried into effect at ten o'clock in the forenoon." Today was Monday. Fewer than five full days to live. Having been tipped off by the guards, the Indians did not seem perturbed. They merely grunted in response, and those smoking pipes continued on.

They could select a spiritual advisor, either Protestant or Catholic, Riggs informed them, who could visit, if they wished, before their judgment day. Colonel Miller urged Christian conversion. "Say to them now," he said to Riggs, "that they have so sinned against their fellow men that there is no hope for clemency except in the mercy of God, through the merits of the blessed Redeemer, and I earnestly exhort them to apply to that, as their only remaining source of comfort and consolation."

The following day, Riggs, fluent in Dakota, spoke with the condemned men. Most proclaimed a miscarriage of justice; they were innocent of any serious crime. But at the same time, they realized with so many white dead, retribution was sure to take place. "This admission was in line with their education," recalled Riggs. "Perhaps it is not too much to call it an instinct of humanity."[32] Any who became agitated were calmed by their companions with soothing words. Riggs, pen and paper in hand, wrote final words to friends and relatives, and others wrote letters themselves. One prisoner, Thunder That

Paints Itself Blue, convicted of arguing in favor of killing captives, wrote bitterly to peace Chief Wabasha, his father-in-law: "You have deceived me. You told me that if we followed the advice of General Sibley, and give ourselves up to the whites, all would be well—no innocent man would be injured. I have not killed, wounded a white man, or any white person. I have not participated in the plunder of their property; and yet today, I am set apart for execution and must die in a few days, while men who are guilty will remain in prison."

White Dog, the man who urged Captain Marsh to cross the river, was a marked man amongst the whites. He complained to Riggs "bitterly that he did not have the chance to tell the things as they were; that he could not have the opportunity of rebutting the testimony brought against him." He admitted that the Dakotas "have done great wrongs to the white people, and do not refuse to die, but they think it hard that they did not have a fairer trial. They want the president to know this."

Riggs spoke to Chaska. Neither realized a mistake had been made and he was not supposed to hang. Chaska described the events of August 18. "His friend shot Mr. Gleeson," he told Riggs, "and he attempted to fire on him, but his gun did not go off. He saved Mrs. Wakefield and the children, and now he dies while she lives." This was Chaska's last known statement before he died.[33]

That night the Indians "extemporized a dance with a wild Indian song." But the officer of the guard, fearful of their fierce antics and cries, ordered their movements restrained by shortening their chains.

On December 24, friends and relatives were permitted a final visit, a last chance to say goodbye. Along with members of the clergy, newspaper reporters were on hand, and one wrote in the *St. Paul Pioneer Press*: "Several of the prisoners were completely overcome during the leave-taking, and were compelled to abandon conversation." But, at the same time, others "affected to disregard the dangers of their position, and laughed and joked apparently as unconcerned as if they were sitting around a camp fire in perfect freedom." On the night before the executions: "The three half-breeds and one or two others, only, were dressed in citizens' clothes. The rest all wore the breech-clout, leggings, and blankets, and not a few were adorned with paint. The majority of them were young men, though several were quite old and gray-headed, ranging perhaps toward seventy. One was quite a youth, not over sixteen. Father Ravoux spent the whole night among the prisoners talking with them concerning their fate, and endeavoring to impress upon them a serious view of the subject. He met with some success, and during the night several were baptized, and received the communion of the Church."[34] Perhaps those Indians who converted felt that being executed the day after Christmas showed little Christmas spirit on the part of the Christian whites. But, if so, they did not show it.

One reporter wrote: "The doomed men wished it to be known amongst their friends, and particularly their wives and children, how cheerful and happy they had all died, exhibiting no fear of this dread event.... They shook hands with the officers who came in among them, bidding them good-by as if they were going on a long and pleasant journey. They had added some fresh streaks of vermilion and ultramarine to their countenances, as their fancy suggested, evidently intending to fix themselves off as gay as possible for the coming exhibition. They commenced singing their death-song, Tazoo leading, and nearly all joining. It was wonderfully exciting."

"I have every hope of going direct to the abode of the Great Spirit, where I shall always be happy," said Round Wind, identified by two German boys as their mother's slayer. But that night Colonel Miller arrived to unshackle the aged warrior and return him to the stockade. The entreaties of Thomas Williamson, along with Round Wind's credible claim of being 10 miles away at the time of the crime, had brought a telegram from President Lincoln. The old warrior's time to join the Great Spirit had not yet come. The number of condemned dropped from 39 to 38.[35]

Friday morning, December 26, the Indians paid close attention as Father Augustin Ravoux and the Reverend Williamson spoke. But at 7:30 all were requested to leave except those involved in the execution. Under Joseph Brown's direction, the prisoners' irons were knocked off and their elbows pinioned by cords behind, while their wrists were tied about six inches apart in front. Even as this took place, most prisoners kept up their singing and appeared content. The job was complete by 9 o'clock when Father Ravoux returned, knelt, and commenced reading from a prayer book in the Dakota language. "During this ceremony nearly all paid the most strict attention," wrote the reporter, "and several were affected even to tears."

White muslin caps were placed on each head, to be pulled down over faces before execution. But this was not the way for a warrior to go. They found the prospect "humiliating," according to the reporter. At 10 o'clock the condemned men were lined up, and marched in procession outside. "The gallows, which were constructed of very square heavy timbers," recalled one observer, "covered an area about twenty-four feet square, and were about twenty feet high. The 'drop' was held by a large rope attached to a pole in the center of the frame."[36]

Captain Redfield led the prisoners between rows of glistening infantry bayonets and cavalrymen with drawn sabers. One thousand four hundred troops were in attendance. Beyond them a crowd of 5,000 civilians looked on. It was an unusually mild and clear day for December—a good day for a hanging, in the eyes of many. Now the prisoners' apparent good spirits returned as they were handed over to Captain Burt, officer of the day. The condemned men jostled each other to be the first to ascend their portal to the Great Spirit, and their death song broke out once more, the chant "Hi–yi–yi, Hi yi-yi,"

On December 26, 1862, the largest mass hanging in American history occurred when 38 Indians were executed. At least one innocent man died by mistake (*Leslie's Illustrated Newspaper*, January 24, 1863).

sounding "truly hideous" to some white ears. "It seemed as if pandemonium had broken loose."

One Indian sang his own song, claiming to be the slayer of a white near New Ulm. He had cut off the victim's head and placed it on a certain "indelicate part of the body." The singer managed to shake his pants loose, and they fell, resulting in an "indecent exposure of his person." This was "an insult to the spectators which it required an Indian to conceive," wrote the reporter, "and a dirty dog of an Indian to execute.... The scene at this juncture was one of awful interest. A painful and breathless suspense held the vast crowd, which had assembled from all quarters to witness the execution."

With the clothing replaced, the noose was adjusted around each neck, then the white muslin caps were rolled down. No doubt they all, like Chaska, regretted having not fled from Camp Release. "Three slow, measured and distinct beats on the drum" were given by Joseph Brown. This was the signal to William Duley, a survivor of the Lake Shetek massacre, to cut the single lead that sprang the drop. The ropes sprung taut as the bodies fell; 38 lives were sent into oblivion. Civilians and soldiers alike gave a loud cheer. But one rope snapped under the strain and the victim thumped to the ground. He appeared lifeless, his neck apparently broken, but he was hastily strung up once more, just in case. "For so many," wrote the reporter, "there was but little suffering; the necks of all, or nearly all, were evidently dislocated by the fall, and the after struggling was slight. The scaffold fell at a quarter past ten o'clock, and in twenty minutes the bodies had all been examined by Surgeons Le Boutillier, Sheardown, Finch, Clark, and others, and life pronounced extinct."[37]

The bodies were taken down and buried in shallow graves by the riverbank—but not for long. Fresh cadavers were in strong demand amongst the medical profession. They were hastily dug up and taken away for dissection and research.[38]

Not present to witness these final acts were Generals Sibley and Pope. Sibley was back home in Mendota, having taken command of the newly formed "Minnesota District" of Pope's military department, and he would soon move to St. Paul. But Indian fighting was not over for him yet. Pope was planning a spring offensive from his new headquarters in Milwaukee, Wisconsin. This was closer to his home state of Illinois, where he had influential allies and friends.[39] The general, no doubt, was still dreaming of a return to the "real war" back east.

Needless to say, Sarah Wakefield was appalled when reading of Chaska's death. Distraught, she wrote letters to Riggs and Abraham Lincoln demanding explanations, and in 1863, she published *Six Weeks in the Sioux Tepees*, defending herself and Chaska. She had two more children before her husband died in 1874, and she lived on in Minnesota till her death in 1899.

12

The Shot That Killed Him

Following Wood Lake, Little Crow headed northwest. Traveling with him were probably no more than 100 warriors; there were about 300 souls altogether, including women and children. Four of Little Crow's wives and his 16-year-old son, Wowinapa, were present, along with other relatives. But Little Crow was not through yet— in his own mind at least. He dreamed of a pact with allied Dakota tribes to the west.[1]

The British, with Dakota help, had fought two wars against the Americans in days gone by. Perhaps, in return, the British could now provide guns and ammunition. With a fresh army, he could return to Minnesota and drive the whites from his Dakota homeland. Failing that, a safe reservation in British territory would do.

Along the way, Little Crow tarried a few days with the Wahpeton Dakotas at Lac Qui Parle. Anxious to gain allies, he spread word that Sibley was hot on their trail, bent on the destruction of any Dakotas, guilty or otherwise. He moved 20 miles north to the village of the influential Standing Buffalo on Big Stone Lake. But Sibley had already sent a letter offering peace to Standing Buffalo in return for Little Crow, dead or alive. The head men debated what to do next.

Finally, Standing Buffalo said he would not hand Little Crow over, but there was no chance of any union between them. "You have already made much trouble for my people," he told the unwelcome visitor. "Go to Canada or where you please, but go away from me and off the lands of my people. You have brought me into great danger without my knowing of it before hand. By killing the whites it is just as if you have waited for me in ambush and shot me down."

Standing Buffalo dispatched a letter to Sibley saying he had no part in the war, and asked for a chance to move his people out of harm's way. But to the chief's alarm, young braves returned the same day with scalps and plunder. Amongst other misdeeds, they had taken part in the attack on Fort Abercrombie. Now thumping drums and the cries of a victory dance were heard throughout the village. This only added to bitterness against Little Crow. The

12. The Shot That Killed Him

unwelcome leader and his entourage moved out, and traveling 200 miles into Dakota Territory, they camped near Devil's Lake.

Following a week's rest and contemplation, they moved southwest 160 miles to a tribe of Yankton Dakotas camped on the Missouri River. Although determined not to join Little Crow's war, they did provide food and shelter while he sought help from other Yankton villages along the river. One band tolerated his presence for almost a month while he harangued warriors to join him in an attack on Fort Pierre. But the Yanktons' only contribution was to send riders warning of the proposed strike. As they could not get rid of Little Crow, they struck their tepees and moved away from him.

On October 3, meanwhile, Sibley replied to Standing Buffalo. He understood many Santees, Upper Sissetons and Wahpetons, had not wanted war, but advised a surrender at this time was not wise. As he put it, "I have a great number of men who are very angry."[2] Instead they should stay in their villages, and he would come to them in good time. Sibley was true to his word. He would arrive the following year with fire and sword.

Little Crow, unable to find support amongst his fellow Dakotas, became desperate. For four days he traveled north up the Missouri River in an attempt to have former enemies, the Gros Ventre, Mandan and Arikara tribes, join him in a war against the whites. Messengers approached one village with traditional signs of friendship; yelling, shooting into the air and displaying a peace pipe. But the dreaded "Sioux" could not be trusted. Warriors opened fire and Little Crow beat a hasty retreat, leaving eight men dead.

As the exiles moved north towards British territory, Little Crow's former labors bore a bitter fruit for the Santee Dakotas. The Sioux-Dakota Act, banishing them from Minnesota to outside reservations, passed Congress on March 3, 1863. A similar Act banishing the virtually innocent Winnebagos had already passed on February 21. During the spring of 1863, about 1,300 Dakotas and 1,900 Winnebagos were shipped from Minnesota by riverboat to reservations along the Missouri River in Dakota Territory.

During May of 1863, Little Crow met with Catholic priest Father Alexis Andre in St. Joseph (now Walhalla), Dakota Territory. He told Andre that he intended crossing the border into Rupert's Land to seek a reservation. He raised a Union Jack over his camp, and warriors donned British medals and decorations awarded to their grandfathers during the War of 1812. The party moved to the border town of Pembina, where an attempt to parley with the local Indians was rebuffed, one chief even draping himself in an American flag.

Having sent word of his coming, Little Crow crossed the border and rode for Fort Garry (now Winnipeg), a Hudson's Bay Company trading post, 60 miles north, the seat of local power since its establishment in 1822. The garrison and inhabitants were protected by formidable stone defense towers and walls, enlarged over the years with earth-filled double timber stockades.

Fort Garry was the center of power in Rupert's land, controlled by the British Hudson's Bay Company. Little Crow arrived there following the Dakota War in hope of gaining British support (author's rendition).

Little Crow rode through the fort gates on May 27, 1863. Leading a colorful throng, the notorious chief was adorned in "a black coat with velvet collar, a breechcloth of blue broadcloth, and deerskin leggings," reported the *St. Paul Press* on June 23. "He wore one fine shawl around his neck and another around his waist as a sash. As a sidearm, he carried a seven-shooter, a fine but delicate weapon."[3] The women in his entourage wore fine dresses plundered from white settlements, topped off with colorful parasols. Despite the confident display, Little Crow appeared "thin and cadaverous," a man worn down by failure with "a heavy price on his head."

Governor Alexander Grant Dallas lent a respectful ear as Little Crow put his case for British arms, provisions and hunting rights in British territory. The chief spoke of Americans breaking treaties and of Indians being hunted by armed troops. He said he would fight "to the knife" against the Americans, but would be most happy to swear allegiance to the British Crown. In return for support during the War of 1812, the British had pledged that "the folds of the red flag of the north would wrap around them and preserve them from their enemies."

But in 1816, following the war's conclusion, the British had deserted their Indian allies. While Dakota lives had been lost, the British provided trifling gifts such as blankets and trade goods in return. Furious, Little Crow's

12. The Shot That Killed Him

grandfather had vented his feelings: "After we have fought for you, endured many hardships, lost some of our people and awakened the vengeance of our powerful neighbors, you make peace for yourself and leave us to obtain such terms as we can! You no longer need our services, and offer us these goods to pay for having deserted us. But no! We will not take them; we hold them and yourselves in equal contempt."[4]

Governor Dallas felt no obligation to now honor promises made and broken nearly half a century earlier. As many as 1000 Dakota refugees had already crossed the border.[5] They were not welcomed by the local Chippewas and Crees. And how were more new arrivals to be fed? During winter, this isolated area was dependent on supplies from the East.

Dallas made it clear that Little Crow, a man with blood on his hands, was not welcome; he should return to the United States. The chief replied that a forced return would see a "war of extermination" upon the Dakotas by the whites. Dallas replied that he would "endeavor to bring their grievances to the notice of the American government, with a view to establishing a better understanding in the future." More empty words, this time from British whites.

Little Crow left the last council meeting on May 29 with provisions and a few presents, a token gesture of friendship. But he was a broken man now. His failure to secure support from Dallas saw the last vestiges of his power slip away. Strangely enough, at least one ex–American soldier thought Little Crow badly treated by the British: "It is a little strange that he could not be recognized," recalled A.P. Connolly, writing in 1896, "when cannibal kings from the islands of the sea can get recognition, and the devotees of royalty will tumble over each other to pay their respects to a lecherous, murderous Turk."[6] This was a reference to Abdul Hamid II's massacre of Armenians in 1895–96.

Little Crow crossed back into Dakota Territory during early June with a mere 18 followers. This tiny band, which included one woman and his teenage son, Wowinapa, was all that was left of the hundreds who had followed him into battle the year before. At Fort Snelling and Sioux City, Iowa, troops were marshaling to hunt him down. Little Crow well knew of the 38 executions the year before. How long could he avoid a similar fate? "When we were coming back," recalled Wowinapa, "he said he could not fight the white men, but would go below and steal horses from them, and give them to his children, so that they would be comfortable, and then he would go away off. Father also told me he was getting old, and wanted me to go with him to carry his bundles." This referred to medicine bundles. Those who carried them were supposedly assured of a happy, long life and health. When a chief handed the bundles to his next of kin, it was the passing of leadership to the younger generation.

In an act of bravado, Little Crow got a message through to St. Paul newspapers informing Sibley and Pope that they "should look for him" at the remains of the old Lower Agency. He added fuel to the fire by telling traders and mixed-bloods that he planned to steal enough horses to mount an army, he would continue to kill whites until he was killed, and he was going to recover a hoard of buried treasure on his way to the Black Hills.

So where was he headed, the Lower Agency or the Black Hills? Little Crow led his band to Devil's Lake, then trekked 350 miles east to home country, the Big Woods, north of the Lower Agency. As though fate had decreed events to go full circle, in late June they arrived near Acton, where the war had started the previous year. On June 29, Amos Dustin was riding in an ox cart near Howard Lake with his mother, wife and three children. The Dakotas struck, killing Amos, his mother and one child. Word got out, and Mrs. Dustin was found barely alive, an arrow in her back, with two surviving children. Amos' left hand had been cut off and carried away, as were both hands of his mother. In a separate encounter, a lone white traveler was killed and stripped. Panic swept the area, a stockade was hastily erected at Rockford,[7] and within a week, Governor Ramsey ordered that a corps of 50 scouts be raised to scour the countryside. They would be paid $1.50 a day and $25 for each male Dakota scalp.

All was not well within Little Crow's small band. Disagreement erupted about what to do next. Several men and the lone woman decided Rupert's Land was their only safe haven; best to return there. Others decided to continue south. Little Crow and his son opted to stay in home country, the Big Woods.

On July 3, 1863, Picket's disastrous charge at Gettysburg helped seal the fate of the Confederacy, and in Minnesota, Kate Dustin died of her arrow wound. Oblivious to these events, white settler Nathan Lamson and his son, Chauncey, had left the Hutchinson stockade to go hunting in the Big Woods. Through the foliage, in a small clearing, they saw two Dakotas picking raspberries. These days, the only good Indians were dead. Nathan edged forward and, steadying his musket, took a bead on the older of the two. A shot echoed through the woods and, with a cry of pain, Little Crow fell.

"He was hit the first time in the side, just above the hip," recalled Wowinapa. "His gun and mine were lying on the ground. He took up my gun and fired it first, and then fired his own. He was shot the second time when he was firing his own gun. The ball struck the stock of his gun, and then hit him in the side, near the shoulders. That was the shot that killed him. He told me he was killed, and asked me for water, which I gave him. He died immediately after." The Lamsons had just granted Little Crow's wish—not to die by a white man's rope. But Nathan had not escaped unscathed, being wounded in the left shoulder by Little Crow's first shot. His son, Chauncey, fired the second shot that killed Little Crow.

"Chauncey crawled away after the second exchange of shots and returned to the stockade in Hutchinson about eleven o'clock that night," recalled young Mary Lamson. "My father remained on the scene of the shooting until morning."

"Where's my papa?" I demanded when Chauncey returned.

"Oh, he's all right," said Chauncey. "He's out there in the woods."

My mother fainted when my brother returned alone and I recall begging the rough old doctor who was attending her not to let my mother die. At daylight my father returned to the stockade and a few hours afterward, Albert, my youngest brother, was born in the rude shelter of poplar poles we called home. Soon after my father came in, bleeding and tired, the mounted soldiers from the fort lined up to go after the body of the Indian. I remember that an older brother of mine was second from the captain as they set out. When they returned they had the body of Little Crow on a blanket in the bottom of a wagon. With other children, I climbed up on the wheel of the wagon to see the Indian. "'Oh, look at the Indian my father shot," I cried.[8]

Wowinapa, meanwhile, had made good his escape after wrapping his father's body in a blanket. He left new moccasins alongside for the chief's last journey to join the Great Spirit.

Once in town, Little Crow's body was put on display. The unidentified corpse was gawked at and scalped. Children lit firecrackers in the ears and nose. The dead man looked familiar to some—Little Crow, wasn't it? Just look at those deformed wrists. But others scoffed at the idea—too good to be true.[9] The body was soon dragged away to be dumped in an offal pit on the edge of town.

Little Crow was not properly identified until after Wowinapa was captured 26 days later and told of his death in the Big Woods. A cavalry officer's saber removed Little Crow's head, and the grim trophy was preserved by Doctor John Benjamin in a kettle of lime. His scalp lock and the deformed wrist bones were put on display at the State Historical Society, to be joined by the skull in 1896. Henry Sibley was not impressed, feeling it "a spectacle which only feed the temper of a barbarous mind, and excite the moral disgust of every man, unblunted by the spirit of revenge."[10] In 1971 Little Crow's remains, courtesy of descendants, came to rest in a South Dakota family plot.

13

The Girl I Left Behind Me

In June of 1863, Generals Pope and Sibley would have been astonished to see the downtrodden Little Crow and his handful of followers traveling south from Rupert's Land. This true picture was a long way from rumors sweeping the frontier. Masses of armed warriors were preparing for a new offensive, so the stories went. Word was that the Dakota Yanktons and Yanktonais, in league with Little Crow, were arming themselves with guns traded from northern buffalo hunters, trappers and traders. The warriors would ally themselves with the Santee Dakotas who had fled Minnesota. The few presents and provisions received by Little Crow at Fort Garry were inflated to substantial supplies that would allow him to rekindle the war.

In October of 1862, Sibley had estimated 2,200 enemy warriors on the loose, but by February of 1863, Pope put the number as high as 7,000.[1] Such a threatening host suited Pope's needs at this time. Sibley had been promoted, but Pope felt that he had not been given due credit for his contribution, consisting mainly of alarmist telegrams and screams for more troops and supplies.

Minnesota Democrat Senators Henry Rice and Morton Wilkinson plotted to have Pope removed—to oblivion. Pope dug in and fought to stay put. Any command was better than none, but he needed a substantial Indian war to put himself in the public eye once more. Perhaps with a successful campaign, he would be recalled to his proper place as a prominent general leading blue-clad divisions against the rebel hordes.

Pope wrote that Senators Rice and Wilkinson were "unscrupulous speculators and traders" who wanted to take control of the department solely for personal profit. The appointment of Henry Rice, a civilian, to command the district, Pope said, would result in many years of border wars and "ruinous Indian treaties and frauds." Rice was a "reckless and ruined speculator and old Indian trader" whose appointment would be based "upon a knowledge of Indians and Indian character, acquired during many years of unlimited concubinage with Indian women."[2] General Halleck saw things Pope's way and made sure he stayed put.

Rice, miffed by the rebuff, predicted the failure of any Indian campaigns conducted by Pope and Sibley. He pulled strings behind the scenes and received authorization to raise a separate cavalry battalion under Major Edwin Hatch. But Pope was having none of this. He demanded that Hatch be placed under his command. Halleck, who had the final say, agreed. Major Hatch found himself exiled to Pembina on the northern border to cool his heels in midwinter while establishing a new military post to impede Indian traffic from British territory. Even a border wall, if such a thing could be built, would make this task impossible.

Attempts to remove Sibley also fell on deaf ears. "The whole thing I regard as a miserable scheme got up by Rice and others who hate Gen. Pope, and do not love me, & who wish to annoy and humiliate us both," he wrote. "I have contempt for the whole humbug, inventors and all."[3]

Given the nod by the War Department, Pope plotted for two military columns to penetrate the depths of Dakota Territory during the summer of 1863. Some 800 Lower and perhaps 4000 Upper Dakotas remained on the loose, he reasoned. Also brandishing the war club were thousands of Yanktons and Yanktonais—he preferred to believe.

One column, mainly infantry commanded by Sibley, would move northwest from Minnesota towards Devil's Lake in Dakota Territory where, it was rumored, hostile tribes massed. At the same time, a second expedition, cavalry under General Alfred Sully, would move from Sioux City, Iowa. This column would ride alongside the Missouri River, and then northeast towards the same point. Indians would be snared by the two forces and crushed with a decisive blow—so the plan went.

A possible flaw in Pope's plan, however, was British territory, which was far too close to Devil's Lake. Fleeing Indians could well head north and claim sanctuary under the Union Jack. Through channels, Pope put in a request to Earl Lyons, representing Britain in Washington, that American troops be allowed to cross the border in pursuit. But the prospect of slashing Yankee sabers amidst the tepees of Indians, guilty or otherwise, living under the Union Jack did not go down well. Pope received a terse wire from General Halleck advising that the president "directs that under no circumstances will our troops cross the boundary line into British territory without his authority." The British had already come close to declaring war on the United States in recent times. In November of 1861, Confederate envoys to London had been seized by a U.S. warship off a British vessel, the *Trent*, on the high seas. The British had been so enraged by this violation that they dispatched troops to Canada in preparation for war. Lincoln, however, wanting "one war at a time," defused the situation by ordering the envoys released.[4]

By mid-July, Sibley had assembled a large force at Camp Pope near the remains of the Lower Agency. Senator Rice and other critics claimed

Minnesota was being stripped of defensive troops, and a large force would be far too cumbersome to achieve anything against elusive Indians on the Dakota plains. On the second point, at least, Pope agreed. He advised Sibley that a column of more than 2000 men would be too unwieldy for the job at hand. But Sibley thought otherwise and mustered 2,200 infantry, 800 cavalry, 100 pioneers, 70 Indian and mixed-blood scouts, and 150 artillerymen. This included John Jones of the Fort Ridgely defense, now promoted to captain commanding the Third Battery of Light Artillery. The officers included many other veterans of 1862 battles, like Joseph Brown, Colonel William Crooks and Lieutenant Colonel William Marshall. The Reverend Riggs was assigned as staff chaplain. In all, Sibley commanded 3,320 men backed up by 225 six-mule-team wagons carrying provisions for 90 days, and hundreds of beef cattle to supply fresh meat. An additional 100 wagons carried medical supplies, camping equipage, ammunition, bridge-building materials, and other stores.

The column marched with colors held high on June 16, 1863, "thermometer 100 degrees in the tent," complained Sibley.[5] It was a late start for the campaign due to a continuing drought that limited the amount of Dakota prairie grass to feed stock. The column, over five miles long, became shrouded in dust, and streams were found to be virtually dry or alkaline. But many soldiers, like Eli Pickett of the 10th Minnesota Infantry, felt the privations worthwhile. He wrote his wife, "I know my hatred of the Indian is great ... so great I believe I could murder the most helpless of their women and children without a feeling of remorse." And he could see economic benefits: "This Indian war will not only rid Minnesota of the Indians, but will bring millions and millions of dollars to our state."[6]

Bugles woke the troops at 2 a.m. every day, and two hours later they set out, marching for an hour till halting for a 10-minute break. The day's march would end at any time from midday till late afternoon, depending on a possible water supply, such as a semi-arid lake or marsh. Often dozens of wells had to be dug to a depth of 10 or 12 feet before drinkable water could be found. What grass was available had to be scythed and brought into camp, as lurking Indians could well swoop and cause a stampede of untethered stock. "It was a season of drought such as was never before known in the west," recalled A.P. Connolly. "The prairies were literally parched up with the heat, the grass was burned up, and the sloughs and little streams were dry. The fierce prairie winds were like the hot siroccos of the desert, and great clouds of dust, raised by the immense column, could be seen for miles and were viewed with wonder."[7]

But things could change with the bat of an eyelid. On June 20, at the old Camp Release site, the soldiers awoke to much different weather. "Drizzling rain and so cold that I suffered with two coats on," complained one soldier. "A most disagreeable day."

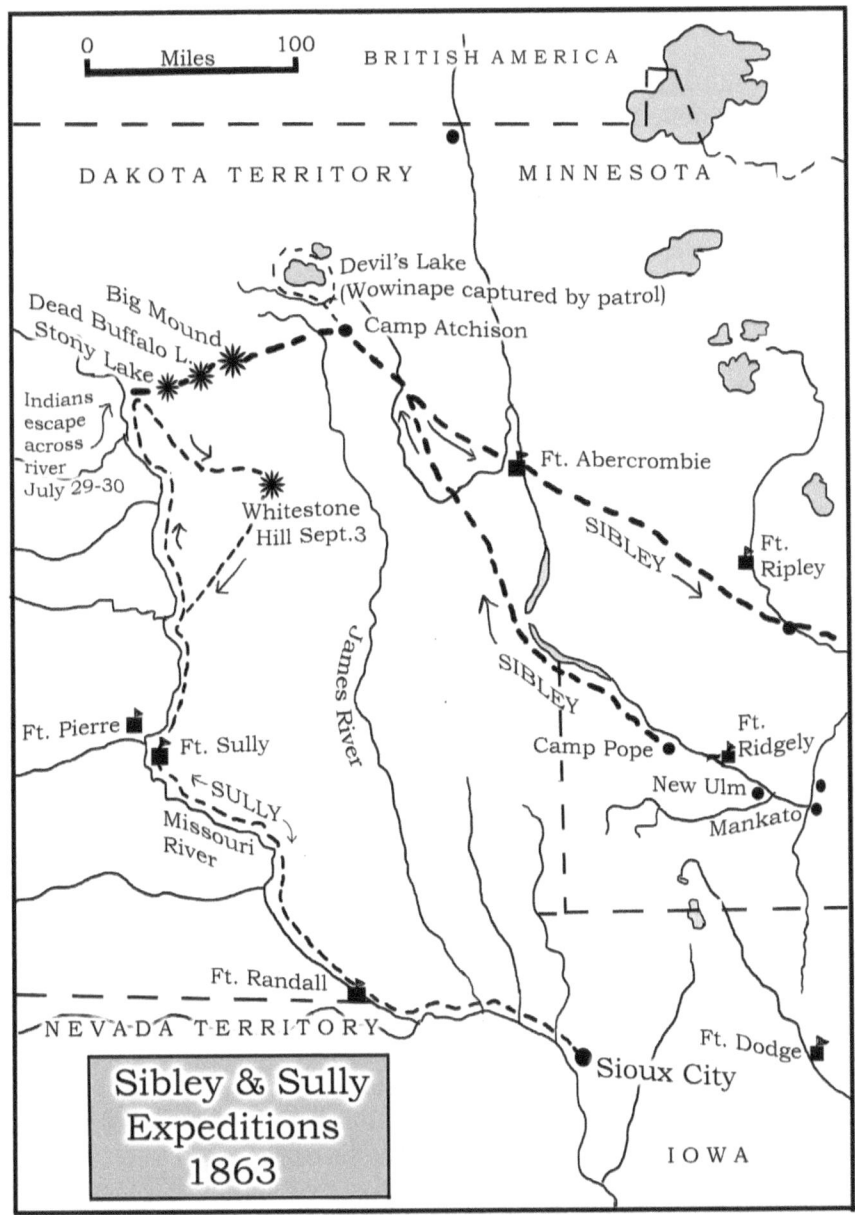

Sibley and Sully expeditions, 1863 (author's rendition).

Only two days later, however, the troops were complaining once more of intense heat. Good water dried up. The stock suffered, and dogs going mad with thirst were put out of their misery with a bullet to the head. On June 24, the Yellow Earth River, "a pretty little stream," finally offered refreshing water in abundance. Soldiers and animals alike lapped it up, canteens were gratefully filled, and fish provided a welcome change of diet. "Our mouths were getting quite sore from eating so much hardtack," complained Amos Glanville.[8]

Ten days and 110 miles after leaving Camp Pope, the expedition crossed into Dakota Territory. The troops took a 3-day break near Lake Traverse while repairs were carried out to wagons and leaking green timber barrels. "Found the remains of four white persons which was killed last fall," Sergeant James Ramer noted in his diary. On July 1 a large threat emerged, but it was no Indian force. "The flames spread, becoming one vast sheet, sweeping over the prairies," recalled Connolly. "A very roaring cataract of fire, the billows of which reached to the clouds…. To arms! To arms! We are called, by bugle and drum, and in the face of this enemy at a 'double quick' we march out to meet it."[9] The horses and mules took fright and the herders had trouble preventing a stampede. A controlled counterfire, however, set by the troops averted the danger, the smoke and flames dwindling away on already burned ground.

Provisions were rapidly running out. Sibley ordered a 600-man wagon detachment north to Fort Abercrombie to procure fresh supplies. While they were gone, another march saw the column arrive at the big bend of the Sheyenne River on July 4, 75 miles from Lake Traverse. The arrival of dark clouds and rain "made us feel like new-born children," recalled Captain Christian Excel. That same day Little Crow's unidentified body was put on display in Hutchinson.

Sibley's guns boomed on Independence Day, and a brass band played as Colonel Crooks was carried around by men of his regiment, the 6th Minnesota Infantry. The sutler did a brisk business with the sale of tinned peaches, sardines, oysters and other delicacies, a welcome if somewhat expensive relief from the usual diet.

A 6-day wait in what was called Camp Hayes saw the return of the detachment from Fort Abercrombie. The troops were happy to receive fresh supplies, but not the news brought back with them, concerning General Lee's invasion of Pennsylvania.[10] Sibley wrote in his diary, "I feel much depressed today, of the gloomy news of the advance of the rebels."

On July 11 the troops broke camp and moved northwest, generally following the twists and turns of the Sheyenne River. It was a barren, desolate march, as recalled by Sibley:

> If the devil were permanently to select a residence upon the earth, he would probably choose this particular district for an abode, with the redskins murdering and plundering bands as his ready ministers, to verify by their ruthless deeds his diabolical hatred of all who belong to the Christian race. Through the vast desert lakes fair to the eye abound, but generally their waters are strongly alkaline or intensely bitter or brackish. The valleys between them frequently reek with sulphur or other disagreeable vapors.

13. The Girl I Left Behind Me

The heat was so intolerable that the earth was like a heat furnace and the breezes that swept along its surface were as scorching and suffocating as the famed sirocco.[11]

Cattle died and men became ill. Many trudging soldiers felt they would see no Indians, and that the expedition was a waste of time, money and effort.

But on July 17 a wave of excitement swept the camp. Three mixed-blood Chippewa buffalo hunters arrived with news of a large Dakota village about 75 miles off, towards the Missouri River. This was the village of Standing Buffalo, who had sent Little Crow on his way the previous year while seeking peace with Sibley. Apart from some willful young braves, Standing Buffalo had managed to keep his people out of the 1862 bloodshed.

Sibley promptly enlisted the buffalo hunters as guides, but as he prepared to march on July 18, a shot echoed through the camp. Lieutenant Fields of the 1st Minnesota Mounted Rangers had killed a mixed-blood private. Private Oscar Wall wrote in his diary, "The Lieutenant will be tried tonight or to morrow if he gets his just dues he will soon depart this life." Other enlisted men felt the same way. Fields, however, claimed the trooper was menacing him with a saber and he fired in self-defense. *Not guilty* was the verdict. And Sibley had separate grief of his own to bear. A young daughter had already died during the expedition, and he received news that a son, Frank, had also succumbed to illness. He was plagued with nightmares for the remainder of the campaign.[12]

On July 18 the column moved 12 miles to Lake Emily and tents arose to create Camp Atchison. Joy swept the troops with the arrival of good war news: Lee's defeat at Gettysburg, and Grant's capture of Vicksburg, both of which had happened two weeks earlier. Throughout the North, bells tolled and salutes were fired. "Grant is my man," said Abraham Lincoln, "and I am his the rest of the war."[13]

Such triumphs for the Yankee cause were a good omen for the Dakota campaign. But the ever-cautious Sibley ordered Colonel Crooks to entrench the camp, and 4-foot-high sod walls went up. Leaving sick men and a guard force behind, Sibley marched on July 20 towards the Indian village. He led a strike force of over 2,000 men, including 500 cavalry. Wagons with rations for 25 days and extra ammunition followed.

On the first day's march, Sibley saw Indians to his front. But they advanced under an American flag, "like Arabs of the desert," recalled William Marshall, to reveal themselves as a large party of mixed-blood Chippewas. They had a buffalo hunting camp three miles to the west. With them was Father Alexis Andre, who confirmed the location of the village, and he wished Sibley good luck. Some Chippewas offered to ride with the troops in return for rations, but Sibley declined. His own force would give the enemy "a whipping they would long remember," he said.

Father Andre claimed 15 to 20 lodges were still at Devil's Lake, and Sibley dispatched two infantry companies and one of cavalry to scout the area. They returned on July 22 with no news of a village, but with a solitary prisoner of great interest. Wowinapa, on a search for kinfolk, had been captured, emaciated and alone. "The scouts found him in the weeds with out any thing to load his gun with he had shot a wolf with the last charge he had," recalled infantryman Thomas Morton.[14] From Wowinapa, Sibley heard first news of Little Crow's death.

Big Mound

The column pushed forward, and shortly after noon on July 24, scouts reported Standing Buffalo's village a few miles to the south. But camped nearby were the hostile bands of Inkpaduta, Lean Bear and White Lodge. Their villages were small compared to Standing Buffalo's large host, but it only takes one shot to start a fight.

Sibley called a halt, and sent scout Joe LaFramboise forward with an offer for talks to take place. While awaiting a reply, Sibley circled his wagons on the east side of a small alkaline lake and dispersed his troops around the camp perimeter, ready for combat. Ten men were detailed from each company to start work with pick and shovel. As the earthworks rose, Indians were seen gathering in force on a rocky range to the east. The largest number appeared around the highest point, called Big Mound by the troops. The ground between there and the camp was dissected by over a mile of rough ground.

The troops watched with interest as a small number of Dakotas rode down the slope and signaled for a parley. Dark clouds gathered overhead, and thunder rumbled as scouts trotted out and met the Indians on a hillock about 350 yards from the earthworks. A chief said his band was peaceful, but warned that some young braves looking on from the bluffs were ready to fight. The army scouts urged a meeting between Standing Buffalo and Sibley. But Scarlet Plume, a Sisseton chief, took mixed-blood army scout Gabriel Renville, his son-in-law, aside. A plot was afoot to murder Sibley and his senior officers, he said. Renville sent word back to camp by Joe Campbell. Sibley replied that he was still prepared to talk, but only within his own lines.

A group of Indians arrived at the camp and conversed with soldiers, who handed out crackers as a gesture of goodwill. But other bluecoats, anxious to fight, fumed at this. Thomas Morton felt that Sibley should have "demanded their surrender and if they refused pitched in and cleaned them out." And Captain Ole Paulson recalled, "There stood the soldiers armed to the teeth, [and we were] burning with the desire to have permission to fire on the blood thirsty savages. But we had to wait patiently until the word of command was given."

13. The Girl I Left Behind Me

Dr. Josiah Weiser of the Mounted Rangers had tended Indians in Minnesota. "Let us go and shake hands with our friends," he said. "I know them." The surgeon, in a major's uniform, rode forward, accompanied by his black servant. He arrived on the hillock and greeted the chiefs in their own language.

Then a fatal shot rang out, and the surgeon fell from his horse.

Tall Crown, of Inkpaduta's band, had ridden behind the doctor and opened fire. Guns were drawn as men scattered and shots were exchanged. Tall Crown jumped from his pony and dodged flying bullets while making good his escape through broken terrain. One scout, Salon Stevens, was wounded and one Indian was hit by return fire.

"They shot Dr. Weiser! They shot Dr. Weiser!" cried the servant as he galloped back to camp. Several old chiefs, decked out with feathered headdresses and coming to talk with Sibley, were caught in the open and shot down.

Bugles blared and drums rolled as Sibley ordered his men to arms. He dispatched three companies of Mounted Rangers under Colonel Sam McPhail to secure Weiser's body. Armed Indians painted for war rode into a ravine running east, but Sibley advanced from camp with a 6-pounder. The gun boomed, flinging case shot at the natural breastwork. Any Indian showing his head was likely to have it taken off. Infantry and cavalry, dismounted due to the rough terrain, moved steadily forward. Under threat from both artillery and troops, the Indians abandoned the ravine, but took position on a hill to the east. A few shells landed in their midst as the cavalry remounted on level ground and charged.

William Marshall followed with the infantry. "Up and on the devils," he yelled. "Give them hell, boys." The outnumbered Dakotas, armed only with a few muskets besides bows and arrows, lacked the firepower and range of the troops, but they were determined to give battle. "Then with a tremendous yell they would discharge their pieces making the dust fly by the sinking of their balls losing distance in front of us," recalled infantryman Charles Bornarth.

"The savages were steadily driven from one strong point to another under a severe fire," reported Sibley, "until, feeling their utter inability to contend longer with our soldiers in the open field, they joined their brethren in one common flight."[15] But the warriors, estimated by Sibley as between one and two thousand, had delayed his advance while the terrified Indian women struck tepees and gathered children. Crossing two miles to reach the last row of bluffs, the troops could see a mass of men, women, and children along with horses fleeing over a mile away. Marshall wanted a cavalry charge, but Colonel McPhail hesitated. "So much for the cowardice of one miserable coward," wrote Sergeant George Clapp to his wife. "Let his name go down to posterity associated with cowards … a hundred or two of the red murderers of men, women and children on our frontier could have been slaughtered."

McPhail, however, did order an advance. But as they moved forward under a sky of black cloud, lightning struck. John Murphy of the 1st Minnesota Mounted Rangers and his horse were killed while others were injured. McPhail's horsemen pursued the retreating Indians as they fought a rear-guard action. A trail of dead warriors and possessions were left in their wake, along with a few old women and infants. Sibley dispatched Major Robert McLaren with several companies to destroy all material left in the abandoned campsite. McPhail's chase ended at Dead Buffalo Lake, where the Dakotas fought back from amidst wild rice and rushes.

Finally, near dark, a few final shots saw the fighting peter out and the Indians disperse. The Rangers counted 31 dead enemy, and felt sure other bodies lay concealed in the dense foliage around the lake and marshes. Sibley estimated Dakota casualties at 42, the real number not known, while the troops lost only three dead and four wounded, one fatally. Killed outright were Dr. Weiser, lightning victim John Murphy, and Lieutenant Ambrose Freeman of the Mounted Rangers. Freeman and others had been out on an antelope hunt when the fighting broke out, and they were attacked by enemy horsemen. The officer was wounded as they dashed for the camp, and died while hiding in bulrushes alongside a small lake. The other three men made it back to safely, but one took four days, drinking brackish water and consuming the odd raw frog.[16]

As darkness set in at Dead Buffalo Lake, McPhail gave orders to set up camp. Some five miles back, William Marshall's 7th Minnesota Infantry, exhausted and disorganized from the pursuit, also began to bivouac. "Our forces were in fact scattered in small squads and without command," recalled infantryman John Danielson, "many not knowing where the next move was to be." Their scant rations were supplemented by buffalo meat left by the Indians, and some grasped discarded buffalo robes to sleep on for the night. The pursuit of the Indians would continue, no doubt, at daybreak by both infantry and cavalry commands.

But Lieutenant Frederick Beaver of Sibley's staff rode into McPhail's quarters. The troops, he said, were to retire back to Sibley's camp near Big Mound. With a groan, the exhausted rangers resaddled their exhausted mounts and began a dispirited ride back. McPhail encountered Marshall along the way and informed him of Sibley's order. The weary infantry shouldered arms and moved off, following the cavalry. The retreating enemy, meanwhile, moved in the opposite direction. Having obtained water scarcely fit to drink from a marsh at the abandoned Indian camp, many weary soldiers plodded back into Sibley's camp at dawn. Had warriors followed, they could have scalped exhausted men sleeping along the way. "I fell over a stone and made no effort to rise," recalled infantryman Thomas Hunt. "No comrade was to be seen or heard, nor was I certain I was going in the right direction; and properly concluding that I should lie there until daylight I went to sleep."[17] Stragglers trudged back into Sibley's camp throughout that morning.

The ill-advised instruction to fall back enabled the Indians to place much distance between themselves and the troops. Sibley later claimed no such order had been given. He had intended for the mounted rangers and infantry to bivouac where they were, and continue the pursuit at daybreak. He said that Lieutenant Beaver had misunderstood the order. The 33-year-old English volunteer would offer no argument, being killed four days later. But Sibley was, in fact, ready to march as the exhausted troops drifted back into camp. He was obliged to allow rest for the day, while the fleeing Indians further widened the gap. It seemed fate had stepped in to save many Indian lives.

Dead Buffalo Lake

Those chiefs like Standing Buffalo, Sweet Corn and Red Plume, who had wished to avoid a clash, split off from Inkpaduta and others who still wished to fight. The peace chiefs were joined by others seeking refuge while traveling north, and in early 1864 some 3,000 Indians crossed the border seeking sanctuary under the Union Jack. They refused to return to the United States, and eventually settled on reservations in the provinces of Manitoba and Saskatchewan.

Sibley, however, had no shortage of warriors howling for his blood. News of the Big Mound fight spread across the prairies like wildfire. Lakotas hunting buffalo east of the Missouri River rode to join Inkpaduta, and along with Yanktonais, about 1,600 warriors gathered to challenge Sibley's advance. Their chief aim was to fight a holding action while noncombatants crossed the broad Missouri River. Once they were across, there seemed little chance the bluecoats would follow. Dependent on wagons for supplies, the crossing, if at all possible, would be slow and difficult.

With the command rested and fed, Sibley gave the order to march before dawn on July 26. The column moved southeast and arrived at the site of the former Indian camp. Although much had already been destroyed, Sibley later reported that a search revealed "vast quantities of dried meat, tallow, and buffalo robes, cooking utensils, and other indispensable articles which were found concealed in the long reeds around the lake, all of which were, by my directions, collected and burned. For miles along the route the prairie was strewn with like evidence of a hasty flight."[18]

Sibley's advance guard of the 6th Minnesota Infantry under Colonel Crooks arrived at Dead Buffalo Lake around noon. Sibley's main column came up, and since this was the last water for many miles, orders were given to set up camp. Then Indians appeared to the front. Two companies moved steadily forward in a skirmish line, supported by pioneers and a battery of

6-pounders. A long-range firefight took place and the Indians fell back, but then warriors appeared on the flanks, and began to move in.

"The savages came swooping down on us," recalled A.P. Connolly, "and it seemed as though they sprang up out of the earth, so numerous were they."[19] Captain Taylor and his Mounted Rangers moved from place to place in support of the infantry, and Sibley ordered Captain John Jones' artillery battery to a hilltop position supported by two companies of the 6th Minnesota. The horse-drawn guns raced up the slope to be unlimbered, swung round, and fired. "There was a heap of Indians made a break for Sibley's wagon train," recalled one warrior, but the cannons returned fire "that would make a noise going through the air, then all load up again and shoot a second time, kill heap more Indians that time."[20]

The firing petered out during the early afternoon, and the gun smoke cleared. It appeared their feathered adversaries had given up for the day. The respite gave time to complete setting up camp. But then hay cutters and teamsters grazing their mules near the lake looked around to see a swarm of mounted warriors galloping to the attack. With wild whoops, they swept in for the kill. But the ranger companies of Captain Eugene Wilson and Captain Peter Davey rode to the rescue, and Major McLaren led six companies of infantry at the double to protect the rangers' left flank. "It was smoky day," recalled Wilson, "and the horses of whites and Indians stirred up the dust, and the contestants mingled with each other, it was often difficult to distinguish friend from foe."[21]

Chief Gray Eagle, "a bold, reckless chief," according to one witness, led a charge right into the soldier camp, but was shot from his horse. Trooper John Pratt's pistol misfired, and he was shot from his saddle by a wounded, dismounted warrior, who was himself shot by Joe Campbell. Despite Sibley's orders, the Indian was scalped by scouts as he died. Several other soldiers were wounded. The final foray lasted about 15 minutes. "The savages, again foiled in their design, fled with precipitation," reported Sibley, "leaving a number of their dead upon the prairie, and the battle of 'Dead Buffalo Lake' was ended."[22]

There was no immediate pursuit. "Our animals were so jaded they could not stand a forced march," recalled Connolly. "The reason was very apparent. We had our regular rations while the horses and mules were on short rations on account of the hot weather burning up the grass, and, besides, the alkali water was as bad for beast as for man."[23]

Stony Lake

Once rested, the dusty troops resumed the pursuit, and on July 27 they arrived at Stony Lake. The tents rose once more; the site was designated Camp

Ambler. The march resumed before dawn, and Sibley rode with the vanguard of the 10th Minnesota Infantry under Colonel James Baker. They were flanked by rows of wagons on either side. The main body of troops followed about half a mile behind. "They are coming! They are coming!" army scouts shouted about two hours later as they topped a rise to the front.[24]

Orders were rapped out, and Baker's troops deployed to left and right. Indians appeared on the crest and one shouted a warning to those following that the troops were ready for them. "But remember our children and families," replied another. "We must not let them get them." Colonel Baker reported, "My whole regiment was deployed, but the Indians covered my entire front, and soon far outflanked on both sides, appearing in numbers that seemed almost incredible, and most seriously threatening the train to right and left of my extended line."[25]

The Indians fanned out, forming a crescent over five miles long, covering about two-thirds of the central march column. On horseback, they dashed about, shaking lances and muskets as they yelled fearful war whoops. They were decked out in war paint and most were naked except for breechclouts. The troops were staggered to see such a threatening host. Sibley estimated their numbers at between 2,000 and 2,500. The Indians displayed an unusual discipline and cohesion, chiefs on hilltops directing certain groups with signal flags.

Two infantry companies deployed as skirmishers, and Baker advanced with the rest of the 10th Minnesota, bayonets fixed, as other regiments were positioned to protect the exposed wagons as they closed up into tight formation. Lieutenant Whipple supported the 10th with his 2-gun battery as they advanced at the double-time. The infantry fired two volleys into the hostile ranks, and three Indians were seen to drop from their ponies, only to be picked up and taken away. Whipple's guns roared, spreading case shot, and the Indians held back from a frontal charge. Sibley ordered Crook's 6th Minnesota, Marshall's 7th, and McPhail's cavalry deployed to protect the wagon trains, and the 10th were ordered to resume their advance in a broad skirmish line, much to the delight of the eager men, frustrated by the halt.

The march continued, the Indians probing for any weaknesses, but the bluecoats held their formations. Armed with superior weapons, they were able to repulse any Indian forays against their lines. Once again Captain Jones' battery did hot work as shot and shell flew towards the enemy lines. It soon became apparent the Indians would be unable to break the bluecoat ranks. On the hilltops, signal flags flew and most warriors rode back towards Sibley's vanguard, the most immediate threat to the Indian women and children. Scouts lying in long grass heard chiefs urging their braves to attempt one last all-out assault, but earlier repulses had taken their heart out of the battle. They could not match the white man's rifle volleys and cannon fire with their outmoded guns, bows and arrows. Sheer bravery was no match for modern weapons.

But they had achieved their primary aim: to slow the enemy while their noncombatants moved towards the Missouri River. With a few final war whoops and shouts of defiance, the Indians fired more futile shots and withdrew. Baker's 10th pushed forward to top the rise where the enemy had first appeared. To their surprise, the Indians had vanished as though never there.

The Missouri

Sibley gave his men two hours' rest, then the troops marched again; the chase resumed. Wary of any ambush, they tramped forward across the dusty plain for 18 miles in combat formation with scouts on the flanks.

But where was General Sully's cavalry? They were supposed to be riding north from Sioux City. Sibley had no word. The Indians were retreating towards the Missouri River, and Sully should be moving in to close the trap.

Sibley's scouts saw a pony amidst a copse of trees. Upon closer examination, they found a young Dakota warrior sound asleep under a buffalo robe. He suddenly leapt up, and taking the robe with him, he ran off in a "zig-zag motion, so that it was impossible to hit him." recalled Connolly. About 30 shots were fired before a scout rode alongside and placed a revolver to his head. He fired, but with split-second timing, the warrior ducked. "He now stopped, dropped the robe, and threw up both hands in a token of surrender."

Taken to Sibley, the prisoner said his father was a Teton Dakota chief from west of the Missouri. They had merely come to watch the fight, not take part. Apparently his story was convincing, as he was released with a letter to his father, praising him for not being involved. But a few days later, the young brave was with Dakotas lying in wait for a party of miners moving by raft down the Missouri. "The young Teton desired peace and rushed towards them waving General Sibley's letter over his head," recalled Connolly. "They, not understanding his signal, shot him to death, when they were at once surrounded by the exasperated Indians, and a battle, short and decisive, was fought, and every man of the miners was killed, but not before twice their number of Indians had shared the same fate, another sad chapter of this unholy war."[26]

The pursuit continued, and Sibley reported that 11 Indian bodies were recovered along the trail. One warrior managed to run off a horse, only to be shot dead when it was recaptured that evening. With Indian scouts on distant hills watching every move, the column set up camp on the Apple River, a tributary of the Missouri. Nine years later, several miles to the north, settlers would establish Bismarck, ultimately the capitol of North Dakota.

"Near our camp in a ravine," recalled Captain Theodore Carter, "a large amount of jerked buffalo meat, buffalo skins and other Indian property, were found and burned. The fleeing families had suffered a great deal from the hardships of their hasty march, as we can see from the number of graves of children we find on the march."

Early on July 29, Sibley ordered McPhail forward to the Missouri with his mounted rangers and two 6-pounders to shell the Indians as they crossed the river. A barrage of arrows from warriors concealed in foliage on the east bank greeted McPhail's advance. The guns were unlimbered, and in short order, shells ripped through the undergrowth, flushing the Indians out. Most, however, had already crossed during the night, many using bullboats, made of buffalo hides stretched over willow frames. The troops arrived to see Indians crossing the river. "They were riding ponies, some ponies carrying a squaw and three or four papooses," recalled John Smith of the 10th Minnesota. "They plunged into the water and swam across." But not all made it. "We drove the Indians across the Missouri and the women and children were drowned, many of them," recalled Newcome Kinney.

Sibley arrived with the bulk of the troops shortly before noon, following a hot 12-mile march under the searing summer sun. "Struck the Missouri about four miles above Burnt Boat Island," Sibley recorded in his diary, "where a natural passage exists, through the bluffs, to the river. The Indian camp was plainly visible on the bluffs opposite, and the hills were lined with savages, watching our line of march."[27]

"We do not want to fight the whites," some yelled from the opposite bank. A scout called back and exchanged words for some time, but a fusillade of bullets greeted soldiers attempting to fill canteens.[28] Eager for action, the troops returned fire as skirmishing continued. A search of the woods by Colonel Crooks' 6th Regiment revealed numerous "carts, wagons and other vehicles" stuffed with Indian possessions. Yet more Indians abandoned the woods and were seen crossing the river, some in bullboats, others clinging to the tails of their horses. They were hit by both artillery and infantry fire. An ineffectual return fire from the opposite bank claimed no white casualties.

Sibley dispatched Lieutenant Beaver, his English aide, with orders for Crooks' men to return. Beaver delivered the order, then "on his way to headquarters," reported Sibley, "he unfortunately took the wrong trail."[29] As darkness came on, both Beaver and Private Nicholas Miller of the 6th Minnesota were reported missing.

Men and animals were exhausted from the day's hot exertions. Mule-drawn ambulances picked up collapsed soldiers, and some stressed horses had to be shot. With "no water to be found on the prairie," Sibley gave orders for his weary command to move a few miles downriver to a site near the Apple River tributary opposite Burnt Boat Island, so named due to the wreck of the steamer *Assiniboine* in 1834. She had been carrying Prince Alexander Phillip Maximilian of Prussia on an expedition of exploration. The prince survived the event to write a book about his American adventures.

During the night, sentries fired at shadows and, in some cases, Indians. A few warriors did manage to get amongst stock, and several mules disappeared into the night. Twice the rattle of drums brought the men from their tents. Flares were sent up. These would not only attract Sully, should he be close, but also the two missing soldiers.

At dawn Sibley dispatched Colonel Crooks back upriver with 11 companies of infantry and dismounted cavalry, and the redoubtable Captain Jones with his 3-gun battery. They had orders to destroy the Indians' carts and wagons found the previous day. Smoke billowed into the blue sky as over 100 vehicles went up in flames. Puffs of gun smoke erupted from the opposite bank, and the troops fired back.

The fate of the two missing men was revealed with the discovery of their bodies, about half a mile apart. Lieutenant Beaver, "after bravely confronting a large party of savages and dealing death in their ranks," reported Crooks, "had fallen, pierced with arrows and bullets, his favorite horse lying dead near him. His was buried in the trenches with the honor due his rank, and every heart beat in sympathy with the family of this brave stranger."[30] Private Miller had lost his scalp in the normal way, while Beaver, his hair being too short, had lost a side whisker from his cheek. An Oxford man, he had come to America in search of adventure, and after two years in New York headed west. He approached Sibley for a commission with letters of recommendation from John Jacob Astor and Hamilton Fish. Ten years after burial, Beaver's body was reinterred in a St. Paul cemetery, his grave maintained at Sibley's expense.[31]

Despite the mass exodus across the Missouri, Sibley's men were given little rest over the two following nights. Warriors had either remained concealed along the east bank, or recrossed after nightfall. On July 30, the darkness erupted into light with the setting of a grass fire, the wind blowing flames towards Sibley's camp. Amidst shouts of panic, the men hastily filled buckets from the river while soldiers desperately thumped the blaze with wet blankets along the burning camp perimeter.

The following night, a party of Indians crawled across the scorched ground to the north and fired a volley, bullets ripping through the camp. The only effects were shredded tents, one dead mule, and a cattle stampede. But this guerrilla warfare unnerved the weary troops, who managed little sleep. Bursts of gunfire continued to flare up until the unseen assailants disappeared with dawn's first light.

Men sweated by day and shivered by night as Sibley remained at "Camp Braden" over the next two days. Cannon boomed and more rockets whooshed in the hope of attracting the missing cavalry command. Sibley felt that Sully,

13. The Girl I Left Behind Me

The death of Lieutenant Beaver in a heroic stand, as imagined by one newspaper artist. This occurred as Sibley shelled Indians crossing the Missouri River (*Harper's Weekly*, September 12, 1863).

"with his comparatively fresh mounted force, could easily have swallowed up the enemy we had so persistently hunted. The long and rapid marches had very much debilitated the infantry," and the horses and the mules "were utterly exhausted." Assuming Sully "delayed by insurmountable obstacles," Sibley gave up hope of any further action against an enemy who could "cross and recross the river in much less time than could my command, and thus evade me."[32] His troops had marched from Minnesota through parched lands and supreme heat, fought three battles and several skirmishes. Now their provisions were depleted. If they did not turn back now, the command would starve.

On July 31, the order to return contained praise for both officers and men. "You have marched nearly six hundred miles from St. Paul, and the powerful bands of the Dakotas, who have hitherto held undisputed possession of the great prairies, have succumbed to your valor and discipline, and sought safety in flight."[33] Sibley called the campaign a "complete success." The failure to link up with Sully received no mention, and many weary soldiers saw things differently. "We are all disheartened that the Indians outwitted us though we drove them from Minnesota and through the Dakota Territory," recalled Edward Patch.

Tents were struck, superfluous wagons burned, and at 5:30 a.m. on August 1, the band struck up "The Girl I Left Behind Me." The troops shouldered arms and marched eastwards into the coming dawn. They were joyful at the thought of returning to loved ones and civilization, but for those glancing back, a depressing sight met their eyes. Warriors had crossed the river, reclaiming their territory, and now followed the retreating troops. Acting as rear-guard, the 6th Minnesota fired a few volleys as a parting gesture, and then trudged on.

Canteens were quickly emptied as the men marched back through scorching heat, mirages playing tricks on their eyes. But late in the day, Apple Creek came into sight; no mirage this time. "We reach the bank, and the Colonel commands: 'Battalion, halt!' but the refreshing water is to near," recalled Connolly, "and the famishing men make a run for it and do not stop until they're in waist deep, and then they drink their fill and replenish their canteens."[34]

On the morning of September 12, 1863, after a trek of over 1,200 miles, the command arrived at Fort Snelling after being greeted with cheering crowds as they marched with colors flying through Minneapolis.

In his report to General Pope, Sibley gave an estimate of the forces arrayed against him: remnants of Minnesota (Santee) bands, 250; Sissetons, 450; eastern Yanktonai, 1200; others including Lakotas from west of the Missouri, 400. A rough total of between 2,300 and 2,500.[35] The Indians estimated their own numbers at 1,600, including 650 Lakotas. As Sibley himself estimated that only 250 were remnants of Minnesota bands, he well knew most Indians being driven across the Missouri under fire had nothing to do with the massacre of 1862.

Indian losses in the campaign are not known. Facing rifles and artillery with inferior weapons. they were decidedly outgunned, and without doubt suffered far greater losses than the troops. Women and children fatalities received no mention in Sibley's report. He claimed the enemy suffered "a loss of at least 150 killed and wounded of his best and bravest warriors, and his beaten forces driven in confusion and dismay, with the sacrifice of vast quantities of subsistence, clothing, and means of transportation, across the Missouri River, many, perhaps most of them, to perish miserably in their utter destitution during the coming fall and winter."[36] But the Dakotas were still there in force the following summer.

Light losses were sustained by Sibley's command. The troops had fared far better than those confronting rebels back east, where more died of disease than combat, many without seeing a shot fired in anger. In all, six officers and men had died in the course of the Indian campaign: Dr. Weiser, shot down at the Big Mound parley; private John Miller, hit by lightning; Lieutenant Freeman, killed while hunting; Lieutenant Beaver and Private Nicholas Miller, killed near the Apple River campsite; and Private John Platt, mortally wounded at Dead Buffalo Lake. Four other soldiers received notable battle wounds, but survived to tell the tale back home.[37]

Other whites died as a result of the campaign, however. A party of white miners in a Mackinaw boat appeared at the very place the Dakotas had been driven across the river. On board were 22 civilians on their way from Boise, Idaho, with up to $100,000 worth of gold dust. The miners knew they were taking a risk. Ten travelers had departed the voyage at Fort Berthold following Indian attacks. But those who pushed on had no idea they would meet such a concentrated Indian force, the result of Sibley's campaign.

As the craft moved downstream, the riverbank erupted in a cloud of gun smoke. Being at close range, the musket balls did far more damage to the miners than they ever had to Sibley's troops. Seventeen of the miners fell, killed outright or wounded. The survivors sprang to action and returned fire, not only with rifles but also a small cannon, inflicting serious damage on the Indians. But then the miners' leader was shot and killed, the powder ran out, and their fate was sealed. The Indians swarmed into the river on horseback and buffalo boats. They were in no mood for mercy, and the remaining whites, including one woman, were speedily cut down. The bodies were stripped, and anything of value taken ashore. Some time later, Indians turned up at Fort Garry with abundant gold dust and greenbacks, and traders were only too happy to supply their wealthy customers with arms and supplies.[38]

14

THE RESULTS ARE ENTIRELY SATISFACTORY

Sibley was back, safe and sound. But what had become of General Sully's command? Sully had not been the first choice to lead the Missouri River expedition. General John Cook, a volunteer officer, had initially been tasked with organizing the job, and met with Yankton chiefs in an attempt to keep them at peace. When Halleck replaced Cook with Sully in May of 1863, General Pope was most displeased. The two men shared a passionate dislike of each other. Sully's regiment had fought under Pope at Second Bull Run, when his boastful predictions of victory had not matched the humiliating defeat.

Sully, like Pope, and unlike Sibley, was a West Point graduate, an army professional. Following graduation in 1841, aged 20, Sully saw action against Seminoles in Florida, to be followed with five years of garrison and recruiting duties. The Mexican War saw a return to action, and he took part in the siege of Vera Cruz in 1847. Sully had other interests, however. Adept with pencil and brush, he painted fine watercolors of army life. His father was the noted artist Thomas Sully, whose portrait of Andrew Jackson provided the basis for the president's image on the $20 bill.

Following the Mexican War, Sully, now 30, was posted to the newly acquired territory of California. Here his next venture was of a more intimate nature, eloping with Manuela Jimeno, the 15-year-old daughter of a prominent Spanish rancher. The father-in-law approved the match, however, and provided Sully with land holdings for development. But strife entered Sully's life when his young wife died during childbirth. The son survived, but only briefly, accidently smothered by his grandmother when she rolled over during sleep.[1] But, despite his becoming somewhat embittered and eccentric by life's pitfalls, Sully's army career did not suffer. His promotion to captain in 1852 saw him take part in the 1853 expedition against the Rogue River Indians of Oregon, and he did service at Forts Ridgely and Pierre. He was tasked with the construction of Fort Randall, Dakota Territory, in 1856, and saw action against Cheyennes in 1860 and 1861.

14. The Results Are Entirely Satisfactory

The outbreak of the Civil War saw him promoted to major, then colonel of the 1st Minnesota Regiment in March of 1862. The Peninsula Campaign, Second Bull Run, Antietam and Fredericksburg saw his rise to brigadier general of U.S. Volunteers. But trouble erupted when six companies of the 34th New York Regiment, claiming their enlistments were up, stacked arms. They refused Sully's orders, and division commander General John Gibbon arrived in camp with the 15th Massachusetts regiment. He told the dissenters that they were mutineers, no better than "the rebels on the other side of the river." The Massachusetts regiment would open fire and "kill every man it could" if they did not follow orders. He then called on the men to step forward if they were ready to do their duty. One by one, they all did, and served for another month.

Seen as weak in handling the situation, Sully was relieved of command, but exonerated with a court of inquiry on May 16, 1863. Despite this, he was sent west to command the Dakota expedition being formed to cooperate with General Sibley. Once again he would be under the command of John Pope. Apart from mutual distrust, both men shared anger at being pulled from the main battlefront to chase Indians out west. Not one for formality, the unconventional Sully chose to dress in corduroy pants, white shirt and white slouch hat when in the field. He carried with his baggage a flock of hens to furnish fresh eggs. "Brevet horses" would appear on his books when mules took the place of proper mounts. A frequent user of "colorful" language, he was short-tempered, and conflict with other officers was part of his creed.[2]

Sully's Dakota expedition consisted of the 6th Iowa Cavalry Regiment, eight companies of the 2nd Nebraska, two companies of Dakota cavalry, and one company of the 7th Iowa. His only infantry were three companies of the 45th Iowa. His artillery was one 8-gun battery. With teamsters and scouts, he commanded about 1,200 men, less than half of Sibley's force.[3]

On June 20, 1863, four

General Alfred Sully, like Pope, fell into disfavor while fighting Confederates and found himself transferred west (author's collection).

days after Sibley marched, Sully rode from Sioux City. The column of 75 support wagons was minimal, horse fodder and other supplies being carried up the Missouri on the steamboats *Alone*, *Shreveport*, and *Belle Peoria*. Many civilians and soldiers doubted the expedition's ability to achieve anything. It was late in the season, and the Missouri's water was dropping fast, making steam navigation difficult. And many of Sully's recruits were most displeased, feeling they had been "recruited under false pretenses." These men from Nebraska and Iowa had joined the army to fight Johnny Rebs, and did not have the same passion for revenge against the Indians as Sibley's Minnesota Brigade.

It took a sluggish three weeks for Sully to cover the 250 miles between Sioux City and Fort Randall. The troops moved too fast for the steamers, the captains having to navigate narrow channels through low water. The march stopped midway until the steamers caught up.

Once at Fort Randall, Sully was infuriated to hear of the Ponca Creek Massacre, in which Indians were the victims, not whites. On June 12, Sergeant Newman went out during the night to look for his missing horse. Indians opened fire and bullets whistled past his head. Next day, Captain Abraham Moreland with a 15-man detachment went out in pursuit. The guilty were long gone, but Moreland came across eight Lakotas who had just been trading at the Yankton Agency. Their leader, Puffy Eyes, had previously saved white prisoners taken from Minnesota by trading horses for them. The small band of Lakotas found themselves surrounded, and handed over their weapons along with a letter from General William Harney which proclaimed the chief to be a good man.

What exactly happened next varies with the telling, but Puffy Eyes' son managed to escape and said the Indians were shot down after being told they were free to leave. The incident was originally reported as a fair fight, but the truth seeped out, and Private Milton Spencer of the 6th Iowa wrote, "I suppose the cowardly wretches who committed that cold-blooded murder feel a little uneasy and so try to give the affair the appearance of a battle." Lieutenant Colonel John Pattee said the victims were "the most loyal and friendly Indians that could be found in the whole country."

Dakotas living on the nearby reservation responded with deep grieving and anger towards the army. Siegmund Rothammer of the 6th Iowa cavalry wrote his wife, "Hereforto plenty of Indians and Squaws would all be around the campfires trading moccasins and Bows.... Today none are visible, and our men begin to think, that trouble may result." Lieutenant Colonel Sam Pollack of the 6th Iowa found himself placed under arrest by the seething Sully. The general felt that bigotry in Pollack's regiment was rampant from the commander down, and he did not want a premature local Indian war on his hands. A board of investigation was set up, but it was found convenient to have the matter shelved.[4]

14. The Results Are Entirely Satisfactory

The column rode from Fort Randall, described by Rothammer as "not worthy of the name, as it really is no fort at all, but only an assembly of loghouses." They paused at the Crow Creek Reservation, where Sully was visited by Winnebago chiefs. Only a few of their young braves had taken part in the 1862 massacre, and they rightly complained of being stripped of their Minnesota lands. The Santee Dakotas had also been packed off to Crow Creek from the Fort Snelling internment camp, and both tribes given poor farming land on adjacent reservations. People died from exposure and malnutrition, and the two tribes did not get along. On viewing conditions, Pastor Sam Hinman wrote to Henry Whipple, "Bishop if I were an Ind[ian] I would never lay down the war club while I lived."[5] In September of 1864, Fort Thompson, complete with stockade and garrison, was established to keep the peace.

Sully's column continued its northwards trek through intolerable heat and dust, buoyed only by the news of the Union victories at Gettysburg and Vicksburg. But on July 25, the proposed date for joining Sibley, they still were hundreds of miles to the south, at Fort Pierre. Originally established as a civilian trading post in 1832, the post had been purchased by the army in 1855. This fort, although rundown, was worthy of the name, apparently, "built in a

The Santees and Winnebagos were exiled from Minnesota to the desolate Crow Creek Agency in Dakota Territory. Fort Thompson was established to keep the peace (author's rendition).

Fort Pierre, an old trading post, as it appeared when purchased by the army in 1855. From here, Sully launched the final phase of his 1863 assault (author's rendition).

square and consisted of four log buildings with log towers, each of which is provided with loopholes for infantry," recalled Rothammer. "On one of these little towers, who like all the buildings in this fort are covered with shingles, is a small gallery for the accommodation of a Sentinel and lookout, and the whole is enclosed by a wall of logs sett perpendicular in the ground projecting about 12 feet out of it."[6]

Some writers in recent times have accused movies of giving a false image of the western frontier fort; they claim that posts with a timber stockade and blockhouses were virtually nonexistent. Fort Abraham Lincoln, for example, in the 1942 Warner Bros. Custer epic *They Died with Their Boots On*, was depicted as a stockaded post, which, in fact, it was not. But immediately following the Minnesota War of 1862, smaller military posts exposed to possible attack by the fearsome "Sioux" were built with stockades and blockhouses, and many existing forts, like Ridgely, Ripley and Abercrombie, were speedily fortified. All the Bozeman Trail forts built in 1866 had stockades and blockhouses. Earlier civilian trading posts, like Fort Pierre, had been established with a stockade from the outset. As time went on, the need became less urgent, and stockades around larger posts like Fort Abraham Lincoln, established in 1872, were not considered necessary. But even this was a concern for some. On one occasion Indians drove off a mule herd from just outside the

14. The Results Are Entirely Satisfactory

post. Custer led the garrison in pursuit and the few left behind feared "that the buildings would be set on fire by the wily, creeping savages," recalled Elizabeth Custer. "It was even thought that the running off of the herd was but a ruse to get the garrison out, in order to attack the post."[7]

At Fort Pierre, Sully was forced once more to wait for the steamers and their precious cargo of grain for the horses. The heat had burned away most of the grass. A reporter for the *Weekly Dakotan* riding with the command wrote, "All that mortal man can do will be done by General Sully, and it is his intent to make one bold stroke at the Indians—grass or no grass." But by August 7, the welcome sight of a riverboat was yet to be seen.

General Pope, in Milwaukee, was not happy. Having received a report from Sully, he replied on August 5, "I never had the slightest idea you could delay thus along the River, nor do I realize the necessity of such delay." Pope reminded Sully that he had "time and time again informed you, how necessary it was that you should be in position on the upper Missouri, or between that River and Devil's Lake, to co-operate with General Sibley.... I never dreamed you would consider yourself tied to the boats if they were obstacles in going up the river. As matters stand it seems impossible to me to understand how you have staid about the River, delaying from day to day, when time of all things was important, and when you have wagons enough to carry at least two months' subsistence for your command."[8]

One steamboat, the *Alone*, arrived very much alone at Fort Pierre, the other two still chugging their way upstream. Sully, stinging from Pope's rebuke, ordered that 23 days of supplies be loaded on mules for a rapid push north, following the Missouri. This news buoyed the troops, who were eager for action after weeks of idle camp life about Fort Pierre. "We in this campaign are all bravados," wrote Henry Pierce back home. The bravado, however, was missing from six men who deserted the night before the expedition's departure. Sully gave orders for the next boat to arrive to keep going and join him upstream. The weather had cooled by the time the column moved out on August 14, and four days later a violent storm with hail "as large as hen's eggs" struck. "Men and horses quickly broke ranks for the shelter of brush," recalled Milton Spencer, "but horses could not stand such a pelting very quietly. Some threw their riders and themselves, others getting wild and crazy ... ran across the flat about half a mile as fast as their legs could carry them."[9]

On August 19, the *Belle Peoria* hove into view. Supplies were loaded into wagons, and any superfluous gear was loaded aboard the steamer along with sick or unmounted troops for return to Fort Pierre. The column moved on, to be struck by another violent rainstorm the following day. Hail pelted the troops for 20 minutes and a wagon rolled over as the column crossed the Little Cheyenne River. Provisions in uncovered wagons were destroyed and troopers were thrown by their panicked mounts. The men pitched wet canvas on bluffs after being forced from the flooded bottomlands. On August 21, the column moved out again, but made slow progress over sodden ground.[10]

Following the Little Cheyenne, the troops moved away from the Missouri River, riding northeast towards Devil's Lake. Now in buffalo country, Sully gave permission for the men to hunt the shaggy beasts that supplied the Plains Indians with virtually all their needs in life. Between 15 and 20 animals were killed, the fresh meat relished over campfires that night. But while hunting the following day, some managed to shoot their own mounts by mistake. Even excellent horsemen could do the same as George Custer recalled in *My Life on the Plains*. He too accidently shot his horse while on a buffalo hunt.[11] Sully ordered that the hunting cease forthwith.

On the same day, scouts arrived in camp with two Dakota women and their children, found while on their way to the Crow Creek Agency. Sully had already heard of Sibley's fights further north, and the Indian women corroborated these stories. Sully dispatched patrols to hopefully contact Sibley, or failing that, to locate Indian villages. Scouts found an elderly Dakota man called Keg, and Sully heard more of Sibley's action, the Indian ambush of the Mackinaw boat, and hostiles recrossing the Missouri to the east side.

A patrol under Captain LaBoo burned ten abandoned lodges, while another squad found the site of the Big Mound fight, Dr. Weiser's grave, and Sibley's return trail back towards Minnesota. These actions had happened more than three weeks earlier, so Sully realized the opportunity to work with Sibley was gone; any action he undertook would have to be self-contained. Scouts corroborated Keg's account of Indian movements and said that the Dakotas, at this time of year, usually camped to the southeast in the Coteau des Missouri. This fertile region was blessed with freshwater lakes, good fishing, and buffalo grazing on tall grass. The Dakotas would hunt and store food, then move for the long winter months back to the Missouri, where the timbered banks provided fuel for fires.

A courier arrived with more orders from Pope: "It is painful for me to find fault, nor do I desire to say what is unpleasant, but I feel bound to tell you frankly that your movements have greatly disappointed me, and I can find no satisfactory explanation of them." Pope ordered Sully to return to the Missouri, load his wagons, and seek Indians west of the river. When winter arrived, he was to distribute his command between Fort Pierre, Fort Randall, and Sioux City. But the order came too late—or was simply ignored.[12] To limp back with Sibley having seen all the action would vindicate the despised Pope's opposition to Sully's having been given command. He needed Indians to attack, and soon, before his supplies ran out. Any Indians would do.

The general ordered a forced march with flankers and an advance guard. The wagons, in two lines, moved 60 paces apart with cavalrymen on each side. All loose stock moved between the wagons, and the cannon battery moved in the center for easy deployment. Indians would be unable to create a stampede, and only a handful of stock were lost after straying during the night.[13]

Whitestone Hill

On September 3, the remains of recently killed buffalo were found alongside a small lake—Indians were not far off. Major Albert House was dispatched with the 3rd Battalion of the 6th Iowa Cavalry, 300 men, to move in advance of the main column. House had orders to engage any small enemy force he may come across, but hold back and send word if a big village was located. Sully would advance at the double under cover of dark for a dawn assault.

At 3 p.m., battalion guide Frank LaFramboise informed Major House that a village of between 400 and 600 lodges lay ahead about the base of Whitestone Hill. This was near the headwaters of Elm Creek, 15 miles west of the James River. The Indians were going about their normal routine, unaware of the troops' approach. House ordered his battalion forward at a fast gait. Sergeant Elkanah Richards of the 6th Iowa recalled, "We knew we were not in Dixie where the enemy took prisoners, but hundreds of miles from civilization where the enemy took no prisoners."

La Framboise and two men were dispatched to inform Sully, now some 10 miles to the rear, but they encountered a party of braves. One warrior called out, declaring "they had fought General Sibley, and they could not see why the whites had come to fight them, unless they were tired of living and wanted to die." The couriers galloped off, and La Framboise arrived at Sully's bivouac shortly after 4 p.m. "The horses at that time were grazing," reported Sully. "At the sound of the bugle, the men rushed with a cheer, and in a very few minutes saddled up and were in line."

One mile from the Indian camp, meanwhile, Major House called a halt and formed his cavalry in line of battle: three companies to the fore with one held in reserve. Concealed by a ridge, they moved steadily forward until about 280 yards from the unsuspecting village. Two officers went ahead to reconnoiter, and returned to report about 400 lodges. The major had no hope of surrounding the village, the tepees too spread out for his 300 men.

"These Indians were partly Santees from Minnesota; Cutheads from the Coleau; Yanktonais, and some Blackfeet who belong on the other side of the Missouri," reported Sully. Also in the village were the "Uncapapas, the same party who fought General Sibley and destroyed the Mackinaw boat."[14] Although Inkpaduta and other war chiefs were present, the vast majority had taken no part in the 1862 massacre.

Then a flag of truce appeared. The troops had been spotted and a delegation of chiefs came forward. They offered to hand over a few leaders who were hostile to the whites. They wanted peace, they said; their only aim was to dry meat for the coming winter months. House, unsure of who had authority to speak for all the Indians, demanded the surrender of the entire village, not a few individuals. The chiefs refused, "and, having sent away their squaws and papooses, together with their stock of provisions, they placed themselves in battle array," reported House. Stories are told of the troops feeling they were about to be annihilated by a savage horde, but according to House, "Our command moved forward, and the enemy retreated precipitately, abandoning everything except their ponies. While we were thus following and scattering the enemy, the Second Nebraska Regiment appeared on the hill."[15]

Colonel Robert Furnas with the 2nd Nebraska had been ordered out in advance. Sully arrived with the main body at about 5 p.m. after a one-hour ride over 10 miles. Colonel David Wilson of the 6th Iowa and Major House thought the Indians fired first,[16] but Furnas claimed the "credit." With daylight almost gone, and no orders from Sully, "I ordered my men to dismount, and after advancing my men 400 yards nearer, ordered the Second Battalion to open the battle by a volley from their Enfields, which they did with precision and effect, creating quite a confusion in the enemies ranks."[17] The 6th Iowa, on the left, also opened fire.

The Indians had been moving into a ravine about half a mile from the village "where there were thousands of men, women and children, ponies and dogs," recalled Elkanah Richards, "and they were a hard looking lot of humanity, I can assure you, after they were surrounded." Death songs were heard from the ravine as warriors prepared to defend their families. One man stepped out wrapped in an American flag, gesturing for peace, "and when he was close to our line, a little Dutchman on the left fired and killed him," recalled Trooper George Belden.

Sully rode through the center of the camp with the battery of four howitzers and three mounted companies. He encountered peace Chief Little Soldier with "some few of his people," whom he placed under guard, then, moving on, encountered "the notorious chief Big Head, and some of his men." With women and children, Sully took captive "over one hundred and twenty human beings. About the same time firing began about half a mile ahead of me, and was kept up, becoming more and more brisk till it was quite a respectable engagement." The troops on both sides of the ravine poured bullets into the Indians. Corwin Lee of the 6th Iowa recalled that the men "fired their guns and revolvers among the Indians who lined the ravine as thick as they could stand, and among whom our Minnie balls told with fearful effect, and the Nebraska boys were pitching into them from the opposite side."

Captain Lewis Wolfe later wrote to the *Iowa City Press* of his surprise that the troops did not suffer higher casualties, as "we were very close to them

14. The Results Are Entirely Satisfactory   173

The Battle of Whitestone Hill, as Sully wished the world to see it. This newspaper illustration was derived from his own work with brush and paint. Sully finally pleased General Pope with his destruction of a Dakota village on September 3, 1863 (*Harper's Weekly*, October 31, 1863).

and the bullets and arrows flew about us like hail." The Indians, he wrote, "fought like enraged men that had nothing but their lives to lose or a victory to gain. Volley after volley flew the leadened hail from our enraged fire."

Colonel David Wilson, commander of the 6th Iowa, ordered his dismounted troopers back onto their saddles. Here was a chance for a glorious mounted assault *Harper's Weekly* would be happy to illustrate. The troops advanced at a fast trot; then, in the gathering darkness, the order to charge was given. With a nudge of spurs, the horses bolted forward at the gallop. In his zest, Wilson found himself far in front of his men, bullets whizzing about, one hitting his horse. He wheeled about and covered the "30 rods" back to his own lines, only to have his horse fall dead. In addition to Indian fire, Wilson's rash action saw men drop from their saddles, hit by "friendly fire" from the 2nd Nebraska, and the charge came to a halt amidst a cloud of dust and bullets.[18] The men dismounted once more, leaving casualties on the field. "The Indians charged right at us, shooting, firing arrows and hurling weapons at us," recalled Trooper Luse of the 6th Iowa. The warriors broke through the bluecoat line, followed by the women and children, who disappeared into the gathering darkness.

Sully, meanwhile, had placed his battery on a knoll overlooking the village. But it was of little use: "I could not use my artillery without greatly endangering the lives of my own men; if I could, I would have slaughtered them.... At this time night had about set in, but still the engagement was briskly kept up and in the melee, it was hard to distinguish my line from that of the enemy. The enemy made a very desperate resistance, but finally broke and fled, pursued in every direction by bodies of my troops."[19]

Private Milton Spencer felt the victory would have been bigger and more easily won without Colonel Wilson's contribution. After the failed charge, "Mr. Indian, seeing the gate open, was not long in going out."[20]

In the dark, confusion reigned supreme. "I became convinced that House's battalion, mistaking my command in the darkness for Indians, were firing into it," reported Colonel Furnas. He ordered his men to remount and get out of range, but the horses became "alarmed and to a considerable extent unmanageable for a short time." They reformed on the crest of a hill as the Indians fled. "But being very dark ... I deemed it imprudent to attempt a pursuit before morning, as it was then 8.30 or 9 p.m."[21]

The Indians disappeared into the dark, and the Battle of Whitestone Hill petered out. Weary troopers unsaddled, ate hardtack and lay on their arms through a long cold night. Wounded troopers, unseen in the dark, lay where they fell, and Indian women came back to take revenge. They "beat their brains out," recalled George Belden, "after which they took a butcher-knife and cut out their tongues." Lieutenant Leavitt, wounded, fought off Indian women with his saber, but was stabbed three or four times. Although still alive when found next day, he soon died of his wounds.

"At length the day appeared," reported Colonel Wilson, "when we found that the enemy, availing themselves of the darkness, had suddenly decamped, but leaving the country strewed for miles around with their dried meats, provisions, packs, robes, tepees, goods and ponies."[22] According to Corwin Lee, other things were left behind: "Squaws, papooses and Indians lay in confusion and blood scattered on all sides." Soldiers took anything they fancied in the way of souvenirs, and the command set out to track the survivors down.

Some, however, while still alive, had not escaped: "We saw a little Indian boy on the field, naked and crying; no one paid any attention to him," recalled Lee. "There were eight or ten little children scattered around. They were collected together and put with the prisoners. At one place there lay two papooses; one of them four or five years old, and the other only a few months. A dead squaw probably their mother, lay with them; the elder would insist on keeping covered saying 'shoot, shoot' whenever uncovered. Another was crying 'Mamma, Mamma!' as pitifully as any white child could."[23]

Sully put on a brave face in his report, thanking both Wilson and Furnas "for the good conduct and cheerfulness with which they obeyed my orders on the occasion." But, despite the "victory," he was hard to please, apparently. He complained of ineptitude amongst the officers of the 6th Iowa, and threatened an examination to test their military qualifications. "That is a trial to which our officers have never been subjected," recalled Milton Spencer, "and as most of them are more familiar with a deck of cards than they are with Cavalry tactics and army regulations, I am afraid it will go hard with some of them."[24] The fact was, with the Civil War raging, Regular Army officers and West Point graduates were in big demand. All sorts of men gained commissions in the volunteer army. Some emerged with flying colors, but not all were up to the job. Sully's misgivings went beyond officers, however. While the enlisted men "conducted themselves well" and were of "the right material," they would only become worthy soldiers with "discipline" and "time."[25]

Smoke rolled skywards as 100 troopers spent two days burning the remains of the Indian camp: 300 tepees, their contents, and over 400,000 pounds of meat, the product of at least 1000 killed buffalos. The "fat ran in streams from the burning mass of meat," recalled wagon master Captain Mason. But not all went to waste, 12 wagons being loaded with meat for the troops. The former owners were now destitute, their winter food destroyed. More prisoners, mostly women and children, were rounded up. Sully's final count was 156 captives, including 32 men.

But, despite Sully's success, the Indians were not through. On September 5 he dispatched Lieutenant Charles Hall of the 2nd Nebraska with 27 men to find out what had become of an ambulance train from their old campsite. The missing vehicles arrived safely that day, but about 15 miles from the battlefield, Hall found his small command attacked by a large war party, 300 in his estimate. He ordered a slow retreat allowing a rear-guard action, returning fire, but "my command was so closely pressed by the enemy that the men increased the rapidity of their retreat, without orders." Hall's efforts to prevent a dash for safety went nowhere, and the Indians circled around in an attempt to cut them off. But most made it back following a 12-mile chase with a loss of six men and four horses killed. If some of the dead had been wounded and left behind, they would have suffered a horrific death. In Indian wars, "Keep the last bullet for yourself" was the going advice. Hall claimed the killing of six Indians and four ponies, "and wounding many others, the number not known."[26]

Also not known was the number of Indian casualties from the big fight two days earlier. Considering the "murderous fire in the ravine" reported by Sully, the "slaughter must have been immense. My officers and guides I have with me think 150 will not cover their loss." Other officers estimated the Indian casualties as high as 200 killed and 200 wounded. Indian accounts, often contradictory, claimed about 200 killed and wounded. Sully reported his own casualties, including the Hall skirmish, as 18 killed and 36 wounded. Other later estimates went as high as 22 killed and 50 wounded.

The Indians claimed Sully's unprovoked attack was a needless massacre, the village mainly populated by those intent on peace, and they only fought back to cover the escape of women and children. The prisoners were dispatched by forced march across the desolate plains to Crow Creek Reservation to join the Dakotas from Fort Snelling. This was remembered by the Indians as a "death march," several dying along the way.

His work done, on September 6 Sully led his command back towards Fort Pierre. On September 11 they rendezvoused with a steamer at the mouth of the Little Cheyenne. Badly needed grain for the horses was unloaded, and wounded soldiers were placed on board. But even this additional food did not prevent many horses and mules from dying while crossing the parched ground on the last leg of the trek. The rear guard shot straggling animals to prevent them from falling into enemy hands.

The column arrived at Fort Pierre in mid-September and prepared to move into winter quarters. A new post, Fort Sully, complete with stockade and blockhouses, was constructed eight miles downstream, thus bringing to a close the long history of Fort Pierre, now deemed inadequate for military needs. Sully and his staff continued south to Sioux City, while the remaining troops were left to garrison Fort Randall and carry out routine patrols.

Sam Brown, the mixed-blood ex-prisoner of Little Crow, was now serving as an interpreter at the Crow Creek Reservation. He heard from the Indian prisoners their version of events, and wrote to his father, Joseph Brown, on November 13:

> I hope you will not believe all that is said of Sully's successful expedition against the Sioux. I don't think he ought to brag of it at all, because it was what no decent man would have done, he pitched into their camp and just slaughtered them, worse a great deal than what the Indians did in 1862, he killed *very few* men and took *no* hostile ones prisoners, he took some but they were friendly Yanktons and he let them go again.... It is lamentable to hear how those women and children were slaughtered it was a perfect massacre and now he returns saying we need fear no more, for he has 'wiped out all hostile Indians from Dakota'; if he had killed men instead of women and children, then it would have been a success, and the worst of it, they had no hostile intentions whatever, the Nebraska 2nd pitched into them without orders, while the Iowa 6th were shaking hands with them.[27]

But General Pope was pleased—even if it did mean eating humble pie. "The results are entirely satisfactory," he wrote Sully on October 5, "and I doubt not that the effect upon the Northwestern Indians will be, as you report, of the highest consequence. While I regret that difficulties and obstacles of a serious character prevented your cooperation with General Sibley at the time hoped, I bear willing testimony to the distinguished conduct of yourself and your command, and to the important service you have rendered to the government."[28]

Pope was right about the "highest consequence." While some Santees

14. The Results Are Entirely Satisfactory

The northeast corner of "Old Fort Sully." This post was abandoned in 1866, the marshy bottomlands having been deemed unhealthy. A new fort of the same name was built 23 miles to the northwest (author's rendition).

attacked by both Sibley and Sully had taken part in the 1862 uprising, most who suffered were other Dakotas innocent of any wrongdoing. They were now scattered throughout the northwest and into British territory. The Yanktonais had learned that the white man's justice was hollow, and in Lakota eyes a war of extermination was underway. They had seen no significant conflict with the U.S. Army since the Grattan fight in 1854, and the retaliatory massacre at Blue Water Creek by General Harney's troops the following year.

General Pope may have been well satisfied with the results of 1863, but some newspaper editors were not. "The hour for striking the avenging blow had arrived, but the blow was not struck," voiced the *Minneapolis State Atlas*. Who was responsible? General Sibley, said the paper, guilty of treason and cowardice. Another expedition would be required in 1864 to finish off the savages once and for all. The *St. Paul Weekly Press* echoed these sentiments: "It will require another season of vigorous and active operations to reduce the fierce and haughty tribes of the Missouri Valley to submission."[29]

Sully wrote a letter for publication which warned settlers in isolated areas to relocate or, at the very least, be vigilant. The destruction of Indian homes and provisions at Whitestone Hill meant the natives were now "destitute and they must necessarily steal or starve this winter." Settlers must have wondered if such a victory was a blessing or a curse.

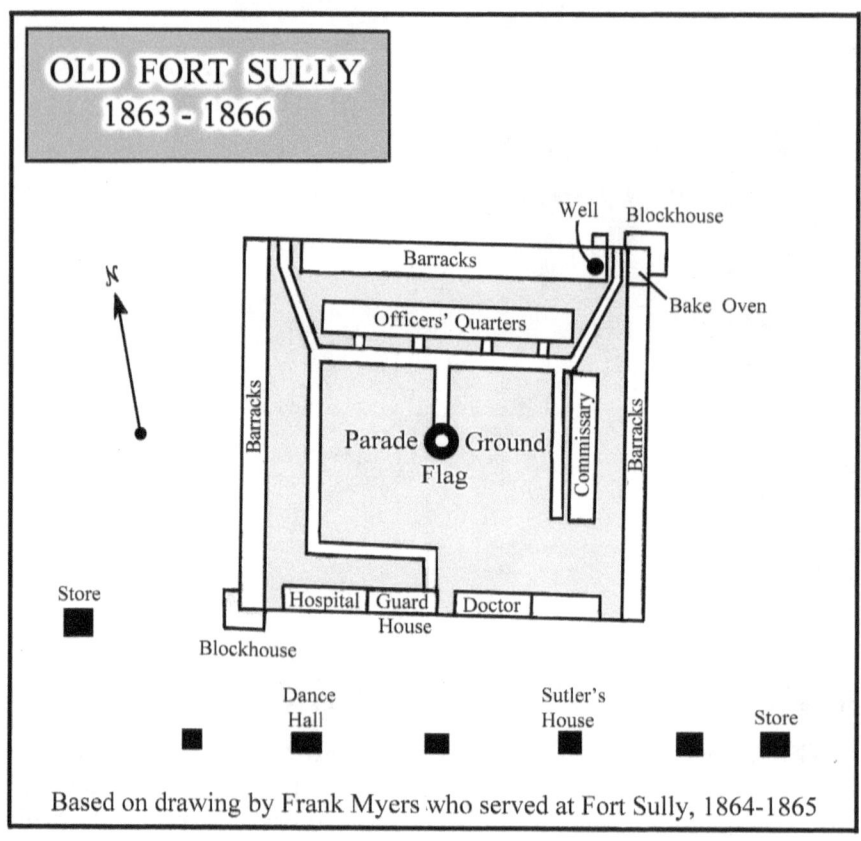

Old Fort Sully plan (author's rendition).

Governor Newton Edmunds wrote to Indian Commissioner Dole, regarding the expeditions: "I am fully convinced that little, if anything, was accomplished towards the subjugation of the Indians.... I am not prepared to say why they were failures; I leave this subject where it properly belongs, to the War Department, to make the enquiry; of the fact, however, I have not the least doubt."[30]

Henry Sibley's force, meanwhile, had been redeployed. Some went south to fight Confederates, while others were stationed at Forts Abercrombie, Ripley, Ridgely, and other smaller posts. Pope planned a defensive line of fortifications with constant patrols to protect the settlers in Minnesota. "Mankato is emphatically a military community," wrote the *Mankato Semi-Weekly Record*. "Our male population is composed of at least two-thirds soldiers." Robert Perry of the 1st Minnesota Mounted Rangers noted, "Along the whole frontier from Iowa to Fort Ridgely, 300 miles, there is camps fortified and garrisoned

… every ten or fifteen miles." The military expeditions and deployments have "enabled several individuals to make fortunes by defrauding the government," wrote Corporal Albert Childs, "and although it has cost thousands and thousands of dollars, not a cents worth of benefit has the government received." Rumors of an 1864 expedition did the rounds. It would be a boon for "those that is speculating out of it," wrote Milton Spencer, and would be most unpleasant "for the poor soldier."[31]

15

An Indian Campaign Is Approved

Guilty or not, many Santee Dakotas who fled Minnesota found a new home in Rupert's Land. But some wintered south of the border, between the Missouri and Red Rivers. Warm log fires would keep the bluecoats at home before the spring thaw would allow active military operations.

Vested interests wished to see a further thrust into Dakota Territory. Apart from lucrative army contracts, a westward push by the iron horse would allow speculators to acquire huge tracts of land for settlement by whites. "If we want war in the spring," Halleck wrote, "a few traders can get one up on the shortest notice."[1] But his priority was to defeat rebels down South. Indians were a secondary consideration, and words being cheaper than troops, he urged Pope to talk with them rather than make war.

But Acting Dakota Governor John Hutchinson declared, "The hostile tribes must be conquered, and must be compelled to make new treaties"— in other words, hand over more land.[2] And of course there was that big prize so desired by whites—gold! It had not been found on the Dakota prairies, but safe passage through Indian lands and up the Missouri River was required to rich strikes in Idaho and Montana. Steamboats thrashed their way upstream to Fort Benton, Montana, where navigable water ceased. They carried miners and equipment before steaming back down again carrying gold, a share of which would finance Union troops fighting rebels down South. An overland migrant trail was established with hopes that the railroad would follow. The Indians, standing in the way of progress, must be pushed aside.

But they were prepared to fight. Alongside the Lakotas and Santees were hundreds of Yanktonais driven to fight the whites following Sully's attack at Whitestone Hill.[3] A scout rode into Fort Abercrombie with news that the Yanktonais were "decided in their hostility," Sibley wrote. "The Yanktonais have invited the disaffected of the other bands of the Sioux to join them, and are determined to attack any boats or parties found within the limits of their country." But, as in 1862, the Indians were not of one mind. During the winter of 1863-64, over 90 Dakotas crossed the border from Rupert's Land and surrendered to Major Hatch at Pembina. In February nearly 300 Yanktonais came into Fort Sully wanting peace. Another 500 to 600 followed, and soon a forest of tepees could be seen from behind the fort walls. On April 20, 1863, two hundred Sisseton lodges arrived at Fort Abercrombie asking for peace.

Dakota war chiefs Shakopee and Medicine Bottle, however, had no intention of surrendering to the tender mercies of American justice. Rupert's Land was now home to them. Lured to the home of a "friend," trader John McKenzie, the wanted men were given alcohol laced with drugs. Tied to sleds, they were covered with furs and taken across the border into the waiting hands of Major Hatch. At Fort Snelling, cursory trials were arranged; the verdicts were in no doubt. On November 10, 1864, the *St. Paul Pioneer Press* commented, "No serious injustice will be done by their execution tomorrow, but it would have been more creditable if some tangible evidence of their guilt had been obtained."[4]

During the early summer of 1864, a small number of hostiles made their way into Minnesota through Pope's defensive line. Given their native skills at camouflage and furtive movement, this comes as no surprise. The line presented a challenge to be breached. March and April of 1864 saw small-scale raids. A 6th Iowa trooper and three civilians were killed, and numerous horses stolen. Then a rumor did the rounds, repeated by Sully, that Lakotas had procured a cannon to fire on riverboats. No such gun existed, of course. Arms dealers north of the border did have their limits. A clamor for action arose against Indian villages on the lower Yellowstone, upper Grand, and Heart Rivers in Dakota Territory. Under pressure, Indian Secretary William Dole gave the nod for offensive operations in 1864. Halleck wired Pope on February 14, "Your plan of an Indian campaign is approved, subject to such modifications experience may suggest."[5]

As with the 1863 campaign, expeditions would set out from Iowa and Minnesota. Both columns of the "Northwestern Indian Expedition" would be commanded, overall, by Alfred Sully. He personally would lead the Sioux City "First Brigade," while the Minnesota "Second Brigade" would be commanded by Colonel Minor Thomas. Sibley had requested that he remain in Minnesota and command troops on the home front. He had done with Indian fighting, apparently. Or perhaps he was miffed at the prospect of being put under the West Point general who, despite falling behind schedule, had been rewarded with the more decisive victory at Whitestone Hill.

As preparations were made, Sibley repeatedly warned Colonel Thomas to advance with extreme caution. "General, I am going to hunt for the Indians," he replied with exasperation, "and if they will hunt for and find me it will save me a heap of trouble." Thomas claimed, possibly to placate Sibley, that the 1863 campaign had "freed all of Minnesota and most of Dakota of their

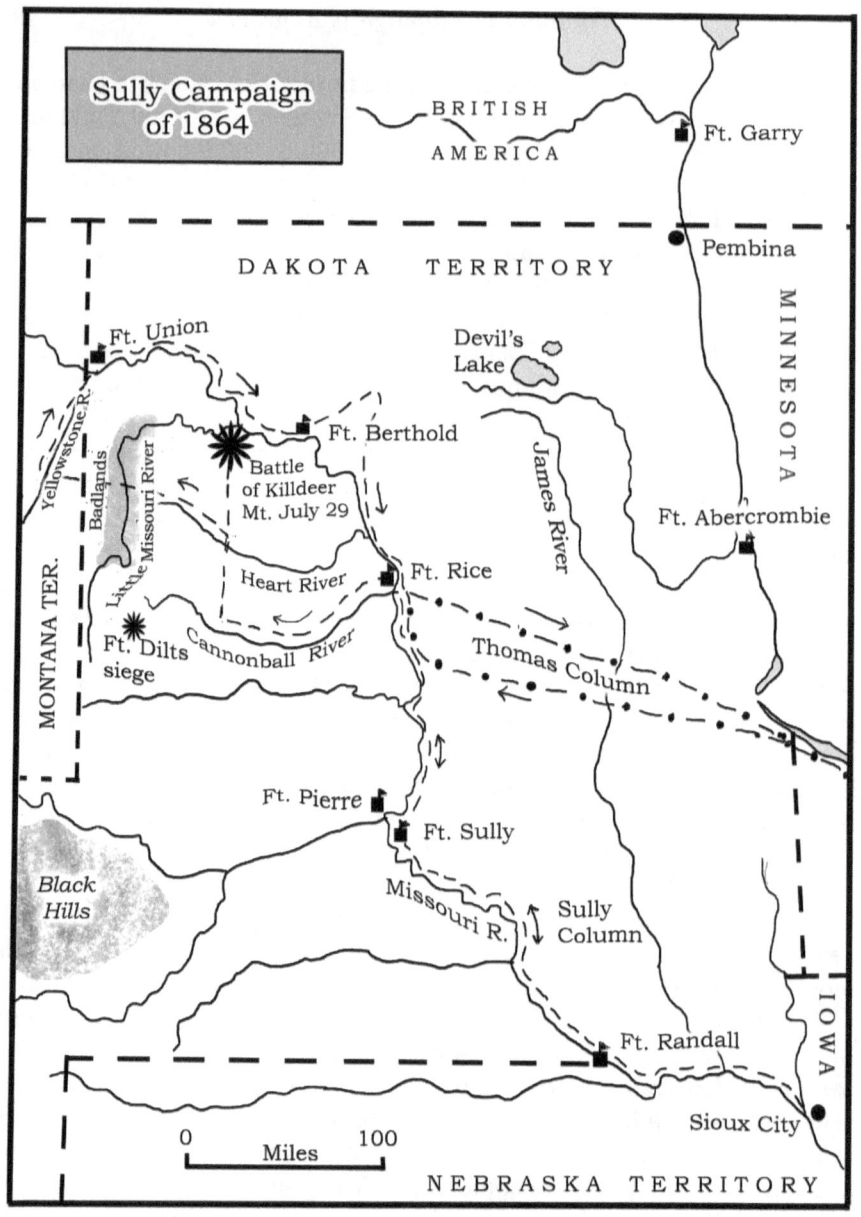

Sully campaign of 1864 (author's rendition).

terrifying presence." But, at the same time, the Indian force was "still strong and defiant, and openly boasted that the white soldiers dare not follow them further."[6]

Thomas' command included the 1000 men of the 8th Minnesota Regiment. Although infantry, they were mounted on Canadian ponies to keep

15. An Indian Campaign Is Approved

pace the 600 men of the 2nd Minnesota Cavalry. One company included 49 "galvanized Yankees," Confederate prisoners given the choice of a prison camp or action on the frontier. The 3rd Minnesota Battery, commanded by Captain John Jones, provided artillery support. Twelve ambulances, 45 scouts, 96 mule teams and their drivers, completed the force, in total, of about 2000 men. They would move against Indians in eastern Dakota Territory.

The First Brigade from Sioux City, under Sully, included the 6th Iowa Cavalry, 880 men, and Major Alfred Brackett's Minnesota Cavalry Battalion, 360 men brought back west from fighting Confederates. Also present were other, smaller local cavalry units, and a battery of four mountain howitzers commanded by Captain Nathanial Pope, a nephew of the major general. With teamsters and scouts, the brigade would muster about 1,700 men.[7] They would march north alongside the Missouri River and pursue Indians in western Dakota.

Both brigades would converge and meet for joint operations under Sully's direction.

Depending upon circumstances, one fort would be built near the termination point of Sibley's previous expedition, and another on the Yellowstone River. These posts would be garrisoned by three to five cavalry companies, and three to four of infantry.[8]

Henry Sibley, meanwhile, would protect the home front with 700 men, a cause for friction between himself and Pope. A substantial force was required, Sibley said. Pope responded on February 11 with a personal jibe, "I think you entirely overestimate the danger from the Indians, as well as the amount needed in Minnesota. If there be the danger you seem to apprehend, surely it may fairly be said that your campaign of last summer accomplished very little."[9]

Both columns would be highly mobile, composed mainly of cavalry and mounted infantry. But the smaller Canadian ponies provided for the infantry in the Second Brigade, while more able to live off the land than the large cavalry mounts, did have their problems. "To mount a regiment of big infantry men on these little animals was a somewhat amusing as well as troublesome performance," recalled Colonel Thomas. Each soldier, generally not an experienced horseman, carried a long rifle, cartridge box, haversack, knapsack, blankets and horse equipment. "Prepare to mount! Mount! and in ten seconds some would be in their saddles, some tearing away, and some all tangled up—man, horse and equipments a confused mass of animation and curses." However: "These ludicrous movements did not last long. The men and horses soon found their place in the ranks."[10]

The flags fluttered and a military band mounted on white horses played as the Second Brigade rode from Fort Ridgely on a fine June day. Determined to be part of the scene, Sibley was present "to superintend the departure in person." He reported that the "column moved on the morning of the 6th, in fine condition."[11]

Thomas marched through terrain that still showed evidence of the 1862 massacre. "The ashes of many houses is all that remain of a once happy family," wrote Ebenezer Rice of the 2nd Minnesota Cavalry. "Father, Mother, Babe youth and manhood gone." Indian graves were found. "Thay Dug up the bodies of the red men and women and kicked them around just as thay pleased and left them above the ground," complained Trooper George Doud. And these "horrid acts" received no reprimand from the officers.[12] As with the previous year, the temperature steadily climbed to over 100 degrees. The water was still "vile," polluted with alkali, which could burn the tongue and cause dysentery.

The First Brigade moved from Sioux City on June 14. As with the previous campaign, General Sully was reliant on steamboats moving up the Missouri. They carried 2,500 spare uniforms, 2,500 spare saddles, 12,000 horse and mule shoes, four months' provisions for 3,500 men, corn for the stock, and, most importantly, 17 barrels of whiskey.

On June 28, Sully neared the mouth of the Little Cheyenne River. Topographical engineer Captain John Fielner, a keen zoologist, rode ahead with two soldiers to collect insect specimens. Sully had offered a larger escort, but Fielner replied with a laugh, "I doubt there are any Indians in the whole country." But as the three men filled their canteens from the river, a blast of gunfire from foliage saw the captain fall with a bullet through his lungs, and another man wounded. Their horses bolted as the Indians attempted to grasp their bridles, and the soldiers made their way back to camp on foot. Fielner died at 10 o'clock that night.

Troops sent out chased the Indians for several miles before catching them in a dry creek bed. Two escaped while three others died in a barrage of bullets. The soldiers returned to camp with guns, bows and arrows, but Sully, not satisfied, sent a squad back. Unlike Sibley, he had no qualms about mistreating dead Indians, and Sergeant Benjamin Estes decapitated the three dead Indians with a large butcher's knife. At the crack of dawn next day, "General Sully directed me to hang the heads on poles on the highest hill as a warning to all Indians who might travel that way," recalled Sergeant Abner English.[13] But, he noted, "General Sully's brutal and reprehensible conduct, instead of acting as a warning and as a restraint on the Indians, worked quite to the contrary and made them furious and determined upon reprisals."

On the same day, June 29, Sully fired signal rockets to attract the Second Brigade. They made contact the following day west of Swan Lake (near present day Akaska, South Dakota). But Sully was appalled to find that an immigrant train of 123 wagons carrying 200 miners, women and children had fallen in with Thomas' command. The disgruntled general had no time for

15. An Indian Campaign Is Approved   185

this intrusion on a military expedition, but was obligated to offer protection. A few days' rest in camp followed as army wagons were dispatched to the Missouri to take on supplies from eight recently arrived steamboats.

Word arrived that an Indian force, comprising Lakotas, Santees and Yanktonais, was gathering between the Cannonball and Heart Rivers. On July 3 the First Brigade marched north, followed by the Second Brigade one day later. Word arrived that the Indians had crossed to west of the river and occupied an area of rolling hills in a sweeping bend of the Little Missouri about 200 miles to the west. Scouts reported more Lakotas moving from the Black Hills towards the gathering point. The Indians were well aware of the beheading of the three warriors, and Inkpaduta cajoled the warriors to make a stand, despite the formidable size of the bluecoat force.

It took three days to ferry 500 wagons, troops and gear across the Missouri by steamer to the west bank. On July 7, Sully laid out Fort Rice, a new post eight miles above the mouth of the Cannonball River (30 miles south of present-day Mandan, North Dakota). Six steamboats arrived with construction materials and four companies of the 30th Wisconsin Infantry under Colonel Daniel J. Dill. It would be their job to garrison the post. With the large workforce at hand, the fort, in its original form, went up in two weeks.

Fort Rice, first established by General Sully during his 1864 expedition, as it appeared in 1870. It was a major post till being abandoned in 1878 (author's rendition).

Lieutenant Colonel John Pattee described the post as log buildings, 80 feet long, "around a square that measured 400 feet on each side. The 24 feet between each building was filled in with a stockade with a gate near the center of the east, west and north site large enough to drive a wagon through."[14] The fort would be expanded during the following years and serve as a major post till abandoned in 1878.

As Fort Rice went up, a small train of five wagons made its way from Kansas towards Idaho. The travelers had been assured at Fort Laramie that all was quiet on the western front; no chance of Indian attack. But on July 12, after crossing Little Box Elder Creek in present day Wyoming, they learned differently. "I was a member of a small company of emigrants, who were attacked by an overwhelming force of hostile Sioux, which resulted in the death of a large proportion of the party, in my own capture, and a horrible captivity of five months' duration," recalled 18-year-old Fanny Kelly, traveling with her husband Josiah and her adopted daughter, 7-year-old Mary Hurley, her sister's child. "Without a sound of preparation or a word of warning, the bluffs before us were covered with a party of about two hundred and fifty Indians, painted and equipped for war," recalled Fanny. They "uttered the wild war-whoop and fired a signal volley of guns and revolvers into the air."

The wagons were corralled for defense as the Indians circled. "If you fire one shot," Fanny told her husband, "I feel sure you will seal our fate, as they seem to outnumber us ten to one, and will at once massacre all of us." Ottawa, the Ogallala Lakota war chief, rode forward. "How! How!" he said, which the whites understood to "mean a friendly salutation." Striking his breast, he said, "Good Indian, me." He pointed around. "Heap good Indian, hunt buffalo and deer." Ottawa assured the immigrants of his "utmost friendship for the white people," and the Indians crowded around, shaking hands "until our arms ached, and grinning and nodding with every demonstration of good will."

But the good will did not last. First the Indians cajoled Josiah Kelly to swap his best horse for one of theirs, then demands were made for food and clothing, readily provided. Talking partly by signs and partly in broken English, "They grew bolder and more insolent in their advances," recalled Fanny, "One of them laid hold of my husband's gun, but, being repulsed, desisted."

Ottawa told the whites they could proceed. But, as the wagons moved off, the Indians stayed alongside. The trail ahead moved into a dark, rocky glen, and Josiah Kelly, anticipating "a murderous attack, from which escape would be utterly impossible," refused to proceed. Ottawa asked the travelers to prepare supper, to be shared with his people. They would then move off into the hills to sleep for the night, he said. The whites readily agreed. But as preparations were underway, "our terrible enemies threw off their masks and

15. An Indian Campaign Is Approved

displayed their truly demoniac natures. There was a simultaneous discharge of arms, and when the cloud of smoke cleared away, I could see the retreating form of Mr. Latimer and the slow motion of poor Mr. Wakefield, for he was mortally wounded." Others lay dead and wounded, but two men, including Fanny's husband, managed to escape while "the Indians quickly sprang into our wagons, tearing off covers, breaking, crushing, and smashing all hindrances to plunder, breaking open locks, trunks, and boxes, and distributing our goods with great rapidity, using their tomahawks to pry open boxes, which they split up in savage recklessness."[15]

Fanny Kelly, taken prisoner by the Dakotas, wrote a vivid account of life during her 6 months of captivity (portrait from *My Life of Captivity Amongst the Sioux Indians*, 1873).

Fanny, daughter Mary, and Sarah Larimer and her son were taken prisoner. The Indians took their captives northeast to join a large concentration of Dakotas—the same Indians being hunted by General Sully.

It is possible that these Dakotas had heard of Sully's beheading of the three warriors a little less than two weeks earlier. But Indians professing friendship and sharing food before attacking was described by others on the frontier, including Abbie Gardner, a survivor of the Spirit Lake Massacre.[16]

Three days later, July 15, Sully wrote to Sibley from Fort Rice: "I write you a few lines to inform you we are getting on well. We are now loading wagons with stores, as we have been delayed by the non-arrival of some necessary stores. We see Indians now and then, and some have sent word they want to give themselves up, but I have not time to attend to them. I shall push on to the camp near the Yellowstone, where I expect a fight. The troops are in good health. The post is a beautiful location for Dakota Territory, but grass is rather light this year."[17]

On July 18, Sully marched towards Rainy Buttes, the reported location of the enemy village. He was still encumbered with the migrants. "I'm damn sorry you are here," he informed them, "but so long as you are, I will do my best to protect you." Four hundred men were ordered to defend the civilians as far as the Yellowstone River, after which they would have to look after

The Attack and Capture of Our Train, July 12th, 1864.

"The Attack and Capture of our Train, July 12th, 1864" (*My Life of Captivity Amongst the Sioux Indians*, by Fanny Kelly, 1873).

themselves. "Keep together," he advised, "for in union there is strength." On the second day's march, another civilian traveler arrived. Aptly named Dakota, the baby girl was newly born to a miner's wife.

On July 24 the column arrived at the Heart River, the temperature peaking at 110 degrees. The hot and exhausted humans survived, but 22 animals died that sweltering day. "I never experienced such a hot day in all my travels," recalled Robert McLaren, promoted to colonel the previous January. "Men were sun-struck, dogs died by the roadside, and oxen were left to die." Frank Myers found the "river contained very poor water for drinking, strongly impregnated with coal and minerals."[18]

Sully established a base camp with the immigrant wagons corralled, and rested his men for one day. He believed a village of 1,600 lodges was only two days away, on the Knife River. The plan was for a fast forced march with a mule train carrying a minimum of supplies. But the mules raised problems, bucking and throwing their packs due to the harsh leather straps incorrectly supplied for the task. But now the unwelcome migrant train could be put to good use. Wagons of light construction were "pressed into service," each loaded with 1,000 pounds of stores. The original ox teams were replaced with mules, four to each wagon.

Killdeer Mountain

Sully finally set off at 3 p.m. July 26. With him rode 2,200 men, a strike force from both brigades. He estimated an enemy force of over 5000 warriors. The Indians themselves later claimed no more than 1,600, a more believable figure.

Indian scouts reported Sully's progress to Inkpaduta, and on his advice the village was shifted to what the Indians called Falling Springs, a favorite hunting ground. Here a central, dominating rise could serve as a focal point for defense. The Lakotas called it Tahchakuty, "the place where they killed the deer" —Killdeer Mountain to the whites. Around the base, the undulating ground and ravines, abundant with brush and timber, could deflect enemy troop movements, cavalry in particular. In this terrain a village some four miles long arose. Any bluecoats approaching during daylight could be seen on flat prairieland stretching for miles around.

On July 26 a band of about 30 warriors encountered a party of Sully's scouts 16 miles from the Indian camp. Their inebriated commander, Captain Christian Stufft, ordered a retreat. His lieutenant refused. Stufft promptly pulled his pistol and repeated the order, and most of the command, about 30 men, beat a hasty retreat back towards camp. The remaining 15 held their ground. Stufft arrived on a panting horse and reported his command "cut to pieces." On his way out, Major George Brackett, dispatched with a relief squad, swung his saber at Stufft in a gesture of contempt. Upon arrival, Brackett found the gun smoke cleared and the 15 stalwarts still very much alive. An arrow had brought down one scout's horse and another man received a knee wound. Three Indian ponies had been killed, and goods including buffalo robes and an Enfield rifle captured. A Crow Indian prisoner with the hostiles broke free during the fight, but his companion had been killed. Stufft, meanwhile, found himself placed under arrest.[19]

Sully deployed his men in battle formation, the wagons driven single file, flanked by mounted troops. Scouts followed the trail of the war party who, it was hoped, would lead them straight to the Indian village. No hostiles were seen during that day's march, but no fires were allowed in camp that night, and nervous sentries firing at shadows kept the command on edge. Dawn's first light saw the troops in the saddle heading northwest. Thirty-five miles later, a spring near the Knife River provided water for the next campsite. But again, little sleep was had, Sully ordering his men to mount up shortly after midnight on July 28. Scouts were put on the alert. Perhaps the Dakotas were closing in for a dawn assault.

But as the column rode, no Indians were seen. Following a 6-hour march, the troops stopped for breakfast. Some wondered if this were not a wild goose chase, with no warriors out to defend their hunting grounds in this part of Dakota at all. The troops saddled up and continued on across the wilting, dry grass under the hot summer sun. One hour later, a small dust cloud was seen. Interpreter Frank La Framboise and several scouts rode up; a huge Indian village lay 10 miles ahead, they said. A ripple of excitement spread through the troops as Indian scouts changed from native dress into military blue to avoid falling victim to "friendly fire."

The Indians, meanwhile, were well aware of Sully's advance. But they felt Wakan Tanka was with them this day. The warriors donned war paint and breechclouts, and there was no panicked striking of tepees for a headlong flight, as usually occurred when troops approached. And many soldiers were not confident of surviving the coming fight. Watches and other valuables were handed to civilian employees to be sent back home if the worst occurred.

Known as the "Kit Carson of the Northwest," Sergeant George Northrup had enlisted in the Union Army to fight rebels. He carried out dangerous scouting missions deep behind Confederate lines. When reassigned to Sully's expedition, he wrote his sister that it may be "the unpleasant duty of comrades to chronicle the loss of my hair." He wrote articles for the *St. Paul Press* and gave his most recent pages to a comrade. "Send these home," he said, "and write my obituary when I'm dead."[20]

Sully, not ready to die just yet, surveyed the scene. He could see why the enemy had selected Killdeer Mountain to make a stand. With cavalry action virtually impossible amidst the rough ground and trees, he dismounted the bulk of his command. As was the usual practice, four horses were held by one man while three comrades joined the firing line.

Sully deployed six companies of the 6th Iowa and three of the 7th Iowa Cavalry to the right, and two companies of the 8th Minnesota Infantry to the left. Captain Pope's battery, supported by cavalry, was deployed in the center. The remaining troops were arrayed behind these men, with Jones' battery and four cavalry companies as a reserve. "The few wagons I had closed up," reported Sully, "and the rear guard, composed of three companies, followed. In this order we advanced, driving the Indians till we reached the plain between the hills and mountains. Here large bodies of Indians flanked me." He reported them as "Unkpapas, Sans Arcs, Blackfeet, Minneconjous, Yanktonais and Santee Sioux." They were armed with bows, arrows, spears, clubs and muskets.

By midday, Indians were seen on the flanking hilltops, and a long line of warriors spread across their front. Inkpaduta was present, along with rising leaders like Sitting Bull and Gall. Insults were flung back and forth between the warriors and Sully's Indian scouts. Some came from the same tribes. But no shots were fired. The scene was tense, all awaiting some hostile move from the other side.

Lone Dog, a young Lakota brave, decided to break the impasse. "About this time an Indian very gaily dressed," recalled Lieutenant Colonel John

Pattee, "carrying a large war club gorgeously ornamented appeared out front of the 6th Iowa Cavalry and called loudly to us and gesticulated wildly about one half-mile away." Lone Dog rode down the slope and raised dust as he galloped across the bluecoat front. "He ran close to the soldiers," recalled White Bull, nephew of Sitting Bull, "and gave them the chance to shoot first." Three shots rang out. All missed. Major Wood arrived at Pattee's side. "The general sends his compliments and wishes you to kill that Indian for God's sake." Two sharpshooters tried their luck with Springfield rifles, but missed, as the bold warrior "immediately stretched himself out flat along the horse's back and plied his left heel vigorously against the flank of his pony and disappeared from my sight over the hill." Sully, however, on higher ground, claimed the warrior fell from his pony on the opposite side, where he "was put on his horse by other Indians who were on foot and held there till they reached the mountains, then about four miles away." But Pattee said his soldiers' bullets "passed over the hill." Wishful sightseeing by Sully, perhaps?

"These were the first guns fired," Pattee recalled. "From this on there was a sort of go-as-you-please firing all along the line." A howitzer commanded by Captain Pope fired the first shell of the day. Most of the Indians had never seen cannon fire. Upon hearing the rush of the "incoming," they fired into the air in hope of bringing the monster down. The shell exploded and another battery opened fire. A series of blasts rent the air 80 feet above the Indians. With shrapnel flying, the Indians began to fall back. Artillery was a demon no bravery could counter. While the large village remained mostly intact, some women lost faith and hastily dismantled tepees, which were "carried into the brush, together with the poles, camp kettles, [and] packs of dried buffalo meat," recalled Pattee.[21]

But the fight had just begun. "Everything changed," recalled Colonel Minor Thomas. The Indians opened fire and charged. "It looked awful," recalled James Fisk. "Thousands of Indians were rushing down on us, in a dead run. It looked to me as though they couldn't stop if they wanted to, and that we would be run over and have hand to hand fighting with the savages. There was no use denying it—I was badly scared."[22] But a long-range volley from the troops brought the charge to a grinding halt. "We gave it to them good," recalled Fisk. The Indians turned back, and the bluecoat march towards the village resumed.

The Dakotas regrouped, and parties broke from the pack, emitting wild whoops. When in range, they would open fire, then wheel about, gallop back, reload, and charge again. But the poor Indian weapons, including many old flintlocks, were no match for those of the troops. Despite claims that Sitting Bull had taken part in earlier fights, the chief recalled, "I had never seen white troops fight before. The number of guns and the amount of shooting was much more than I had ever expected."[23]

In the Indian camp, an old man crippled from birth, Man-Who-Never-Walked, decided this was a good day to die. His friends gave him weapons and led him out on a travois to confront the advancing troops. His unfortunate horse died in a shower of bullets, and soon the old warrior too was riddled. Man-Who-Never-Walked earned a new name from his admiring friends: Bear Heart.

"Captain Pope passed out on my left with the four howitzers in front of the second brigade and disappeared behind a high hill," recalled Pattee, "but was soon called back by the general, and informed that a battery was not a good thing to scout with."

A large party of Indians appeared in the troops' rear after riding in from the plains beyond, attracted by the sound of gunfire. In tight formation, the warriors made a good target. One of Jones' big guns belched fire and smoke, and a shell exploded in their midst. Six warriors and five horses went down, and the others scattered.

When a brave was killed or wounded, Sitting Bull later said, his companions would "feel sorry and cry," and do all in their power to remove him from the field. But "when a white soldier gets killed, nobody cries, nobody cares; they go right on shooting and let him lie there. Sometimes they even go off and leave their wounded behind them."[24] Four Horns, Sittings Bull's uncle, was badly wounded. Sitting Bull and White Bull led him back to the village, where Sitting Bull had "medicines on hand at all times and put some on the sore," recalled White Bull. He "gave him some to drink then bandaged the hole."[25] Sitting Bull stayed by Four Horns' side till time came to abandon the campsite.

Indians were seen massing on a hill to the front right flank. Major Brackett led his four companies in a furious mounted charge. According to Pattee, they "piled up 27 Indians in one pile, 10 of them killed with a sabre." The others scattered through the brush and timber.[26] But this left Brackett exposed. Warriors were seen massing for an assault, but again Jones' guns barked and several Indians fell amidst dust and smoke. They were quickly picked up by their comrades and taken off. Brackett, wounded in one hand, made it back safely to the bluecoat lines, but the "Kit Carson of the Northwest," George Northrup, fulfilled his gloomy prediction. Struck by a bullet and three arrows, he died on the field. But his scalp remained intact as his body was brought in. Eight other men were wounded, and one soon died.

The troops, despite repeated attacks, intense heat and thirst, marched relentlessly towards the village, firing, reloading, then firing again. The Indians' main thought now was to save the women and children, and the village was abandoned as they fought back from the cover of foliage and ravines. On the western flank, Sully ordered his men to swing round, bypassing Indians to their front, and head straight for the village. The cannons roared and shells

15. An Indian Campaign Is Approved 193

exploded over the ravines, showering the warriors with shrapnel that ripped through trees, flesh and bone.

Brackett's battalion with Jones' battery advanced on the right, and the bluecoat line pushed forward. But the light was beginning to fade, and Sully ordered a halt to allow cannon fire with canister and shells to flush the enemy out. "It was amusing to see the desperate efforts made by the Indians to get out of the reach of the cannon," recalled Frank Myers.[27] And Sully had no qualms about firing on noncombatants. "A magnificent sight," recalled Colonel Thomas, "1,600 lodges filled with women and children, dogs, horses and all paraphernalia of their homes, and their attempting to save them with the shells bursting about them, carrying destruction in their path."[28]

As the light faded, over 200 Indians appeared on the mountaintop. They had regrouped and come back as a decoy while women and children made their escape. Four companies of the 8th Minnesota under Major George Camp scrambled up the slope and poured in several volleys, killing 12 warriors and wounding more before the Indians retreated down the opposite slope. Other squads moved into the ravines to kill off any warriors holding their ground. Captain Stufft, despite his previous lackluster performance, had been restored to duty. "The Indians fired on us," he reported, "killing one of my horses and wounding another. I immediately ordered the men to dismount ... and made a charge on the enemy, firing into the dense thicket, killing two Indians and wounding one, which my Winnebago boys afterwards killed, scalped and beheaded."[29]

With the fleeing Indians was their white prisoner, Fanny Kelly. "General Sully's soldiers appeared in close proximity," she recalled, "and I could see them charging on the Indians, who, according to their habits of warfare, skulked behind trees, sending their bullets and arrows vigorously forward into the enemy's ranks. I was kept in advance of the moving column of women and children, who were hurrying on, crying and famished for water, trying to keep out of the line of firing."[30] Fanny's adopted daughter Mary had escaped the first night of their capture. Unknown to Fanny, however, she had been tracked down and killed. Her body had been found pierced by three arrows and scalped. Sarah Larimer and her son had successfully escaped under cover of dark.

The triumphant troops occupied the desolated village, strewn with discarded possessions and debris. How many Indians died depends on who told the story. Estimates vary from 100 to 208, although Henry Wieneke claimed 1,000 bodies were burned along with the village.[31] Sully's report read that the number killed, "from what we saw, was from 100 to 150. I saw them during the fight carry off a great many dead and wounded." The rugged terrain "prevented me from killing more."[32] As usual, how many women and children died received no mention.

The exhausted, thirsty and hungry troops slept on the battlefield that night, many sheltering in abandoned Indian lodges. Despite victory, they were not in a charitable mood. Men from the 8th Minnesota found a helpless old man, whom "our boys dispatched to the happy hunting ground with as little compunction as if he had been a tiger," recalled Thomas Hodgson. Two young boys, however, were spared— for the moment. They were given hardtack to eat, "which the little fellows ate with avidity and relish," recalled one soldier. But then Indian scouts arrived and "struck their tomahawks into their brains."[33] A baby, only a few months old, was found. Who would care for the infant? A quick bullet solved the problem. According to Sully's orders, all wounded braves captured were to be treated as prisoners of war. But no prisoners were taken at Killdeer Mountain. One wounded brave found in the brush was hauled to the edge of the village to be peppered with bullets as a file of soldiers rode by.

The column moved out before daylight the following morning. Seven hundred men of the 2nd Minnesota Cavalry under Colonel McLaren were left behind to burn tepees and shoot the hundreds of Indian dogs on the loose. Encumbered with wagons and artillery, Sully could not cross Killdeer Mountain and was obliged to march around the base. Six miles later, the broad trail left by the fleeing Indians was seen in the distance, but the intervening rough terrain made any immediate chase impossible. Sully climbed the mountain and scanned the countryside through his telescope for 30 miles around. The landscape was "was cut up in all directions by deep ravines, sometimes near 100 feet deep, filled with timber, the banks almost perpendicular."[34]

The troops retraced their steps to the Indian village, where McLaren's men were hard at work. Their task was overwhelming, so another 500 men were detailed to help out. Over 1,000 tepees went up in flames along with 40 tons of dried buffalo meat, tanned buffalo hides, dried berries, antelope and elk hides, brass and copper pots and pans, saddles and blankets.

Most of the Indians had fled westwards towards the rugged, dry terrain known as the Dakota Badlands. "Many days in succession I tasted no food, save what I could gather on the way," recalled Fanny Kelly. "A few rose leaves and blossoms was all I could find, except the grass I could gather and chew, for nourishment.... Women and children were crying for food; it was a painful sight to witness their suffering." As dogs and horses died, "their bodies were eaten immediately."[35]

But not all Indians had departed the battle site. Some wished to stop further bloodshed. A white flag was seen on a nearby bluff, but before Sully could intervene, the bearers disappeared amidst a volley of shots fired from the camp.

Late that day, the troops pulled out. Behind them a trail of smoke rose from the hot, glowing remains of the former Indian village. Their march was

15. An Indian Campaign Is Approved

watched by bitter warriors bent on revenge. The column moved two miles southeast to Spring Creek, an ideal place to establish camp. Shortly after sunset, Indians swooped down on the horse and mule herd. A mounted picket was wounded as his horse went down amidst a shower of arrows, but he managed to escape by crawling through long grass. Orders were shouted and guns grasped as the camp went on full alert. Stampeded animals were rounded up by herdsmen and secured for the night. Sergeant William Campbell, in charge of the pickets, did his rounds. Private Winget opened fire on the approaching figure, proving his marksmanship as the sergeant fell dead. Two other pickets, meanwhile, had disappeared into the night. Their bodies were later found bristling with arrows, minus their horses, sabers and guns.

Before dawn the troops moved out. Two days and 65 miles later, they arrived amidst a heavy downpour at the Heart River corral to receive a warm welcome. The soldiers and civilians there had feared the Indians may bypass Sully's strike force and attack them instead. More rifle pits had been dug and a wooden log used to fabricate a "Quaker" cannon. But after dark, a peaceful sleep was still not possible. Wolf howls and flitting movements, possibly Indians, had sentries firing into the darkness, keeping all on edge.

Sully wrote his report. He had achieved his aim, he said, to punish the combined Indian bands and destroy their means of subsistence, all with the loss of only 10 wounded and five dead, including the three killed at the Spring Creek campsite.[36]

But, despite Sully's success, the enraged Indians were not through yet.

16

AM I FREE, INDEED FREE?

"It was grand, dismal and majestic. You can imagine a deep basin, 600 feet deep and twenty-five miles in diameter, filled with a number of cones and oven-shaped knolls of all sizes from twenty feet to several hundred feet high, sometimes by themselves, sometimes piled large heaps on top of one another, in all conceivable shapes and confusion. Most of these hills were of a gray clay, but many of a light brick color, of burnt clay; little or no vegetation.... Viewed in the distance at sunset it looked exactly like the ruins of an ancient city."[1] So Alfred Sully described the Dakota Badlands. In order to complete his mission, the establishment of a new fort on the banks of the Yellowstone River, the general had to cross this daunting ground while still escorting the immigrant train. A shortage of rations meant this was the only practical route. Sully had to rendezvous with supply steamers in early August, but crossing the Badlands seemed an impossible task. One Indian scout, however, had crisscrossed the rugged terrain with hunting parties on previous occasions. He knew of one pass wagons could traverse, he said, providing troops worked with pick and shovel leveling the way.

The column moved out from the Heart River site on August 3, and, on reduced rations, marched westward for two days. Mounted enemy scouts were seen on the bluffs watching their advance as they moved along the river bank. On August 5 the gently rolling hills came to an abrupt halt as the daunting Badlands appeared. The rugged landscape extended more than 20 miles on each side of the Little Missouri River. Short of good water and grass for the stock, the command bedded down for the night on a promontory overlooking the forbidding terrain. In the dark, one trooper managed to fall 200 feet to his death. After sunrise his body was found, "an unrecognizable mangled mass of broken bones and bloody flesh," recalled Nicholas Hilger.[2]

Many felt they were about to enter a hornets' nest from which there would be no escape. The Indian scouts, however, assured Sully all would be well. But Old Fool Dog sensed trouble ahead. Sully would "smell the blood of his enemies within two days," he warned.[3]

On the morning of August 6, the apparently impossible trek began. The long, winding column moved along a narrow, rocky path. At times straining ropes had to be used to slow the wagons down dangerous slopes. Sweating troops in advance leveled rocks and clay as they toiled beneath the hot, climbing sun. While scanning the terrain for Indians, Sully had time to take in what he termed "a most wonderful and interesting country. It was covered with pieces of petrified wood, and on the tops of some of the hills we found petrified stumps of trees, the remains of a great forest. In some cases these trees are sixteen to eighteen feet in diameter. Large quantities of iron ore, lava and impressions in rocks of leaves of a size and shape not known to any of us."[4]

Twelve miles in, with no Indian attack, the column arrived at the banks of the Little Missouri. Sully was now in the very center of the Badlands, and he began preparations to set up camp. "Having dug our way down to this point," he reported, "it was now necessary to dig our way out."[5]

Next day, Sunday, August 7, Sully ordered a day of rest to allow stock to feed on bottomland grass. That morning, without orders, some troopers led their horses into the thick cottonwoods along the riverbank. They were so complacent they left not only saddles behind, but weapons as well. A blast of gunfire from the brush caused a horse stampede as the soldiers ran for their lives. The pickets also ran, with the exception of Private John Beltz, who stood his ground and opened fire with carbine and revolver. The Indians managed to snatch a few horses before riding off. A company of cavalry galloped in pursuit, but returned empty-handed, the Indians having disappeared like will-o'-the-wisps between the crags and mounds of clay.

The column remounted and moved to bivouac on better grasslands three miles ahead, and a party of four companies under John Pattee crossed the river and went to work leveling the way ahead. When returning to camp, part of Pattee's command was left behind. A burst of gunfire echoed though the crags, and the missing troopers galloped into camp, Indians in hot pursuit. Almost cut off, the soldiers had been fired on from the hills as they dashed for safety through a deep gorge along the track just leveled. As they breathlessly dismounted, the pursuing warriors appeared on a bluff looking down on the camp. They began haranguing the troops, saying they had been reinforced, and now had 10,000 braves. They boasted about their white captive, Fanny Kelly, and dared the troops to attempt her rescue. The whites would be massacred in the morning, they said, and soldiers taken prisoner would be forced to eat one another.

Jones' guns were quickly swung round and the warriors scattered as a few solid cannonballs bounced harmlessly off the hill. Seeing no damage, the Indians regrouped. Jones, however, was merely getting his range. A third shot was fired, and the Indians ran to the rolling ball. Bad mistake, as it transpired. Several braves went to Wakan Tanka when the shell exploded, and the rest took to their heels.[6]

A nervous night followed, all kept on edge with howls from both Indians and wolves. A burst of gunfire from the immigrant train caused Sully to issue a threat. Their wagons would be shelled if they did not cease firing on his pickets as they were being changed.

That night, Sully, suffering from dysentery and rheumatism, had Colonel Thomas visit his tent. He would have to take effective command the following day, Sully told him. "Have everything ready to move at six o'clock in the morning, in perfect fighting order. You will meet them at the head of the ravine, and have the biggest Indian fight that ever happened on this continent."[7]

Next day, August 8, Thomas' Minnesota Brigade led the way as the troops splashed crossed the Little Missouri. Alert for hostiles, they made a slow, grinding progress along the track cut by Pattee's men. A fresh contingent labored in the van, rocks and clay being shoveled aside. The train became spread out over three to four miles as the slow, plodding oxen pulling the civilian wagons moved at a snail's pace. "I felt more apprehension for their safety than that of my command," reported Sully, "for they had with them a large number of women and children." He felt the Indians could "dash onto any point of my train" from the steep-sided ravines.[8] He had companies dismount and take position on the heights until relieved by the troops in their rear.

Captain Jones' battery moved in the center, and the wagons moved in single file, with flanking cavalry, alongside the steep cliffs and weirdly shaped cones. Where possible, the wagons would double up, moving side by side to shorten the train. Several First Brigade companies came up at the rear along with Captain Pope's four guns. Three miles along, Indians appeared in masses across the front and on top of the rocky, steep slopes of a deep gorge. They opened fire, and leading army Indian scouts turned and ran until one man, Nicholas Hilger, rode forward, pulled a pistol and ordered their leader back.

But one vital ball struck the main Indian guide in the chest. This brought the column to a halt as the badly wounded man was put aboard an ambulance. But, without his guidance, the column would be trapped. Fortunately for Sully, he was still able to point the way forward. Jones' guns, meanwhile, lobbed shells amidst the Indians on the heights and they fell back. Several bloodstained, riderless Indian ponies trotted into the white lines.

The column pressed on as the Indians reappeared, war whoops echoing through the ravines and buttes as they opened fire. Under escort, the troops digging the roadway labored on, forging the way, as arrows and bullets flew. A cloud of gun smoke rose from the gullies as the troops fired volleys at elusive warriors on foot who darted from canyon to rise. More smoke climbed as several disabled wagons were torched by the rear-guard troops. Ailing stock, the victims of heat and thirst, were put out of their misery with a quick bullet.

16. Am I Free, Indeed Free?

White Bull later recalled a Yankton army scout calling out to the Dakotas, "We are thirsty to death and want to know what Indians you are."

"Hunkpapas, San Arc, Miniconjou, Yanktonai, and others. Who are you?" replied Sitting Bull.

"Some Indians with the soldiers."

"You have no business with the soldiers. The Indians here have no fight with the whites. Why is it the whites come to fight the Indians? Now we have to kill you, too, and let you thirst to death."[9] Colonel Thomas recalled, "The Indian shotguns and bows and arrows were no match for the accurate aim and long range of our rifles and carbines, and when the artillery sent shells into their assemblies on the hills and into their retreats in the ravines, the cowardly rascals soon learned that they were no match for soldiers that had come 1,000 miles to fight them."[10] One can only wonder what Thomas thought in 1866 and 1876 when these very same "cowardly rascals" wiped out Fetterman and Custer. Neither command had artillery. "Owing to the inferiority of their arms we could keep the savages at a tolerably safe distance with our long range guns and the artillery," recalled Nicholas Hilger. "Otherwise there might not have been a man left alive, so numerous were they and so persistent in their attacks."[11]

An Indian assault against the rearmost wagons was repulsed when Company A of the Dakota Cavalry counter-charged, and the Indians fell back with the loss of two braves. A second attempt saw the loss of another two when dismounted troops under Pattee opened fire from behind cover, halting the charge at 20 paces. Using the Indians' own tactics, squads went out into the ravines as decoys, drawing Indians into small ambushes whenever they gave chase.

The road diggers and their escorts, meanwhile, were delighted to come across a large, shimmering pond in a rocky basin. They had now marched 10 miles and nine hours since leaving the previous bivouac, and this welcome oasis would provide a suitable campsite for the night. But both ravenous stock and soldiers quickly splashed in, thrashing the water to something more like mud. Those coming behind were obliged to offer a dollar a canteen for the unpalatable concoction that scarcely passed for water.

As canvas was erected, Indians appeared on the surrounding bluffs, and troops from the 2nd Minnesota moved out to provide protection around the camp. One company ventured a little too far and soon found itself surrounded. The outnumbered soldiers dug in behind rocks and fired back as bullets and arrows flew. Colonel Thomas dispatched several companies to the sound of the guns, and the brief siege was lifted. No soldier had been killed, and only a few had received arrow wounds.

As the earthy Badlands glowed red under a setting sun, hundreds of warriors made one last assault. Drums rattled as soldiers sprang to action and the Indians were driven back by cannon and rifle fire. Judging by his colorful report, Colonel Thomas may well have had literary ambitions: "Over buttes, through ravines, rocks and stones, the wild yells and rapid dashes of the savages, the troop pressed forward with a courage and untiring energy that rapidly overcame all obstacles, and night closed the wild wake, and the men laid down on their arms in line of battle, eager for the morning's light, to again commence the work of death."[12]

Acute vigilance and constant changing of pickets kept both civilians and soldiers on edge, grabbing what little sleep they could, but the night passed with relative quiet.

The following morning, August 9, the column set out once more, led by two companies of the 6th Iowa under Major House, and the Dakota Cavalry under Captain William Tripp. The other troops were deployed along the flanks with Pope's battery near the van, and Jones' battery with the wagon train. Taking their turn at eating dust, Thomas' Minnesota Brigade marched at the rear.[13]

Again Indians appeared. But the skirmishing was light. The chiefs could see there was no real way to stop the bluecoat juggernaut; the bones of the hated whites would not bleach Badlands rock and clay as they had hoped. A half-hearted assault on the rear guard was easily thrown back with a few well-aimed volleys. "The enemy were repulsed on all sides," reported Sully. "A few miles brought us to an open country, and the last we saw of the Indians was a cloud of dust some six or eight miles off, running as fast as they could."[14]

The Battle of the Badlands was over. Sully said he could not estimate the number of Indian dead, as the battle had been fought in skirmishes over a long distance. But he proceeded to do so anyway, placing the figure at "certainly over 100." His own command had come off very lightly, with about a dozen wounded and only one man killed, an Indian scout who ventured too far from the column on the final day's march.

The Indians were gone, but so was the grass, thanks to "myriads of grasshoppers, who had eaten everything. My animals were almost starved." More ailing stock had to be shot along the way. Six miles further on, the column came upon the Indians' former campsite, one mile long and half a mile wide, with smaller bivouacs dotted about. "I should judge all the Indians in the country had assembled there," reported Sully. Nicholas Hilger recalled, "Their fires were yet burning and many of their effects, including the undisposed bodies of dead warriors, were left in camp to tell of the hasty and unexpected flight."[15]

Indian trails could be seen to the northeast and southwest. As was their custom, they had split up to baffle pursuit. Many Indians crossed to the eastern bank of the Little Missouri before splitting into still smaller parties.

16. Am I Free, Indeed Free?   201

Hunkpapa Lakota bands, including that of Sitting Bull, moved southeast to hunt buffalo, at this time still abundant on the western plains.

By the time the famished troops approached the Yellowstone River on August 12, their daily rations, according to Frank Myers, was "one hardtack a day, although we had plenty of bacon; but without vegetables or bread; is a poor diet." Tongues swelled and lips split from lack of water. But that morning, it seemed fate had stepped in to save the command. The soldiers awoke alongside "a beautiful spring of water gushing out of the side of a bluff. It was strongly impregnated with minerals, but pure and cold and accepted by man and beast as a precious boon from a kind providence."

Scouts reported the Yellowstone just ahead. A cheer went up when an artillery salvo was answered by rifle shots. The *Alone* and *Chippewa Falls*, the first steamers to navigate the Yellowstone, carried a welcome 100 tons of supplies. But most corn for the stock had gone down with the *Island City* when she struck a ruinous snag near Fort Union on the Missouri.

The joyous troops broke ranks. "All discipline was forgotten," recalled Harlan Bruch, as "men and animals rushed into the stream and swallowed life inspiring fluid and joy and happy shouts took the place of misery."[16] The horses drank their fill before feeding on tall green grass along the riverbank. Hunting parties went out and brought down deer and elk, fresh meat for the campfires, and men with dysentery were fed on fresh berries picked from bushes on the fertile bottomland.[17] That night the regimental bands gave a concert in honor of the victorious troops' safe arrival—and the fall of the Confederate capital of Richmond, eight months before it actually happened. Fake news has always been about.

The shortage of good animal feed, the loss of the *Island City*, and falling water levels forced Sully to abandon any further plans for pursuit, or the construction of a new fort. The existing steamers would not be able to carry freight to the intended location, the confluence of the Yellowstone and Powder Rivers, about 200 miles to the southwest.[18]

On August 14 the expedition crossed the swirling waters of the Yellowstone to the west bank, which was no easy task with a civilian train in tow. At least two miners and one soldier were drowned, along with numerous stock, while steamers carried the heavy freight across. The column set out for Fort Union, a civilian trading post owned by the Northwestern Fur Trading Company, 35 parched miles downstream to the northeast. Due to low water, the steamers were forced to unload freight to cross rapids, and Indians reappeared to hinder Sully's advance by setting fire to woods in the line of march.

They arrived at Fort Union on August 17, and two days later, Sully was relieved to see the last civilian wagons raise dust as they moved away. A guide had been hired to lead them to Fort Benton and the Montana mines. But something was amiss. Sully was obliged to send a squad in pursuit to retrieve

Fort Union was established by the American Fur Company in 1822. Although a civilian post, it hosted troops when required, including a contingent during 1864–1867 (author's rendition).

government stock and arms bartered from soldiers who had been plied with drink. A party of deserters was also with the immigrants, the lure of gold outweighing their meager army pay of 11 dollars a month for a private infantryman or 12 for a cavalryman. A veteran who proved his worth over time could expect 17 dollars a month.[19] As the troops approached the train, the deserters galloped off, only to clash with a Dakota war party. One man was killed before they rejoined the train.[20]

The proposed Powder River fort had been scrapped, and Fort Union was a civilian post. Sully felt a government fort at the confluence of the Yellowstone and Missouri Rivers, near Fort Union, could well serve military needs. With Fort Rice it could help keep the Missouri River traffic free of Dakota assault, maintain overland traffic, and generally be a thorn in the Indians' side. Building materials for the proposed new fort had been stored at Fort Union on June 13, guarded by a company of the 13th Wisconsin Infantry. Sully dispatched Captain H. Van Minden to survey a new site, and Fort Buford, complete with stockade, would be built in 1866. Sitting Bull would attack the post while it was under construction, but would finally surrender there five years after the Little Bighorn.

On August 21, following two days' rest, Sully's column headed down the north bank of the Missouri, marching east towards Fort Rice. Along the

16. Am I Free, Indeed Free?

Fort Berthold, as it appeared in 1864, a trading post owned by the American Fur Company. It replaced an earlier post built in 1845. As with Fort Union, it was garrisoned from 1864 till 1867 (author's rendition).

way he encountered the Mandan, Arikara and Gros Ventre tribes that lived around Fort Berthold, another civilian trading post. Weakened by the ravages of smallpox, they asked Sully for protection against their old enemies, the Lakotas. Captain Abraham Moreland's 6th Iowa company was given the task, along with responsibility for establishing a line of communication between Fort Union and Fort Rice.

To avoid trouble, Sully set up camp five miles from Fort Berthold, where whiskey merchants plied their trade. But where there's a will there's a way, and during the night determined souls managed to slip by the pickets. "I am told by reliable persons that the Indians had it in their tents for sale," reported Sully. "It is said they get it from the English half-breeds, who appear to have control of the country.... An expedition into their country would have a very beneficial effect."[21]

The column moved on August 30, but then veered northeast. Inkpaduta's band had been seen at Dog Den Butte in the Mouse River Valley. Perhaps there was still a chance to snare the perpetrator of Spirit Lake. On September 1, Sully made a forced march of 60 miles, his wagons left behind. He arrived only to find the warm ashes of his quarry's campfires, but no "scoundrels" in sight. Once again the old chief had been one step ahead. Realizing Inkpaduta could easily escape across the northern border, Sully gave up the chase and turned back.

Two officers, Major Rose and Captain Paine, stayed behind to hunt buffalo. But had the Dakotas flown the coop, or merely stayed out of sight? The dreaded war whoop was heard as warriors appeared. Having shot two Indians from their ponies, the officers made a mad dash for safety, the enemy in hot pursuit. The firing was heard by Sully's rear guard, and Captain Davy's company of 2nd Minnesota Cavalry galloped to the rescue, driving the Indians off.[22]

Riding through immense buffalo herds, the column arrived opposite Fort Rice on September 8. The command crossed the river the following day, delighted to receive mail from families and news of the world outside. Sully praised the work carried out by Colonel Dill and his garrison of 13th Wisconsin troops. When complete, "the post will be one of the best in the west," he reported.

"Fort" Dilts

But Sully received other news that set his teeth on edge. One day earlier, Lieutenant Smith and 14 men had arrived at Fort Rice with a letter from Captain James Fisk. His wagon train was surrounded by Indians and under attack. Fisk's "Montana and Idaho Expedition" of 88 wagons and 200 souls had passed through Fort Rice on August 23. Fisk, of the quartermaster corps, was a loose cannon, according to some. But his expedition, to open overland routes to the western gold mines, was approved by Secretary of War Edwin Stanton. The army brass had no control, and worse still, they were obliged to provide Fisk with an army escort if required. Although advised at Fort Rice to go no further, Fisk had insisted on proceeding, and Colonel Dills provided an escort of 47 men of the Dakota Cavalry under Lieutenant Smith. Sully felt the men with Fisk's train were draft dodgers, who "curse and ridicule the expedition and officers in command.... Fisk, I am reliably informed, was the loudest talker in this respect; he ridiculed the expedition and particularly me in the loudest terms, so now he sends back word he is corralled about 200 miles west and wants help, as he says, to go forward, for it would be ruinous to him to turn back."

Sully was infuriated that women and children were put at risk "who were innocent of the folly of so small a party going into an enemy's country, who had lately been badly whipped, and would do all they could to take revenge if possible."[23] Perhaps Sully's fury was inflamed by the fact that, despite Killdeer Mountain, it was still the "enemy's country." Captain Fisk had crossed swords with General Sibley the year before with a similar wagon train venture. Sibley considered him "too reckless and too ignorant to be trusted." General Pope would write to General Halleck, "As Captain Fisk is beyond my control, I trust that the War Department will take such action in his case as the gross military offenses charged against him by Generals Sully and Sibley warrant."[24]

Sully also had little time for Lieutenant Smith. "This is the same lieutenant that the President dismissed for low, outrageous conduct." But, he added, "Captain Fisk reports him of the bravest of men. He may be." The recently reinstated Smith told Sully the train was surrounded by 1,000 Indians. But troopers in his command, upon questioning, suggested 300, a more realistic figure.

The assault, led by Sitting Bull, had commenced on September 2, 1864. One wagon had overturned while crossing a deep gulch. Another wagon pulled over to assist, and a small party set about helping to right the vehicle, with nine soldiers acting as guards. Then about 100 Hunkpapa Lakotas appeared. They charged, and Sitting Bull rode right into the whites. But one soldier fired his pistol at almost point-blank range, the bullet entering the chief's left hip and exiting the small of his back. Sliding over the side of his pony, Sitting Bull made his escape with the help of White Bull and two others. Jumping Bull bandaged the wound, and with the bleeding stopped, Sitting Bull was taken back to their village, about two miles away.

The small party, however, were cut down by arrow and tomahawk with the exception of one man who managed to escape. Making for the train, he encountered a party of 50 men coming to the rescue after hearing firing to the rear. Leading the rescue charge was Corporal Jefferson Dilts, who rode straight into the Indians as they looted the captured wagons. With revolver and carbine blazing, he shot down at least two startled warriors.[25] Out of ammunition, he turned back and galloped towards his companions, but the enraged warriors brought him down, mortally wounded, with three arrows in his back. Through a haze of gun smoke, the rescue party fought off the Lakotas until sunset, when they managed to make their way back to the corralled wagon train. The whites had lost two soldiers and two teamsters killed outright, while four more soldiers died of their wounds.

That night the Indians made no hostile moves, and a party made their way back to the skirmish site, where they buried two dead. They returned safely, but a late thunderstorm made life a dismal, damp affair. By morning, the immigrants were sploshing around in three inches of muddy water covering the low-lying ground.

The Lakotas, meanwhile, had been delighted to find valuable prizes amongst the booty. One captured wagon contained several rifles and 4,000 rounds of ammunition, and the other revealed boxes of liquor, tobacco and cigars. At dawn the wagon train moved out with alcohol-fueled warriors, puffing on cigars, riding around the flanks. The Indians launched the occasional wild assault, showering the prairie schooners with bullets and arrows. Fisk ordered the wagons corralled once more only two miles down the track. Here the travelers stayed through the following night, vigilant and nervous with little sleep.

Across the prairie, meanwhile, the word spread. War paint was daubed and more Indians arrived to join the assault. Here was a chance for revenge, as Sully feared, for Killdeer Mountain, the Badlands, and the battles of the previous year.

Next day the wagons moved out once more, but ever-increasing numbers of warriors appeared on the bluffs. Forced to fend off probing assaults, Fisk searched for suitable ground to make a determined stand. A few miles east of the Little Missouri, a spring was found. Fisk corralled the wagons again and gave orders for every able-bodied man to get to work. Picks, shovels and dirt flew as a sod breastwork arose from the ground, four feet thick and four feet high, right round the wagon corral. A trench was dug to the spring 50 yards away.[26] The thoughtful Fisk had brought along a mountain howitzer for just such an occasion. This could be moved from embrasure to embrasure as required. Now the defenders had a regular fort, they felt, and a fort requires a name. Fort Dilts was decided on, in honor of the brave corporal who had lost his life on September 2.

September 5 saw Fort Dilts under long-range attack, but the whites answered with rifle fire, and the howitzer boomed. There were no casualties behind the sod walls. How long, however, could this go on? No doubt Fisk winced when realizing he was going to have to send for help from Fort Rice, where he had derided Sully and the troops he now needed to save his hide.

Under cover of a stormy night, Lieutenant Smith and 13 soldiers quietly made their way out and headed towards Fort Rice, about 170 miles away. The siege, meanwhile, continued, the Indians unable to dislodge the whites, who were amply supplied with provisions, water and gunpowder. A few days following Smith's departure, a large party of Indians were seen "on an eminence of prairie one mile away," recalled Fisk, "and in full sight of the camp. There came from the crowd three unarmed warriors towards the train, holding up a white flag which they planted in the ground about seven hundred yards off, and then retired.... I sent Mitchell, my brave and efficient officer of the guard, with two Sioux-half breed interpreters to ascertain the meaning of the overture."

Mitchell returned with a note written by the white captive, Fanny Kelly. With the Indians not being able to read English, but dictating and watching carefully, she had fudged the words to get her own message across: "Try to release me, for mercy's sake." The wagons were free to go on in exchange for 40 head of cattle, Fanny wrote, but she knew the Indians had other plans. "I fear the result of this battle. The Lord have mercy on you. Do not move." Other letters were exchanged, four wagons being added to the Indian demands. Fisk replied that he was an officer of the government not authorized to give "any thing but destruction to the Indians who try to stop me on my march. However, I will, for your release, give three of my own horses, some flour, sugar, and coffee, or a load of supplies."[27]

No agreement was reached. Mrs. Kelly remained a prisoner of the Indians—for the time being, at least.

Fifty-six hours after leaving the sod enclosure, Lieutenant Smith's party arrived at Fort Rice. The furious Sully ordered Colonel Dill out with a rescue force of 900 soldiers and two howitzers. But only 100 men were mounted. "I would have sent only a cavalry force," Sully reported, "but this I could not; my animals were too weak to stand a rapid march, having marched 1,500 miles in the last three months, sometimes with little or no grass, and the worst of alkali water."[28]

The rescue force marched from Fort Rice. What would they find? Hacked bodies of men, women and children, the wagons looted and ablaze? The mounted advance guard arrived on September 20 to cheers and shouts of joy. Fort Dilts, such as it was, had held out. By the time the footsloggers arrived, it would appear the train was in party mode. "It was one vast whiskey camp," recalled infantryman Thomas Hodgson. "It was a first-class fraud. The government had been bamboozled into a grand scheme for shipping whiskey to Idaho, the men along were in a grand scheme for plunder."[29]

Many Indians, tiring of the 16-day siege, had departed to hunt buffalo. Those remaining did not fight, but the 6th Iowa Cavalry lost 14 precious horses when a party of Lakota braves swooped at dawn.

Fisk had been saved by the very troops he had disparaged. Chagrin turned to fury when he was informed that they were not to escort him westward, but return the train to Fort Rice. Upon reaching the post on September 30, the train disbanded and the would-be immigrants scattered, having lived through an episode that looked like a dime novel plot. Fisk returned to Minnesota, where he would to be involved in disputes over money and other issues while pushing for another expedition. Despite being despised by the army brass, he retained political support and led two more wagon trains to Idaho in 1865 and 1866. Former military officer William Larned, a member of the 1864 expedition, criticized Fisk for his drinking habits and general irresponsibility, but added, "I still like him, for his great good nature covers a great many defects."[30]

Sully felt more military posts were needed, including the one on the Yellowstone. In the meantime, he suggested they employ "all the Indians north of the Missouri, above the Big Bend ... it would be policy and economy for the Government to expend a few thousand dollars and get these Indians into a war with the hostile portion of the Sioux, and to assist them also with troops, till all the posts are permanently established."³¹ This idea did not bear fruit.

The campaign over, Colonel Thomas marched the Second Battalion back home to Fort Ridgely. They arrived on October 8 after a 1,625-mile round trek taking four months and three days. The battalion was split up, the infantry being sent south to fight Confederates, while the 2nd Minnesota Cavalry remained at home to protect settlers from Indian raids.

Sully marched south, leaving a strong garrison to hold Fort Rice. Over 400 men had lost their horses during the campaign, and they traveled 1,000 miles in eight barges from Fort Rice to Sioux City. From there Pattee's 7th Iowa Cavalry returned to general patrol duty along the frontier. Other units marched to posts in Minnesota and southern Dakota Territory. Unable to establish a new post on the Yellowstone, Sully had arranged with the American Fur Company for troops to be stationed at Fort Union and Fort Berthold. Sibley, meanwhile, had established Fort Wadsworth between Lake Traverse and the James River. With Fort Sully, established the year before, and now Fort Rice, white civilization was driving further west. The Missouri River, a vital link to Montana and Idaho, was made far safer from Indian attack as this route gained importance over the northern land routes.

On the Plains, however, the tribes were by no means subdued, their greatest victories yet to come. One result of Sully's punitive expeditions was to drive numerous Dakotas further south, where they carried out raids along wagon trails. Southern Cheyenne and Arapahos, receiving the blame, became the target of troops. In July of 1864, mixed-blood George Bent lived with Cheyennes along the Solomon River in Kansas. Despite being at peace, he said they were repeatedly harassed. Goaded beyond endurance, the Cheyennes struck back, raiding stage stations and wagon trains.³²

But, further north, the military invasions had been a sobering experience. As the winter of 1864 approached, several Dakota chiefs arrived at military posts to discuss peace. Halt all attacks on whites, they were told, and peace would be theirs. Arrangements were made to talk with General Sully at Fort Randall, and Pope informed Halleck that he expected peace this winter, his only concern that Indians, backed by British traders, may cross the border and carry out small-scale raids.

On October 23, 1864, about 200 Hunkpapa and Blackfeet Lakotas arrived at Fort Sully. Their leader, Bear's Rib, spoke to Captain John Pell: "We used to laugh when they said the whites were going to try and go through our country to fight us," he said. But now, "we realize that the whites go wherever they want to, that nothing can stop them. That where they want to stay we can no more drive them away than we can a wall of solid rock."³³ Pell brought up the matter of Fanny Kelly, still their prisoner. More expeditions would be launched if she was not returned, he said. The chiefs said they would do all they could. Sully informed Pell, "When they bring in the white woman prisoner you are authorized to give $200, or three unserviceable horses and a lot of rations etc. I calculate horses at the old rate among Indians, i.e., $50 per horse. You are also authorized to make them a good present in rations when they arrive."[34]

What exactly happened next depends on which account is believed, Indian stories often contradicting each other. South Dakota State Historian Doane Robinson spoke to Blackfeet chief Crawler, 77, in 1908. According to Crawler, Brings Plenty, a Hunkpapa, refused Crawler's offer to trade Fanny Kelly for horses, and returned to his tepee. As he sat by a central fire with the young woman at his side, Crawler strode in and sat opposite.

"My friend," said Crawler, "I have come to secure the white woman. I have brought horses to pay for her."

"My friend," said Brings Plenty, "I have no use for your horses. I will keep the captive."

Crawler drew himself closer to the fire, rubbing his hands. "My friend, I would advise you to exchange the captive for the horses."

"My friend, I have no desire to part with the captive."

Crawler leant further over the fire, again offering the exchange, only to be refused a third time. Brings Plenty drew a knife and placed it by his side; then "Crawler suddenly drew his revolver, and flashed it in Brings Plenty's face, and at the same instant, catching the woman by the shoulder, threw her around the fire and back of himself, and still covering the Huncpapa with his revolver, quickly backed out of the tepee, where his confederates, standing at the door, hastily took possession of her and mounted her on one of their ponies." The rescue party made good their escape, leaving the trade horses behind for the furious Brings Plenty.

That night they arrived at the camp of Hollow Horn, and over the following days a large throng of Indians gathered, and made their way towards Fort Sully. According to Doane Robinson, "Mrs. Kelly had received by this time the very erroneous impression that the large party of Indians were going down with the intention of overpowering the military and taking possession of Fort Sully."[35] According to Mrs. Kelly, the Blackfeet Lakotas " kept up an air of friendliness, and communicated frequently with the whites; but, in reality were ready to join any hostile expedition against them, and were with the Oglalla Sioux when our train was attacked at Box Elder."[36]

Fanny convinced a friendly Indian, Jumping Bear, to take a letter to Fort Sully, now garrisoned by three companies of the 6th Iowa Cavalry. Arriving safely, he was taken to Major House, commanding. "I write this letter, and send it by this Indian, but don't know whether you will get it, as they are very treacherous. They have lied to me so often they have promised to bring me to town nearly every day. I wish you could do something to get me away from them. If they do bring me to town, be guarded, as they are making all kinds of threats and preparations for an attack. I have made a pencil of a bullet, so it might be hard to read. Please treat this Indian well. If you don't, they might kill me."[37] Jumping Bear stayed at the fort for a few days, provided with clothes and food, before being dispatched with a reply "which I never received," recalled Fanny, "as I never saw him again."

The night before heading for distant Fort Sully, the chief addressed his warriors, recalling the destruction of their homes by the white invaders. Now familiar with the Dakota tongue, Fanny recalled "as near as I can recollect," his words: "They build forts to live in and shoot from with their big guns. Our people fall before them. Our game is chased away from the hills. Our women are taken from us, or won to forsake our lodges, and wronged and deceived.... Show them no mercy. They are but few, we are many. Whet your knives and string your bows; sharpen the tomahawk and load the rifle. Let the wretches die, who have stolen our lands, and we will be free to roam over the soil that was our fathers.' We will come home bravely from battle. Our songs shall rise among the hills, and every tipi shall be hung with the scalp-locks of our foes."

When nearing Fort Sully in early December 1864, "The Indians paused and dismounted to arrange their dress and see to the condition of their arms," recalled Fanny. "Their blankets and furs were adjusted; bows were strung, and the guns examined by them carefully. They then divided into squads of fifties, several of these squads remaining in ambush among the hills, for the purpose of intercepting any who escaped the anticipated massacre at the fort; the others then rode on towards the fort, bearing me with them."

"One morning, we discovered, back of the Fort on the hill, a large body of Indians," Lieutenant Hesselberger recalled in 1870. "The commanding officer was notified of the fact. He immediately gave orders to prepare the fort for defense. Since the warning received from Mrs. Kelly, we had been unusually watchful of the Indians. The fort was poorly constructed, having been built by soldiers for winter quarters. The Indians were notified not to approach the Fort, and only the chiefs, who numbered ten or twelve, were allowed to come inside the gates, bringing with them Mrs. Kelly, and when inside the fort, the gates were immediately closed, shutting out the body of the Indians, who numbered about 1,200 to 1,200."[38]

Fanny, ill clad for the freezing conditions, rode through the gates. "My emotions were inexpressible, now that I felt myself so nearly rescued," she recalled. "At last they overcame me. I had borne grief and terror and privation; but the delight of being once more amongst my own people was so overpowering that I almost lost the power of speech, or emotion, and when I faintly murmured, 'Am I free, indeed free?' Captain Logan's tears answered me as well as his scarcely uttered 'Yes,' for he realized what freedom meant to one whom had tasted the bitterness of bondage and despair."

16. Am I Free, Indeed Free? 211

How exactly had Fanny Kelly been treated during that bondage? In 1869 she swore out an affidavit to Congress while seeking financial compensation for loss of possessions. She stated that she was "forced to become the squaw of one of the O-gal-lah-lah chiefs, who treated her in a manner too horrible to mention, and during her captivity was passed from Chief to Chief, and treated in a similar manner." But in her 1871 published memoir, she wrote that she did not suffer "the slightest personal or unchaste insult." Based on the experiences of other young women, it would appear she whitewashed her captivity. The previous year, four Dakota chiefs had signed an agreement for damages to be paid from their annuities.[39] The whitewash would appear to be part of the deal, in addition to avoiding the Victorian-era stigma of having been intimate with those considered an inferior race.

The day following Fanny's arrival, Major House concluded a deal with the chiefs. They accepted three horses and $50 worth of presents, some provisions, and the promise of a future treaty with General Sully. "The Indians remained nearly two weeks about the fort, and during that time efforts were made to induce her to leave the fort and visit them at their lodges," recalled Fanny, writing in the third person, "doubtless with the design of recapturing her." She was happily reunited with her husband, who traveled to Fort Sully upon hearing of her release.

"I believe, and it is the opinion of others, that the advice and warning of Mrs. Kelly was very valuable to us," concluded Lieutenant Hesselberger, "and was instrumental in putting us on our guard, and enabled us to ward off the threatened attack of the Indians. In my opinion, had the Indians attacked the fort, they would have captured it." This was backed up by a "Statement of Officers and Men of the Sixth Iowa Cavalry," who "verily believe, from information then gained, and from that which they afterwards learned, it was the intention of the Indians to attack the fort."

But Doane Robinson, in 1908, accepted Crawler's account—there was *no plot* to take the fort, and Fanny Kelly was acting under an "erroneous impression." Having died four years earlier, Fanny Kelly could not defend her version of events. But after five months of capture, she understood the Dakota language, and it was impossible for her to get any erroneous impression. Thus, if her account is incorrect, it was a deliberate lie.

Historian Stanley Vestal repeated Robinson's version in his book *Sitting Bull, Champion of the Sioux*, published in 1932, but also embellished the story by claiming Crawler was ordered into the tepee by Sitting Bull, and it was he who was instrumental in her being saved.[40] At least one history book in more recent times has embroidered this tale even further by stating it was Sitting Bull who argued with Brings Plenty, while Crawler sat on the side.[41] Surprisingly, the author, Michael Clodfelter, quotes Robinson as the reference. But Robinson's only mention of Sitting Bull was: "There was a very large camp of

Huncpapas there, and Sitting Bull, then a young man of 26 years of age, was among them."[42]

Fanny Kelly made no mention of Sitting Bull, Crawler, Brings Plenty or the supposed tepee encounter. The claim that Sitting Bull saved Fanny Kelly is Stanley Vestal's fabrication, wishful thinking taken as fact by many. Fanny's firsthand version was first published in 1871, while the unreliable Indian account appeared decades later. A failed plot due to the actions of a white female prisoner was a humiliation for the warrior race, and something best denied. After Killdeer Mountain, wiping out Fort Sully would have been sweet revenge, a coup to rival the later Fetterman and Custer Fights.

In 1870, Mrs. Kelly was awarded $5,000 by Congress for her warnings to the Fisk train and Fort Sully, and in 1872 another $10,000 for loss of property during the wagon train attack at Little Box Elder.[43]

17

THEY FEAR IT
IS ONLY A TRAP

Fanny Kelly gained her freedom just in the nick of time. News of the Sand Creek Massacre arrived shortly afterwards. She had come close to being burned at the stake in retribution after Killdeer Mountain, and Sand Creek may well have seen the threat carried out.

On November 29, 1864, an American flag fluttered above a peaceful Cheyenne village on Sand Creek in Colorado. The calm was shattered with a blaze of gun and cannon fire. The Colorado militia under peacetime minister Colonel John Chivington carried out horrific acts matching those of the Santees during the Minnesota Massacre. Trophies such as scalps and other body parts were exhibited in Denver following the "victory."[1]

New spread like wildfire. This is what could be expected from the whites while attempting to make peace. The Plains Tribes raised the tomahawk, bent on revenge. In early 1865 the Cheyenne struck back, while other tribes from Montana to Texas carried out raids along wagon trails and ripped down miles of telegraph wires. Settlers died while homesteads went up in flames.

On January 7, about 1,000 Lakota, Cheyenne and Arapaho struck Julesburg, Colorado. Buildings were sacked as the 50 inhabitants, men employed tending a stage station, telegraph office and other facilities, fled to nearby Fort Rankin. A cavalry detachment, lured out by decoys, was saved from annihilation when young braves fired from ambush too early. During a desperate retreat, 14 soldiers and four civilian volunteers died. The fort's 18-foot-high sod walls saved those inside from meeting the same fate. The Indians rode off, but returned on February 2 to sack the settlement once more, this time leaving it a smoldering ruin.

The Beaver Creek Station and various ranches went up in flames. Several men were killed and two women and a child carried off. Nine men from the 3rd Colorado Cavalry were caught by a war party while traveling east. Luggage was ripped open to reveal scalps taken at Sand Creek. Their bodies were soon found hacked beyond recognition as human beings.[2]

In Minnesota, residents panicked when news broke out of more Indian murders. On October 2, the Jewett family were found dead near Mankato. Jack Campbell, a mixed-blood brother of one of the 38 Indians hanged at Mankato, had managed to elude army patrols and lead his band of Dakotas back to home turf on a looting foray. Following the attack, Campbell separated from his men and headed for Mankato with incendiary plans in mind, only to be captured and placed in jail. Following a trial, he was lynched by an angry mob in a Mankato street.

His former followers, meanwhile, escaped into Dakota Territory, but the military sent out a party of fellow tribesmen who hunted them down. "There were but five savages in the party," reported Henry Sibley on May 26, "four of whom were dispatched, and the remaining one only escaped by plunging into a lake after losing his horse and all his effects. One of them before being disposed of was captured, and made a confession of the whole proceeding. He pled for mercy on the ground that he was a good Indian and a member of the church, but the scouts took the ground that if so he was in a proper frame of mind to go to the happy hunting grounds, and he went."[3]

The Civil War came to its official close on May 10, 1865, with the capture of Confederate President Jefferson Davis.[4] But the war on the plains continued unabated. On July 26, twenty-nine soldiers died when the garrison at the Platte Bridge Station came under attack, and an approaching military wagon train was surrounded and wiped out.

Sully, meanwhile, had been hard at work garnering men and supplies for an 1865 campaign. The original plan was to head west from Sioux City and cooperate with an expedition led by General Patrick Connor to attack Indians along the Powder River in present-day Wyoming. But the Jewett murders brought about a howl for action against hostiles supposedly camped at Devil's Lake in northern Dakota Territory. Not only civilians but army officers including General Sibley predicted more mayhem on the Minnesota frontier. Pope had planned to protect Minnesota with 18 companies of cavalry and four of infantry, about 1,300 soldiers. He felt this an adequate force—if properly led. Pope wrote to Halleck's replacement, General Ulysses S. Grant, that Sibley's claims "exhibit a panic which I hardly know how to deal with, except by asking you to send me an officer to command in Minnesota who is not subject to such uneasiness."[5]

News trickled in from scouts and friendly Indians that some hostile northern Dakota chiefs were prepared to come in and talk peace at Fort Rice. A show of military force in that area may well induce others to follow. The plan for Sully to cooperate with Connor's Powder River campaign was dropped, and he was ordered to march for Devil's Lake via Fort Rice. In Minnesota, fearful settlers welcomed the news. With the Civil War over, however, and the country in huge debt from four years of war, priority in government ranks quickly became spending as little as possible on military matters, and the disbandment of volunteer regiments commenced.

While 1864 had seen two columns mustering a total of about 3,700 men, Sully's 1865 force was only about 1,000 men. This included soldiers, teamsters, scouts, herders and other civilian employees. Governor Newton Edmunds of Dakota Territory favored pacifying wild hearts bent on revenge with annuities and gifts. General Pope, on the other hand, wanted no gifts. More of the fire and sword diplomacy of the past two years would be their reward should Indian raids not cease. Indians deliberately went on the warpath, Pope reasoned, to be bribed into peace with payments and gifts. While Edmunds had been given leave by Congress to treat with the Dakotas, Pope declared the same tribes to be openly hostile, thus they were a military concern. But Sully's relatively small force could hardly make effective war on the tribes. Establishing peace must be the prime objective this time round.

Shortly before marching, Sully wrote to Pope that plans were afoot amongst Indians "to hold the upper country, which is well filled with buffalo and other game, and in order to do this they are going to commence to clean out all posts.... Indians continue to annoy Fort Rice, they are Cheyennes and others. A sentinel was badly wounded on the night of the 10th, and on the evening of the 22nd a large force drove the men from the saw-mill into the block-house."[6] Sully had ordered a sawmill built on a hill commanded by guns in the fort. Close by was an outer blockhouse garrisoned by a small guard to protect the mill and horse stables beyond the walls.

On July 7, Sully marched from Sioux City. Thousands of Indians were headed to Fort Rice, 470 miles away, for proposed peace talks—so Sully was told.

The ambitious and resolute 23-year-old commander at Fort Rice, Colonel Charles Dimon, made no secret of his view towards Indians: all were hostile as a matter of course. On March 30 he had dispatched a squad to pursue Dakotas seen on the east bank of the Missouri. Santee chief Big Thunder and a companion took refuge in a camp of Yanktonais, friendly to the whites. Chief Two Bears, wanting no trouble, handed them to Dimon. The captives, armed with "English guns," said they had merely come to hear the news, but on April 12 a war party of Santees and Yanktonais struck the herds outside the fort. Two soldiers were killed while the warriors escaped with "13 horses, 19 mules, 35 cows, and 1 ox."[7] That evening Dimon helped even the score by placing his two prisoners, not involved in the raid, before a firing squad.

The thousands expected at Fort Rice did not appear. Only 250 lodges were on hand when Sully arrived on July 13, and none of the head men were principal chiefs. "They are Uncpapas, Blackfeet and Yanktonais," recalled Sully. "They report more coming in, but they have great difficulty in getting away from the camp. The hostile party wish to keep them by force." Mistrusting the whites, the Indians "are fearful that I have some trap set for them." Apart from Sully's own fire and sword record, fear of Colonel Dimon reinforced their suspicions. Matters were not helped when Dimon fired a salute to welcome Sully as he crossed by boat to the fort from the east bank. Hearing the boom of guns, Indians heading towards the fort scattered back into the hills.[8]

The Sioux "are not very well satisfied with having Fort Rice in the heart of their Country," wrote Lieutenant Colonel Pattee to the *Chicago Tribune* on July 21. "It is a great eye sore to them and during the last winter it has been governed by the 1st U.S. Bat. This regiment was made up from a camp of rebel prisoners near Norfolk, Virginia, and officered by men from Massachusetts who knew but little of Indian ways and they have not got along very smoothly."[9] As regards the "Sioux Nation," Pattee observed, "there are but few in this nation that know what the word Sioux means. Among themselves they are called Dakota or La-ko-ta. The Indians on the west side of the Missouri are called Tetons."

Pattee wrote that he was brought up on the frontier and had observed many tribes, including "the Wyandots, Shawnees, Chippewas, Potowatomis, Otoes, Delawares, and others but there is no doubt that the Sioux are the most degraded set of savages on this continent.... How often have I thought of Longfellow's Hiawatha and his band of Dakotas; Land of handsome women. How he must have drawn upon his imagination in describing the 'Mountains of the Prairie' where 'Getcha Manitou the Mighty' came down and sat and smoked as a 'signal to the Nations.'"

Pattee had little time for easterners "who cry out against every attempt to chastise these vagrants as their past conduct merits. I think if some of them could visit this country and eat hard bread and bacon and lay out on these broad prairies without a tent and that too, when the mercury was from 22 to 36 degrees below zero, as I have done, they would cease their senseless sympathy and cease their cry about Mr. Lo, the poor Indian." One can see Pattee's point of view. The troops, living under harsh conditions, cleared the way for the cozy homes and farms of the white settlers who would follow. But what about that "poor Indian" who had nothing to do with Minnesota massacre, and saw his tepee go up in flames, his belongings and family destroyed? Perhaps Pattee's view of the Dakotas as "the most degraded" was influenced by their prominence in opposing white invasion of Indian lands.

Making peace with the poor Indian was not the brigade's only problem. Other logistical matters, major and minor, always dogged military operations, and Pattee felt the paymaster's unit did a poor job. They paid the troops in the field instead of before marching, leaving families at home without money. Once the campaign was over, "some of these additional pay-masters can apply themselves to their old callings or singing negro ballads and tending bar or some other ornamental or useful occupation for which some of them seem admirably qualified."

Indians told General Sully "1,000 lodges of hostile Sioux" were camped on the Knife River within reach of the civilian trading post Fort Berthold, about 95 miles north of Fort Rice. The Indians camped about Fort Rice, already nervous, struck tepees and fled when an unknown white man galloped through their camp yelling that a supply boat crossing the river concealed troops intending "to kill them all that night."[10] Dimon went to the camp and assured those remaining that they were quite safe. But they soon made it clear to Sully that no peace treaty was possible within range of Dimon's guns. Sully decided to relocate the peace talks to Fort Berthold, where supplies could be shipped up the Missouri by steamboat.

But what to do about Colonel Dimon? Three chiefs "made a story set against the Commanding officer of this post," recalled Pattee, "and seemed to have an unfavorable opinion of his skill in managing a Post in Indian Country." Even before Sully had marched from Sioux City, he had written "unofficially" to General Pope regarding the young colonel. While admiring his "energy and pluck," Sully felt that Dimon "is too young—too rash—for his position, and it would be well if he could be removed. He is making a good deal of trouble for me, and eventually for you, in his overzealous desire to do his duty." Sully thought "an older and cooler head" should command at Fort Rice.[11]

Pope, now head of the larger Department of Missouri with headquarters in St. Louis, wrote back, "Act as you think best." According to Pattee, Dimon conveniently applied for a leave of absence for 20 days. Sully said he was not empowered to grant leave, but anxious to have Dimon gone, gave him permission to travel to St. Louis and apply directly to Pope.[12] Dimon received his furlough, but would briefly command the post once more before he and his regiment were mustered out of service on November 27, 1865.

Sully marched from Fort Rice on July 23. Left behind in command was the "older and cooler" head of John Pattee. It was garrisoned by four companies of the 1st "galvanized" U.S. Volunteers, two companies of the 4th Volunteers, and one company of the 6th Iowa Cavalry. "The command of Fort Rice was no easy task," recalled Pattee. "All the officers and men were strangers to me, but I found them generally quiet and well equipped for their various duties. A large number of the officers were well educated and very bright men."

But 80 soldiers had died during the winter and there were 22 currently in the post hospital. Pattee inspected the provisions and supplies. Perhaps bad food was the problem. But he found "there was a large supply of subsistence stores in good condition." And, furthermore, "The fort was well built. The 30th Wisconsin Infantry must have been largely from the timber region and good axmen, for they had done their work well." The howitzers had been mounted in blockhouses by a galvanized Yankee ex-naval gunner, who put his expertize to good use. "The guns could be swung around, run out for firing, and withdrawn with one hand."[13]

As per orders, Sully's column headed towards Devil's Lake, 130 miles northeast of Fort Rice, in search of Indians to make peace with—or fight, if necessary—providing they did not skip over the border to the north.

While marching, they found plenty of buffalo, antelope and "lakes filled with ducks and geese," ideal hunting country, but there was not an Indian in sight. Perhaps this came as little surprise.

Lieutenant Colonel John Pattee, considered an "older and cooler head" by Sully, replaced Colonel Charles Dimon as commander of Fort Rice during the 1865 campaign.

The Indians had learned hard lessons about confronting troops with superior arms. But, following a trail reported by scouts, Sully felt he may be able to bag traders illegally selling ammunition to hostiles. He took "completely by surprise" a camp of 1,500 corralled carts owned by "half-breeds" traveling from British territory towards the Missouri. "They had with them their women and children and even their priest," reported Sully. "There was also traveling with them a French nobleman lately from Paris."

Sully had the camp searched, but found no evidence of contraband. He informed the leaders that they must cease coming into American territory as "they were killing all our game. From their own report they had killed 600 buffalo in one day. They answered me that they knew no line or frontier. The half-breeds on the north of the line were all one family; they were intermarried, and that in their camp were many who live in the United States, while they lived in the British Possessions. They all spoke the same language (French); that they paid no taxes, had no laws; but each camp or colony made their own laws, appointed a chief and two councilors, a police, &c. They handed me a written copy of their own laws, among which I saw was a fine of five pounds to sell ammunition to Indians." They claimed they would starve without coming south, and mixed-bloods on the American side hunted for valuable furs in British territory. Sully gleaned valuable information as to

Indian movements, and quite a few hunters asked to join him, their only pay plunder from hostile camps. But this was refused, as "I was afraid they would require my men to fight while they interested themselves in the plundering."[14]

Sully arrived at Devil's Lake on July 29. This is where hostiles were gathered, just awaiting their chance to wreak havoc along the Minnesota frontier—so the story went. But there was not an Indian in sight. The water was found to be brackish, and the men went to work digging wells. But the animals were not so fussy, and "appear quite fond of it," as were the many fish in the lake. The great explorer, John C. Frémont, once described Devil's Lake as "a beautiful sheet of water, the shores being broken into pleasing irregularities by promontories and many islands."[15]

Sully reconnoitered for a future post site, and in 1867 Fort Totten would be built. He marched towards Fort Berthold, about 140 miles to the west, passing lakes "beautiful to look at, but so strongly impregnated with alkali and other substances that it would about take the skin off your lips to drink it." The Mouse River provided a respite, "a beautiful stream of clear running water, filled with fish."

The hot, tired column arrived at Fort Berthold on August 8, and Sully sent word to the Indian village of over 2,000 lodges on the Knife River, about 50 miles away. "Sioux of different bands, Cheyennes and various others" were there, and he estimated 10,000 warriors, or about five warriors per lodge. (John Pattee, on the other hand, based on his observations, estimated two warriors per lodge as a rule, a far more realistic figure. Other estimates put the number at three per lodge.)

Sully said those who wished to make peace could come in for talks, but he would make war on those who wished to fight. Several days later, the runners returned to report considerable division among the chiefs. "They are convinced there is no use of fighting with any prospect of success, but yet they fear it is only a trap I have set to capture and slay them; that at one time the feeling was very strong to come in and surrender, but that a chief (who wishes to lead the war party) called Sitting Bull, hearing this on his return to camp, went through the different villages cutting himself with a knife and crying out that he was just from Fort Rice; that all those that had come in and given themselves up I had killed, and calling for the nation to avenge the murder. In consequence of this 500 warriors went to Rice to see if it was true and to avenge the massacre."[16]

Fort Rice

On the morning of July 28, just before breakfast, John Pattee inspected a cattle yard 200 yards from the north gate. All was serene, but suddenly the war whoop was heard as a squad of soldiers under arms dashed from the fort. Pattee was horrified to look around and see several warriors galloping straight for him. "The chances were ten to one against me," he recalled. But his scalp was safe, since the Indians were far more interested in a small herd of ponies grazing nearby. They drove the animals off, killing one trooper guarding the herd, Private James Hufstudler. Hit by an arrow, he was then beaten from his horse by a daring warrior.

Private Andrew Burch, mounted, spurred after the culprit, who joined three companions. "I ran them up a hill some 400 yards," recalled Burch, "and shot at him five times with my revolver, but did not hit him. I should if my horse had not been frightened by his war rigging. His pony was hung with red tassels; he himself had a red blanket around his waste, his shoulders were naked and painted red, his hair was hanging loose, two feathers fluttering in it. He had a rifle or shotgun in a fringed covering hanging on his back and in one hand his bow and arrow. His horse was streaked with red paint over his haunches. When he ran behind the hill, I pursued him to the top and saw over the hill 25 or 30 Indians—they kept pretty well concealed, as I could only see their heads."[17]

Pattee, meanwhile, ran through the west gate and scrambled up the lookout station. From there he saw what he thought to be "thousands of Indians on three sides." Looking around, he saw soldiers atop the buildings watching the action. "Fall in!" he yelled. The drum rolled and the soldiers ran onto the parade ground, guns in hand. Pattee rapped out orders to company commanders. They were to take position outside the fort, but no further than 200 yards away. He mounted up and rode outside to find "the companies strung out around the fort," but not at 200 yards. They were at least half a mile away.

A howitzer banged, and one Indian was seen to go down along with his horse as the shell exploded. Pattee dispatched a rider to order Captain Sewell's exposed company, back from the northwest; then he saw one group of about 25 men under Sergeant Hoffman ascending a hill. He sent an orderly to call them in, but too late. They arrived at the crest and came under attack.

Captain Abraham Moreland, meanwhile, officer of the day, led his 10 best men in a mounted dash from the fort. They galloped past the sawmill and over a small bridge spanning a creek. He charged the Indians, who fell back as the rest of his company, led by Sergeant Hobbs, arrived to back him up. But now some of the soldiers' Canadian ponies, unused to gunfire, became skittish, and Hobbs was obliged to abandon his mount.

On the hilltop, Sergeant Hoffman was attempting to hold off the Indians, and, joined by Hobbs on foot, they retreated back down the hill fighting a rear-guard action with their revolvers. "I was approaching from the south as fast as my horse could bring me, and in plain sight," recalled Pattee, "and saw more than one Indian fall before those brave and dauntless men and their deadly weapons. Hoffman went down to his death with an arrow through his body." Hobbs and the other men managed to make it to Lieutenant Beckerman's advancing company, and the Indians fell back. Pattee sent a squad to retrieve Hoffman's body. "Captain Moorland's company made ten distinct charges on the Indians, he being frequently 100 to 200 feet in advance of his men."

The Indians were now gathered behind three hills about half a mile apart. The troops pushed forward and followed them for four miles before giving up the chase. Satisfied with the day's work, they returned to the fort, so ending the Battle of Fort Rice.[18] Two soldiers had been killed, Hoffman and Hufstudler; the Dakota losses were unknown. During the fight, Indians had been seen dressed in military garb carrying "new patent firearms" and riding "American horses" rather than their usual, smaller ponies.[19] Sully, upon hearing of the action, assumed they were spoils from the Platte Bridge fight and attack on Julesburg, the year before.

The Indians were gone, but that night jumpy sentinels gave the alarm. "In ten minutes a company was at each of the gates fully armed with guns loaded ready for action," recalled Pattee. "Howitzers were run out and five balls were thrown from the guns that lighted up the whole country for half a mile in all directions." But there was not an Indian to be seen.

Frontier Scout was a small newspaper published at Fort Rice. According to the October 12, 1865, edition, three Hunkpapa leaders, Iron Horse, Grinstone and Red Horse, seeking peace with the whites, stated that Sitting Bull and The Man-That-Has-His-Head-Shaved led the warriors who initially drove off the ponies outside the fort. But then they departed with their spoils, taking no further part in the fight. For this Sitting Bull, was whipped when he returned to camp. According to their account, only two horses were captured, and these were killed, "thus satisfactorily arranging the division of plunder." (Sully would hear from Indians that 12 horses had been driven off, more in line with Pattee's account of "a small band of ponies.")

The three chiefs also told of attacks made against General Connor's expedition in the Powder River country. "Their stories are very conflicting, and to be received with a grain of salt," stated the writer.[20] It was possible that the chiefs, seeking peace, vilified Sitting Bull to gain favor with the whites. His supposed aversion to fight seems out of character, especially after having instigated the attack on Fort Rice.

Sully bided his time at Fort Berthold. His dire threat to attack the Knife River village of 2,000 lodges was a mere bluff. "They are camped in a strong position I know very well," he reported, "and easy to retreat from by breaking into small parties and scattering into the Bad Lands of the Little Missouri." With his relatively small force, Sully's only hope of any successful attack was to entice a large number of Indians from the village beforehand. And before such an attack, he would need steamboats to cross the Missouri. The only alternative was the use of rafts, which would take a week to construct. If his command failed to rout the Indians and fell back, the enemy would claim a victory, Sully feared. And if he departed Fort Berthold having made no attack, "matters will be nearly as bad."

Custer would attack a village of similar size on the Little Bighorn 11 years later. The 7th Cavalry would count only 647 men, including soldiers, scouts, mule packers and interpreters. And, unlike Sully at Killdeer Mountain, Custer would divide his command.[21]

Sully's problem of how not to lose face with either defeat or retreat was solved by the fight at Fort Rice. Once news arrived at the big village, the whole camp "fled south," Sully reported on August 13, "the friendly Indians feeling sure I would never make peace with them after the Rice affair." A trusted Indian scout followed their trail, which headed south towards the Powder River. This news was telegraphed to Fort Laramie to be dispatched to General Connor.[22] Following an attack on an Arapahoe village on August 29, Connor's troops would be harried by the hit-and-run tactics of the combined Indian tribes. Stragglers were picked off, and Connor was forced to burn his own wagons as stock died off. The troops limped back to civilization, considering themselves lucky to be alive. Apart from establishing a makeshift post called Fort Connor, the only real result was the hostility of the Arapahos. They would now fight alongside the Dakota and Cheyenne. (Fort Connor, on the Bozeman Trail, would be renamed Fort Reno and rebuilt with a solid stockade and blockhouses the following year during Red Cloud's War.)

The Indians had fled south, and Sully knew it was time for him to march in the same direction. But not chasing Indians. His campaign of 1865 was over, with results far less tangible than those of the two previous years. "The result of General Sully's expedition during the summer of 1865 had proved a dismal failure," recalled John Pattee. The "fine body" of veterans had marched a total of 1,315 miles, "the entire summer consumed in this useless expenditure of time, to say nothing of the cost in money."[23]

Cost indeed. Over twenty million dollars had been spent during the summer of 1865 on the Sully and Connor campaigns. Including other deployments, about 6,000 soldiers had tramped across the dry, dusty plains on horse and foot in a futile attempt to crush the Plains tribes. Another 4,000 troops who had enlisted to fight Confederates had been sent west on defensive duties.[24] With the Civil War over, many angry men simply shed their uniforms and headed home.

Sully saw the futility of military columns chasing an elusive foe across a rugged landscape they called home. The Indians had learned the hard way that the best form of defense was to keep on the move, one step ahead of plodding troops encumbered with wagon trains. A more effective method of

17. They Fear It Is Only a Trap 223

subduing Indians, Sully suggested, would be a bounty for "every hostile Indian captured, or his scalp, which would be cheaper and more effective than sending large bodies of troops, who can never be successful in hunting small bodies of Indians in their broken, mountainous country."[25] He had previously written to Pope, "I would like authority, as I had last year, to take into service a small body of Indians, paying them the same as soldiers and giving them rewards for every scalp they bring in—say, $50 per scalp. I have Indians I know I can trust in this business, for I have so compromised them with their nation that it is in their interest to serve me."[26]

18

THE INDIAN NO LONGER HAS A COUNTRY

Following the Civil War, the much-reduced United States Army was deployed mainly in the defeated South to enforce Reconstruction. Here the troops chased lawless bands of freebooters, diehard rebels and others still on the loose. The result was, in 1866, when troops were sparsely deployed at various posts out west, a mere 700 soldiers were expected to protect travelers along the Bozeman Trail between Nebraska and Montana, over 500 miles long.[1]

Despite widespread use of repeaters during the war, the troops were handed outmoded muzzleloaders to do the job. They rebuilt Fort Reno and constructed Forts Phil Kearny and C.F. Smith, but 81 men died when lured into an ambush by 2,000 Lakotas. The following year, the tables were turned when Indians lost heavily in the Wagon Box and Hayfield fights, the troops belatedly equipped with modern breechloaders. Following an inquiry, the government adopted a new "Peace Policy." The reluctant army brass felt civilization had just taken a blow when ordered to abandon the Bozeman forts. The Stars and Stripes came down, the troops marched out, and the posts went up in flames at the hands of the victorious Lakotas. Chief Red Cloud had won his war.

What of the Santees who had been tried and found guilty, but escaped the noose thanks to Abraham Lincoln? They were imprisoned at Camp McClellan, near Davenport, Iowa, where 120 died over the next three years. By 1866, Minnesota settlers no longer felt under threat. The Santees at Fort Snelling had been banished to Crow Creek, and Lincoln's successor, Andrew Johnson, pardoned them all, including the surviving Davenport prisoners. Little Crow's son, Wowinapa, sentenced to hang, was among those who walked free.[2] Between one and two hundred "friendlies" of the Fort Snelling captives had been spared the journey to Crow Creek. Resettled near Big Stone Lake, bordering Minnesota and Dakota, some warriors rode as scouts with Sibley's 1863 campaign.

Under the urging of Bishop Whipple, others were allowed to return, and on February 9, 1865, Congress appropriated $7,500 "for the relief of certain friendly Indians of the Sioux Nation, in Minnesota." Whipple, however, felt it inappropriate that one-third of the money went to John Other Day, the savior of 62 whites.[3] Dakota annuity monies, and additional funds, were paid out to cover damage claims by white settlers for property destroyed.

In 1865, the Winnebagos were relocated from Crow Creek to the reservation of friendly Omahas in Nebraska, where they were given their own land. Many had already moved there without official sanction. The following year, most Santees were moved to more prosperous land in northeastern Nebraska, although the Crow Creek Reservation remained intact.

Still at large, however, were many Santees who had fled to Dakota Territory in 1862. In 1867 they were provided with reservations at Devil's Lake and Lake Traverse, Dakota Territory. Others eventually resettled in Minnesota near their old homes. Many who had taken refuge in British territory never returned.

A gold strike in the Black Hills in 1874 led to an illegal invasion of Indian lands guaranteed by the Fort Laramie Treaty of 1868. Troops took the field, but against Indians, not white trespassers. In 1876, Americans were shocked by the greatest Indian victory west of the Mississippi when Custer and the 7th attacked a huge Lakota and Cheyenne village at the Little Bighorn. The Dakotas, however, were ultimately crushed with a renewed offensive by U.S. troops. Sitting Bull fled to Canada, but, his people starving, he returned in 1881. For four months during 1885 he toured with Buffalo Bill's Wild West show. In 1890 more trouble erupted, and Sitting Bull was killed by Indian police shortly before the massacre of Lakotas at Wounded Knee in 1890.

The resolute Inkpaduta was never captured, having died in Canada in 1881.

Henry Sibley was brevetted major general of volunteers on November 29, 1865, and mustered out of the army on April 30, 1866. Over the years, he was involved with various business pursuits and was president of the St. Paul Chamber of Commerce. He served in the state legislature, and as president of the Board of Regents of the University of Minnesota. He died in St. Paul on February 18, 1891, two days before his 80th birthday. He is remembered through various place names, including Sibley County, Hastings township, Sibley State Park, and Henry Sibley High School.

With the disbandment of the volunteer army, Alfred Sully's rank lapsed to that of lieutenant colonel in the regular army. In September of 1868, the 7th Cavalry's usual field commander, George Armstrong Custer, was on suspension for having been AWOL, and Sully led nine companies of the 7th Cavalry and one of the 3rd Infantry on a foray into Indian Territory (later Oklahoma) from Fort Dodge, Kansas. On September 12, the command faced a force of

Cheyennes, Kiowas and Comanches at Wolf Creek, but no decisive engagement took place, and the column was forced to retreat, harassed by Indians along the way. Sully's officers, most displeased with the results, complained of his traveling in an ambulance. Based on ailments endured during earlier campaigns, the ambulance travel may have been a necessity.

George Custer returned to duty on October 7, and on November 15 both Sully and Custer led another expedition into Indian Territory. The command established Camp Supply in preparation for a winter campaign against the Cheyenne. Both were lieutenant colonels in the regular army, but, according to Edward Godfrey of the 7th Cavalry, Custer overrode Sully by virtue of his brevet rank of major general as opposed to Sully's of brigadier general. The antagonistic joint command came to an end with the arrival of a Custer admirer, department commander General Phil Sheridan. Sully was sent back to Fort Harker, Kansas, and Custer went on to command the attack on Black Kettle's Cheyenne village on the Washita River, November 27, 1868.[4]

The following year Sully was appointed Superintendent of Indian Affairs for Montana. In 1873 he was promoted to full colonel, commanding the 21st U.S. Infantry. He died at Fort Vancouver, Washington, on April 27, 1879, aged 58.

John Pope finally got his wish: a command back east, but not until well after the Civil War was over. In April of 1867 he assumed command of the Reconstruction Third Military District with headquarters in Atlanta, Georgia, where he ruffled Southern feathers with dictatorial decrees. He was replaced later the same year, and given a command well to the north: the Department of the Lakes, based in Detroit, Michigan. In 1870 he returned to the west to command the Department of the Missouri, which saw further involvement in Indian wars, and the relocation of Southern Plains Tribes to Indian Territory.

In 1879, Pope's 1862 defeat at Bull Run came back to haunt him. A board of inquiry concluded that General Fitz John Porter had been unfairly convicted of cowardice and disobedience, and that Pope and General Irvin McDowell were the prime cause of the Union defeat. Porter's supposed insubordination had, in fact, saved the Union Army from a far bigger disaster. But Pope had proved himself an able administrator since the war, and he was promoted to major general in 1882 with command of the Military Division of the Pacific. He retired in 1886, and died at Sandusky, Ohio, on September 19, 1892, aged 70.

Although an angry intolerance of "hostiles" never left his mind, a fairer side of Pope's nature did appear with the passage of time. While commanding the Department of the Missouri the second time around, he made enemies in Washington by recommending improvements in the administration of Indian Affairs, and denounced corruption. This earned him the reputation as a controversial "reformer" and "Indian lover," claims he was happy to accept.[5]

18. The Indian No Longer Has a Country

As early as August of 1865, as Sully reconnoitered the site of the future Fort Totten at Devil's Lake, Pope wrote, "The Indian, in truth, no longer has a country, his lands are everywhere pervaded by white men; his means of subsistence destroyed and the homes of his tribe violently taken from him, himself and his family reduced to starvation, or to the necessity of warring to the death upon the white man, whose inevitable and destructive progress threatens the total extermination of his race."[6]

Appendix: Timeline of the Dakota War of 1862–1865

March 1857—Spirit Lake Massacre. Outlawed Dakota Chief Inkpaduta leads the killing of over 40 white settlers in Iowa, a prelude to bigger events yet to come.

1858—Santee Dakota Reservation halved by a new treaty. Under pressure, the Indians relinquish lands north of the Minnesota River.

January 1, 1862—Special Commissioner George Dole writes to President Lincoln reporting fraud amongst traders and Indian agents.

May 20, 1862—Homestead Act signed off by Lincoln, encouraging an influx of settlers to Minnesota.

August 17, 1862—Five settlers killed by Dakotas at Acton, Minnesota.

August 18, 1862—Violence breaks out at the Lower Agency and the wholesale slaughter of settlers commences. Troops are badly beaten at Redwood Ferry.

August 19, 1862—Indian attack on New Ulm township is repulsed. In St. Paul, Henry Hastings Sibley is appointed to crush the revolt.

August 20, 1862—Fort Ridgely is attacked, the Indians driven off.

August 22, 1862—A second attack on Ridgely also fails.

August 23, 1862—Second attack on New Ulm with larger numbers of Indians, but again they are repulsed.

August 23–September 29, 1862—Fort Abercrombie. News arrives of the outbreak and dead victims are found in a nearby settlement. On August 30, Indians drive off stock outside the fort and commence a siege lasting four weeks. At one time a frontal assault sees outbuildings captured. The defenders keep the Dakotas at bay until help arrives, and on September 29 the Indians disperse.

September 2, 1862—Battle of Birch Coulee. First clash involving troops expressly mobilized to crush the outbreak. The Indians are driven off, but troops suffer heavy losses.

September 23, 1862—Battle of Wood Lake. Little Crow is defeated, his power broken, and he flees with a few hundred followers next day.

September 26, 1862—Sibley enters "Camp Release" and 269 prisoners are set free. Over 1,000 Indians surrender, and others come in over time.

November 28, 1862—The trials of 392 Dakota warriors commence. They are presumed guilty unless they can prove otherwise. Sixteen are given prison terms and 303 are sentenced to death, but Lincoln ultimately authorizes the execution of only 38.

December 26, 1862—The condemned men hang at Mankato in the largest mass execution in American history.

March 3, 1863—The Sioux-Dakota Removal Act passes Congress, negating all former treaties. The Santees are to be banished from Minnesota to reservations elsewhere. A similar Act banishing the Winnebago tribe has already passed on February 21.

May 27, 1863—Little Crow arrives at Fort Garry in British territory and pleads his case to Governor Dallas for British support. Refused, he rides back into American territory with a handful of followers to continue the war as best he can.

July 3, 1863—Little Crow is shot and killed by settler Nathan Lamson and his son Chauncey. Nathan is awarded the $500 bounty on Little Crow's head.

July 26–30, 1863—General Sibley's punitive infantry expedition into Dakota Territory fights Indians at Big Mound, Dead Buffalo Lake and Stony Lake. On July 30, the Indians, under fire, escape across the Missouri River, making further pursuit impossible. The troops return to Minnesota and the Indians regain their lost ground.

September 3, 1863—Battle of Whitestone Hill. A cavalry expedition from Iowa under General Alfred Sully ravages a Dakota village, an action hailed as "entirely satisfactory" by General Pope.

July 28, 1864—Battle of Killdeer Mountain. General Sully battles Dakota warriors before destroying their village and provisions for the coming winter.

August 7–9, 1864—Battle of the Badlands. Sully's expedition is harassed as they march through rugged terrain towards waiting supply boats on the Yellowstone River.

September 2–20, 1864—Siege of "Fort" Dilts. A rough sod enclosure is thrown up around a corralled wagon train in Dakota Territory when attacked on September 2. A party ride for Fort Rice and the siege is lifted with the arrival of troops on September 20.

July 28, 1865—The last shots of the Dakota War are fired when Fort Rice, Dakota Territory, is attacked, and a horse herd driven off. Troops skirmish with the Dakotas outside the post.

Sully, meanwhile, is at Fort Berthold to the north, seeking peace talks. Upon news of the attack on Fort Rice, the Indians decamp and head south. Sully retraces his steps to Sioux City, Iowa, and the final expedition of the Dakota War is considered a "dismal failure."

Chapter Notes

Chapter 1

1. Minnesota Historical Society document, *Martell: A Pioneer Gone*, 1.
2. Michno, *Dakota Dawn*, 110.
3. Carley, *The Dakota War of 1862*, 15.
4. Minnesota Historical Society document, *Martell: A Pioneer Gone*, 2.
5. Curtiss-Wedge, ed., *The History of Renville County, Minnesota*, 157.
6. Humphrey, *Boyhood Remembrances*, 345.
7. *Ibid.*, 339.
8. Anderson and Woolworth, eds., *Through Dakota Eyes*, 51.
9. Bishop report, *Minnesota in the Civil and Indian Wars*, 168.
10. Wall, *Recollections of the Sioux Massacre*, 66.
11. Anderson and Woolworth, eds., *Through Dakota Eyes*, 51.
12. *Ibid.*, 93.
13. Humphrey, *Boyhood Remembrances*, 346.
14. Curtiss-Wedge, ed., *The History of Renville County, Minnesota*, 157.
15. Wall, *Recollections of the Sioux Massacre*, 68.
16. Bishop report, *Minnesota in the Civil and Indian Wars*, 170.
17. Williams, *Frontier Forts Under Fire*, 107.
18. Anderson and Woolworth, *Through Dakota Eyes*, 155.

Chapter 2

1. Transcript of L. Taliaferro journal, Vol. 15, p. 48, Collections (online).
2. "The Spirit Lake Massacre," History Net (online).
3. Beck, *Inkpaduta: Dakota Leader*, 89, 90.
4. Empson, *A Street Where You Live—St. Paul*, 66.
5. Beck, *Inkpaduta: Dakota Leader*, 105.
6. Anderson, *Little Crow, Spokesmen for the Sioux*, 45.
7. *Ibid.*, 46.
8. Clodfelter, *The Dakota War*, 21.
9. *There Once was a Kaposia Village*, St. Paul Historical Society (online)
10. *Ibid.*
11. Holcombe, *Minnesota in Three Centuries*, Vol. 11, 315.
12. Michno, *Dakota Dawn*, 14–15.
13. *Ibid.*, 11.
14. Itinerary of Delegates, Peabody Museum, Harvard U. (online).
15. Carley, *The Dakota War of 1862*, 4–5.
16. "Urania S. White's Story," Renville County (online).
17. Michno, *Dakota Dawn*, 14.
18. George E.H. Day to Abraham Lincoln, U.S. Dakota War of 1862 (online).
19. McClure, *The Story of Nancy McClure*, MHS Collections, 444.
20. Anderson and Woolworth, *Through Dakota Eyes*, 8, 9, 12, 13.
21. Tarble, *The Story of My Capture and Escape*, 56.

Chapter 3

1. Michno, *Dakota Dawn*, 1.
2. Report of the Commissioner of Indian Affairs, 1862–55, 56.
3. "Big Eagle," Digital History (online).
4. "Urania S. White's Story," Renville County (online).
5. Report of the Commissioner of Indian Affairs, 1863–270, 271.
6. "Big Eagle," Digital History (online).
7. *Ibid.*

8. Michno, *Dakota Dawn*, 29.
9. Curtiss-Wedge, *History of Redwood County*, 110.
10. Anderson and Woolworth, *Through Dakota Eyes*, 30.
11. "Big Eagle," Digital History (online).
12. *Ibid.*, 108.
13. Michno, *Dakota Dawn*, 34–36.
14. Anderson and Woolworth, *Through Dakota Eyes*, 32.
15. Renville, *Dispatches from the Dakota War*, 55.
16. Anderson and Woolworth, *Through Dakota Eyes*, 56.
17. Wakefield, *Six Weeks in the Sioux Tepees*, 63, 64.
18. Report of the Commissioner of Indian Affairs, 1863–273, 274.
19. Michno, *Dakota Dawn*, 31.
20. Eggleston, *The Tenth Minnesota Volunteers*, 11.
21. Wakefield, *Six Weeks in the Sioux Tepees*, 62.
22. Report of the Commissioner of Indian Affairs, 1863–274.
23. *Minnesota in the Civil and Indian Wars*, Vol. 11, 177.
24. Williams, *Frontier Forts Under Fire*, 140.
25. Michno, *Dakota Dawn*, 40.
26. *Ibid.*, 33–38.
27. Wakefield, *Six Weeks in the Sioux Tepees*, 62.
28. *Minnesota in the Civil and Indian Wars*, Vol. 11, 178.
29. Report of the Commissioner of Indian Affairs, 1863–274.

Chapter 4

1. Brown, *Bury my Heart at Wounded Knee*, 170.
2. Michno, *Dakota Dawn*, 45.
3. "Urania S. White's Story," Renville County (online).
4. Report of the Commissioner of Indian Affairs, 1863–275.
5. Anderson and Woolworth, *Through Dakota Eyes*, 25, 26.
6. *Ibid.*, 30.
7. Nix, *The Sioux Uprising in Minnesota*, 83.
8. *St. Paul Daily Press*, Sept. 12, 1862, 2.
9. *Minnesota in the Civil and Indian Wars*, Vol. 11, 178.
10. Curtiss-Wedge, *History of Redwood County*, 122.
11. Anderson/Woolworth, *Through Dakota Eyes*, 35.
12. Curtiss-Wedge, *History of Redwood County*, 122, 123.
13. *Ibid.*, 123.
14. Michno, *Dakota Dawn*, 52.
15. Anderson/Woolworth, *Through Dakota Eyes*, 35.
16. *Ibid.*, 36.

Chapter 5

1. Berg, *38 Nooses*, 32.
2. Lynd, *History of the Dakotas*, 147.
3. Anderson and Woolworth, *Through Dakota Eyes*, 54, 55.
4. *Ibid.*, 56.
5. Michno, *Dakota Dawn*, 66.
6. McClure, *The Story of Nancy McClure*, MHS Collections, 448–452.
7. Wakefield, *Six Weeks in the Sioux Tepees*, 66.
8. Anderson and Woolworth, *Through Dakota Eyes*, 120.
9. Carley, *The Dakota War of 1862*, 20.
10. Michno, *Dakota Dawn*, 188.
11. *Ibid.*, 181.
12. Eggleston, *The Tenth Minnesota Volunteers*, 21.
13. Haymond, *The Infamous Dakota Trials*, 24.
14. Schultz, *Over the Earth I Come*, 82, 83.
15. Brown, *In Captivity*, 3.
16. *Ibid.*, 5.
17. Tarble, *The Story of My Capture and Escape*, 24–35.
18. Michno, *Dakota Dawn*, 121.
19. Schwandt, *The Story of Mary Schwandt*, MHS Collections, 468.
20. Brant/Murch, *A History of the Great Massacre*, 340.
21. Heard, *History of the Sioux War and Massacres of 1862 and 1863*.
22. Haymond, *The Infamous Dakota War Trials of 1862*, 153–154.
23. Michno, *A Fate Worse Than Death*, 224.
24. Wakefield, *Six Weeks in the Sioux Tepees*, 123.
25. Drimmer, *Captured by the Indians*, 317.
26. Letters regarding the 1862 Lake Shetek Massacre, MHS (online).

27. Michno, *Dakota Dawn*, 249, 250.
28. Letters regarding the 1862 Lake Shetek Massacre, MHS (online).
29. Haymond, *The Infamous Dakota War Trials of 1862*, 153.
30. "Julia Wright Was a Forgotten Survivor," *Star Tribune* (online).
31. Drimmer, *Captured by the Indians*, 329.
32. Carley, *The Dakota War of 1862*, 23, 24.
33. Brown, *In Captivity*, 8.

Chapter 6

1. Folwell, *A History of Minnesota*, Vol. 11, 361.
2. Carley, *The Dakota War of 1862*, 32, 33.
3. *Ibid.*, 33.
4. Michno, *Dakota Dawn*, 193.
5. Keneally, *Abraham Lincoln*, 67.
6. Bryant and Murch, *Indian Massacre in Minnesota*, 179.
7. Michno, *Dakota Dawn*, 196, 197.
8. Bryant and Murch, *Indian Massacre in Minnesota*, 180, 181.
9. Folwell, *A History of Minnesota*, Vol. 11, 363.
10. Flandrau, *Minnesota Historical Collections*, 786.
11. Carley, *The Dakota War of 1862*, 25.
12. *Ibid.*, 26.
13. Zdon, Article in *Allies*, MHS newsletter, Summer 2013, 1–4.
14. *St. Paul Daily Press*, September 12, 1862.
15. Zdon, Article in *Allies*, MHS newsletter, Summer 2013, 3.
16. Timothy J. Sheehan, "The U.S.-Dakota War of 1862" (online).
17. Anderson and Woolworth, *Through Dakota Eyes*, 172.
18. Michno, *Dakota Dawn*, 227.
19. *Ibid.*, 231.
20. *Ibid.*, 233.
21. Anderson and Woolworth, *Through Dakota Eyes*, 155.
22. *Ibid.*, 236.
23. Carley, *The Dakota War of 1862*, 29.
24. Sheehan's report, *Minnesota in the Civil & Indian Wars*, Vol. 11, 170.
25. Anderson and Woolworth, *Through Dakota Eyes*, 156.
26. Wakefield, *Six Weeks in the Sioux Tepees*, 78.
27. "Time Passages: Quiet Heroine of Fort Ridgely" (online).
28. Michno, *Dakota Dawn*, 303.
29. Wakefield, *Six Weeks in the Sioux Tepees*, 79.
30. Sheehan's Report, *Minnesota in the Civil & Indian Wars*, Vol. 11, 171.
31. Anderson and Woolworth, *Through Dakota Eyes*, 149.
32. *Ibid.*, 157.
33. Sheehan's Report, *Minnesota in the Civil & Indian Wars*, Vol. 11, 172.
34. Michno, *Dakota Dawn*, 306.
35. Tarble, *The Story of My Capture and Escape*, 42–44.
36. Anderson and Woolworth, *Through Dakota Eyes*, 157.
37. Carley, *The Dakota War of 1862*, 38.
38. Flandrau, *History of Minnesota*, 150.
39. Michno, *Dakota Dawn*, 315.
40. Buck, *Minnesota History Bulletin*, Vol. 1, 449, 450.
41. History Net, "Deadliest Attack on a Western Town" (online).
42. Michno, *Dakota Dawn*, 322, 341.
43. Flandrau, *History of Minnesota*, 152.
44. Daniels, *Reminiscences*, MHS Collections, Vol. XV, 331.
45. Michno, *Dakota Dawn*, 335.
46. Flandrau, *History of Minnesota*, 153, 154.
47. Buck, *Minnesota History Bulletin*, Vol. 1, 451, 452.
48. Daniels, *Reminiscences*, MHS Collections, Vol. XV, 330.
49. Flandrau, *History of Minnesota*, 155.
50. Letter of W.H. Hazzard, 1897, 10.
51. *Minnesota in the Civil and Indian Wars*, Vol. 11, 206.
52. Buck, *Minnesota History Bulletin*, Vol. 1, 452, 453.
53. Michno, *Dakota Dawn*, 343.
54. Flandrau, *History of Minnesota*, 156.
55. Daniels, *Reminiscences*, MHS Collections, Vol. XV, 333.
56. History Net, "Deadliest Attack on a Western Town" (online).

Chapter 7

1. *Official Records*, Vol. 13, 590–591.
2. *Minnesota in the Civil and Indian Wars*, Vol. 11, 196.
3. *The Daily Dispatch*, September 6, 1862.
4. *Minnesota in the Civil and Indian Wars*, Vol. 11, 165

5. Berg, *38 Nooses*, 108.
6. West, *Ancestry, Life and Times of Henry H. Sibley*, 87.
7. Berg, *38 Nooses*, 110.
8. Schultz, *Over the Earth I Come*, 21.
9. Tarble, *The Story of My Capture and Escape*, 45.
10. Beck, *Columns of Vengeance*, 29.
11. *The Free Press*, December 27, 1913.
12. Carley, *The Dakota War of 1862*, 48, 49.
13. Riggs, *Mary and I: Forty Years With the Sioux*, 165.
14. *Bibliography of Minnesota*, Vol. 111, Part 1, 84–85.
15. Berg, *38 Nooses*, 105–107.
16. *Minnesota in the Civil and Indian Wars*, Vol. 11, 215–216.
17. *Ibid.*, 212b.
18. *Ibid.*, 220.
19. Anderson and Woolworth, *Through Dakota Eyes*, 163–164.
20. *Minnesota in the Civil and Indian Wars*, Vol. 11, 213.
21. Carley, *The Dakota War of 1862*, 44.
22. West, *Life and Times of Henry H. Sibley*, 266.
23. *Minnesota in the Civil and Indian Wars*, Vol. 11, 219.
24. Shultz, *Over the Earth I Come*, 212.
25. *Minnesota in the Civil and Indian Wars*, Vol. 11, 212d.
26. *St. Paul Daily Press*, January 30, 1863.
27. Carley, *The Dakota War of 1862*, 45.
28. "The U.S.–Dakota War/Battle of Acton," *Tri-County News* (online).
29. *The Free Press*, December 27, 1913.

Chapter 8

1. McPherson, *Battle Cry of Freedom*, 532.
2. *Minnesota in the Civil and Indian Wars*, Vol. 11, 225.
3. Folwell, *A History of Minnesota*, Vol. 11, 176.
4. Schultz, *Over the Earth I Come*, 201.
5. West, *Life and Times of Henry H. Sibley*, 266.
6. Schultz, *Over the Earth I Come*, 212–213.
7. *Minnesota in the Civil and Indian Wars*, Vol. 11, 225.
8. Schultz, *Over the Earth I Come*, 216.
9. West, *Life and Times of Henry H. Sibley*, 206.
10. Berg, *38 Nooses*, 116.
11. Wakefield, *Six Weeks in the Sioux Tepees*, 100.
12. Berg, *38 Nooses*, 136.
13. Hatterway and Jones, *How the North Won*, 54, 55.
14. *Minnesota in the Civil and Indian Wars*, Vol. 11, 232.
15. Carley, *The Dakota War of 1862*, 55.
16. The Siege of Fort Abercrombie, Friends of (online).
17. *Minnesota in the Civil and Indian Wars*, Vol. 11, 253.
18. *Ibid.*, 236.
19. *Ibid.*, 225.
20. Schultz, *Over the Earth I Come*, 224.
21. *Minnesota in the Civil and Indian Wars*, Vol. 11, 238.

Chapter 9

1. West, *Life and Times of Henry H. Sibley*, 207.
2. Anderson and Woolworth, *Through Dakota Eyes*, 239.
3. Schultz, *Over the Earth I Come*, 47–49.
4. *Ibid.*, 229.
5. Wakefield, *Six Weeks in the Sioux Tepees*, 105.
6. Beck, *Columns of Vengeance*, 29.
7. Brown, *In Captivity*, 9.
8. Anderson and Woolworth, *Through Dakota Eyes*.
9. *Ibid.*, 243.
10. *Ibid.*, 236.
11. Brown, *In Captivity*, 9.
12. Anderson and Woolworth, *Through Dakota Eyes*, 236.
13. *Ibid.*, 258.
14. *Minnesota in the Civil and Indian Wars*, Vol. 11, 245.
15. *Ibid.*, 246.
16. *Ibid.*, 242–243.
17. *Ibid.*, 245.
18. Anderson and Woolworth, *Through Dakota Eyes*, 236.
19. *Ibid.*, 223.
20. *Ibid.* 237.
21. *Ibid.*, 258–259.
22. *Minnesota in the Civil and Indian Wars*, Vol. 11, 249.
23. Wellman, *Death on the Prairie*, 21.
24. Anderson and Woolworth, *Through Dakota Eyes*, 240.
25. Schultz, *Over the Earth I Come*, 222.

26. Anderson and Woolworth, *Through Dakota Eyes*, 222.
27. Schwandt, *The Story of Mary Schwandt*, MHS Collections, 470.
28. Brown, *Bury My Heart at Wounded Knee*, 57–58.
29. Renville, *A Thrilling Account of Indian Captivity*, 213.
30. *Minnesota in the Civil and Indian Wars*, Vol. 11, 249–250.
31. Berg, *38 Nooses*, 158–159.

Chapter 10

1. Wakefield, *Six Weeks in the Sioux Tepees*, 110–111.
2. *Ibid.*, 108.
3. Anderson and Woolworth, *Through Dakota Eyes*, 247.
4. Schultz, *Over the Earth I Come*, 239.
5. Anderson and Woolworth, *Through Dakota Eyes*, 224.
6. *Bibliography of Minnesota*, Vol. 111, Part 1, 87.
7. West, *Life and Times of Henry H. Sibley*, 276.
8. Wakefield, *Six Weeks in the Sioux Tepees*, 115.
9. Schwandt, *The Story of Mary Schwandt*, MHS Collections, 471.
10. Anderson and Woolworth, *Through Dakota Eyes*, 257–258.
11. Riggs, *Mary and I: Forty Years with the Sioux*, 179.
12. Schultz, *Over the Earth I Come*, 245.
13. Reilly, *Frontier Newspapers and the Indian Wars*, 11–12.
14. Wakefield, *Six Weeks in the Sioux Tepees*, 114.
15. Berg, *38 Nooses*, 165.
16. Reilly, *Frontier Newspapers and the Indian Wars*, 8.
17. Anderson and Woolworth, *Through Dakota Eyes*, 225.
18. Haymond, *The Infamous Dakota War Trials of 1862*, 74.
19. Williams, *Rebel Guerrillas*, 190.

Chapter 11

1. West, *Life and Times of Henry H. Sibley*, 278.
2. Schwandt, *The Story of Mary Schwandt*, MHS Collections, 467.
3. Berg, *38 Nooses*, 220–221.
4. Heard, *History of the Sioux War and Massacres of 1862 and 1863*.
5. Haymond, *The Infamous Dakota War Trials of 1862*, 71.
6. Heard, *History of the Sioux War and Massacres of 1862 and 1863*, 271, 272.
7. Wakefield, *Six Weeks in the Sioux Tepees*, 115–116.
8. *Ibid.*, 118.
9. Berg, *38 Nooses*, 187.
10. Nichols, *Lincoln and the Indians*, 96.
11. *Ibid.*
12. Buck, *Indian Outbreaks*, 216.
13. Schultz, *Over the Earth I Come*, 252.
14. Berg, *38 Nooses*, 193–194.
15. Schultz, *Over the Earth I Come*, 252.
16. Berg, *38 Nooses*, 304–305.
17. Schultz, *Over the Earth I Come*, 254.
18. Berg, *38 Nooses*, 197.
19. Anderson and Woolworth, *Through Dakota Eyes*, 227.
20. Thomas Rice Stewart, *Memoirs*, MHS Collections, 1519.
21. Berg, *38 Nooses*, 289.
22. *Ibid.*, 249.
23. *Ibid.*, 213–214.
24. West, *Life and Times of Henry H. Sibley*, 286.
25. Bryant and Murch, *Great Massacre by the Sioux Indians*, 469–470.
26. Schultz, *Over the Earth I Come*, 257–258.
27. Berg, *38 Nooses*, 209.
28. Reilly, *Frontier Newspapers and the Indian Wars*, 13.
29. Report of Commissioner Dole, December 3, 1862.
30. West, *Life and Times of Henry H. Sibley*, 288.
31. Burlingame, *Abraham Lincoln: A Life*, 483.
32. Riggs, *Mary and I: Forty Years with the Sioux*, 185.
33. Berg, *38 Nooses*, 230.
34. Heard, *History of the Sioux War and Massacres of 1862 and 1863*.
35. Schultz, *Over the Earth I Come*, 263.
36. Tarble, *The Story of My Capture and Escape*, 63.
37. Heard, *History of the Sioux War and Massacres of 1862 and 1863*.
38. Carley, *The Dakota War of 1862*, 75.
39. Berg, *38 Nooses*, 235.

Chapter 12

1. Schultz, *Over the Earth I Come*, 265.
2. Beck, *Columns of Vengeance*, 43.
3. *St. Paul Press*, June 23, 1863.
4. Berg, *38 Nooses*, 268.
5. Schultz, *Over the Earth I Come*, 268.
6. Connolly, *A Thrilling Narrative*, 212.
7. "Dustin Massacre," *Herald Journal* (online).
8. *The Free Press*, December 27, 1913.
9. Carley, *The Dakota War of 1862*, 86.
10. West, *Life and Times of Henry H. Sibley*, 333.

Chapter 13

1. Clodfelter, *The Dakota War*, 88–89.
2. Pope to Halleck, *Official Records*, Vol. 12, part 3, 826.
3. Sibley to Col. John Kelton, *Official Records*, Vol. 22, part 2, 371.
4. McPherson, *Battle Cry of Freedom*, 390.
5. West, *Life and Times of Henry H. Sibley*, 304.
6. Beck, *Columns of Vengeance*, 86.
7. Connolly, *A Thrilling Narrative*, 205.
8. Glanville, *I Saw the Ravages of an Indian War*, 117.
9. Connolly, *A Thrilling Narrative*, 209.
10. Beck, *Columns of Vengeance*, 94.
11. *Minnesota in the Civil and Indian Wars*, Vol. 11, 305.
12. Beck, *Columns of Vengeance*, 96.
13. McPherson, *Battle Cry of Freedom*, 638.
14. *Ibid.*, 98.
15. Sibley Report, *Minnesota in the Civil and Indian Wars*, Vol. 11, 298.
16. Clodfelter, *The Dakota War*, 100.
17. Beck, *Columns of Vengeance*, 110.
18. West, *Life and Times of Henry H. Sibley*, 504.
19. Connolly, *A Thrilling Narrative*, 238.
20. Beck, *Columns of Vengeance*, 117.
21. *Ibid.*, 118.
22. West, *Life and Times of Henry H. Sibley*, 505.
23. Connolly, *A Thrilling Narrative*, 239.
24. Clodfelter, *The Dakota War*, 105.
25. Baker Report, *Minnesota in the Civil and Indian Wars*, Vol. 11, 322.
26. Connolly, *A Thrilling Narrative*, 246.
27. West, *Life and Times of Henry H. Sibley*, 314.
28. Lounsberry, *Early History of North Dakota*, 299.
29. Sibley Report, *Minnesota in the Civil and Indian Wars*, Vol. 11, 301.
30. Crooks' Report, *Ibid.*, 315.
31. Lounsberry, *Early History of North Dakota*, 293.
32. Sibley Report, *Minnesota in the Civil and Indian Wars*, Vol. 11, 302.
33. West, *Life and Times of Henry H. Sibley*, 317.
34. Connolly, *A Thrilling Narrative*, 254.
35. Sibley letter, *Minnesota in the Civil and Indian Wars*, Vol. 11, 310.
36. Sibley Report, *ibid.*, 302.
37. Clodfelter, *The Dakota War*, 113.
38. Lounsberry, *Early History of North Dakota*, 292.

Chapter 14

1. Sully, *No Tears for the General*, 63–70.
2. Thrapp, *Encyclopedia of Frontier Biography*, 1389.
3. Lounsberry, *Early History of North Dakota*, 294.
4. Beck, *Columns of Vengeance*, 135–137.
5. Hinman to Whipple, June 8, 1863, Whipple Papers, MHS.
6. *Ibid.*, 140.
7. Custer, *Boots and Saddles*, 132–133.
8. *South Dakota Historical Collections*, Vol. VIII, 112–113.
9. The Letters of Private Milton Spencer, *North Nebraska History*, 249.
10. Executive Documents, no. 1 (Serial 1184), 38th Congress, 555–556.
11. Custer, *My Life on the Plains*, 82.
12. Clodfelter, *The Dakota War*, 125.
13. *Ibid.*, 128–129.
14. Sully Rep., September 11, 1863, S.D. Hist. Collections, Vol. VIII.
15. House Rep., September 3, 1863, S.D. Hist. Collections, Vol. VIII.
16. Chaky, *Terrible Justice*, 201.
17. Furnas Report, September 6, 1863, S.D. Hist. Collections, Vol. VIII.
18. Clodfelter, *The Dakota War*, 137.
19. Sully Report, September 11, 1863, S.D. Hist. Collections, Vol. VIII.
20. Clodfelter, *The Dakota War*, 140.
21. Furnas Report, September 6, 1863, S.D. Hist. Collections, Vol. VIII.
22. Wilson Report, September 3, 1863, S.D. Hist. Collections, Vol. VIII.

23. Beck, *Columns of Vengeance*, 166.
24. The Letters of Private Milton Spencer, *North Nebraska History*, 252.
25. Sully Report, September 11, 1863, S.D. Hist. Collections, Vol. VIII.
26. Hall Report, September 5, 1863, S.D. Hist. Collections, Vol. VIII.
27. Eggleston, *The Tenth Minnesota Volunteers, 1862-1865*, 74.
28. Pope to Sully, October 5, 1863.
29. *St. Paul Weekly Press*, November 19, 1863.
30. Report of the Commissioner of Indian Affairs, 38th Congress (Serial 1220), 403.
31. Beck, *Columns of Vengeance*, 170–172.

Chapter 15

1. Utley, *Frontiersmen in Blue*, 274.
2. Clodfelter, *The Dakota War*, 155.
3. Beck, *Columns of Vengeance*, 179.
4. Haymond, *The Infamous Dakota War Trials of 1862*, 135, 136.
5. Halleck to Pope, February 14, 1864.
6. Beck, *Columns of Vengeance*, 180.
7. Kingsbury, *Sully's Expedition Against the Sioux in 1864*, Vol. 8, 451, 452.
8. Pope to Sibley, January 18, 1864.
9. *Official Records*, Series 1, Vol. XXXIV, Part 11, 303.
10. *Minnesota in the Civil and Indian Wars*, Vol. 1, 388.
11. South Dakota Historical Collections, Vol. VIII, 291.
12. Beck, *Columns of Vengeance*, 190.
13. English, *Dakota's First Soldiers*, Vol. 9, 278.
14. Pattee, *Reminiscences*, 306.
15. Kelly, *Narrative of My Captivity* (1873 ed.), 20–27.
16. Gardner, *History of the Spirit Lake Massacre*, 64–69.
17. South Dakota Historical Collections, Vol. VIII, 293.
18. Beck, *Columns of Vengeance*, 199.
19. Clodfelter, *The Dakota War*, 165.
20. Eggleston, *The Kit Carson of the Northwest*, 28.
21. South Dakota Historical Collections, Vol. V, 309.
22. Beck, *Columns of Vengeance*, 207.
23. *Ibid.*, 208.
24. Vestal, *Sitting Bull: Champion of the Sioux*, 61.
25. Bergemann, *Brackett's Battalion*, 112.
26. South Dakota Historical Collections, Vol. V, 309.
27. Beck, *Columns of Vengeance*, 215.
28. Judd, *Campaigning Against the Sioux*, 9.
29. South Dakota Historical Collections, Vol. VIII, 375.
30. Kelly, *Narrative of My Captivity* (1873 ed.), 99.
31. Beck, *Columns of Vengeance*, 216.
32. Sully Report, July 31, 1864.
33. Beck, *Columns of Vengeance*, 216.
34. Sully Report, July 31, 1864.
35. Kelly, *Narrative of My Captivity* (1873 ed.), 110.
36. Clodfelter, *The Dakota War*, 165.

Chapter 16

1. Pope to Halleck, November 3, 1864.
2. Beck, *Columns of Vengeance*, 221.
3. Pfaller, *Sully's Expedition of 1864*, 57.
4. Sully Report, August 13, 1864.
5. *Ibid.*
6. Pattee, *Dakota Campaigns*, 312.
7. Clodfelter, *The Dakota War*, 183.
8. Sully Report, August 13, 1864.
9. Campbell Collections, *Interviews with White Bull*, 6–10.
10. *Official Records*, Series 1, Vol. XLI, Part 1, 169.
11. Beck, *Columns of Vengeance*, 225.
12. *Official Records*, Series 1, Vol. XLI, Part 1, 169.
13. Clodfelter, *The Dakota War*, 185.
14. Sully Report, August 13, 1864.
15. Chaky, *Terrible Justice*, 203.
16. Beck, *Columns of Vengeance*, 239.
17. Myers, *Soldiering in the Dakotas*, 24.
18. Sully Report, August 13, 1864.
19. Clodfelter, *The Dakota War*, 9.
20. English, *Dakota's First Soldiers*, 292.
21. *Official Records*, Series 1, Vol. XLI, Part 1, 152, 153.
22. Clodfelter, *The Dakota War*, 192.
23. Sully Report, September 9, 1864.
24. Pope to Halleck, October 6, 1864.
25. Michno, *Encyclopedia of Indian Wars*, 152.
26. Beck, *Columns of Vengeance*, 243.
27. Kelly, *Narrative of My Captivity* (1873 ed.), 275–276.
28. *Official Records*, Series 1, Vol. XLI, Part 1, 154.
29. Beck, *Columns of Vengeance*, 243.

30. White, "Captain Fisk Goes to Washington," *MHS Magazine* 228 (online).
31. *Official Records*, Series 1, Vol. XLI, Part 1, 155.
32. Brown, *Bury My Heart at Wounded Knee*, 74.
33. Pell to Sully, October 26, 1864.
34. South Dakota Historical Collections, Vol. VIII, 340.
35. *Ibid.*, Vol. IV, 115.
36. Kelly, *Narrative of My Captivity* (1873 ed.), 195–196.
37. *Ibid.*, 280.
38. *Ibid.*
39. *Ibid.*, 270–271.
40. Vestal, *Sitting Bull: Champion of the People*, 65–66.
41. Clodfelter, *The Dakota War*, 200.
42. South Dakota Historical Collections, Vol. IV, 114.
43. Naparsteck, *Sex and Manifest Destiny*, 132.

Chapter 17

1. Brown, *Bury My Heart at Wounded Knee*, 87–92.
2. Wellman, *Death on the Prairie*, 75–76.
3. *Official Records*, Vol. XLVIII, part 2, 616.
4. McPherson, *Battle Cry of Freedom*, 853.
5. Clodfelter, *The Dakota War*, 207.
6. *Ibid.*, 800–801.
7. *Official Records*, Vol. XLVIII, part 2, 851.
8. Clodfelter, *The Dakota War*, 209.
9. South Dakota Historical Collections, Vol. V, 331.
10. *Official Records*, Vol. XLVIII, part 2, 1109.
11. *Ibid.*, 434.
12. South Dakota Historical Collections, Vol. V, 339.
13. *Ibid.*
14. *Official Records*, Vol. XLVIII, part 2, 1147.
15. Berg, *38 Nooses*, 243.
16. *Official Records*, Vol. XLVIII, part 2, 1173.
17. Brown, *The Galvanized Yankees*, 129.
18. South Dakota Historical Collections, Vol. V, 341, 342.
19. *Ibid.*, 1181.
20. *Frontier Scout* 1, No. 15, 3.
21. Williams, *Custer and the Sioux, Durnford and the Zulus*, 80.
22. *Official Records*, Vol. LVIII, part 2, 1182.
23. South Dakota Historical Collections, Vol. V, 343–344.
24. Clodfelter, *The Dakota War*, 214.
25. Annual Report of the Commissioner of Indian Affairs, 1865, 211.
26. *Official Records*, Vol. XLVIII, part 2, 852.

Chapter 18

1. Williams, *Frontier Forts Under Fire*, 203.
2. Berg, *38 Nooses*, 285.
3. Carley, *The Dakota War of 1862*, 81.
4. Barnes, *The Great Plains Guide to Custer*, 84.
5. Berg, *38 Nooses*, 296.
6. *Official Records*, Vol. XLVIII, part 2, 1151.

Bibliography

Government and Historical Society Documents

Adjutant General's Report, Executive Document, 1863.
Annual Report of the Commissioner of Indian Affairs, 1862–1865.
Annual Report of the Secretary of War, 1861–1865.
House Executive Documents, 23rd, 37th and 38th Congresses.
Minnesota Historical Society Dakota Conflict of 1862 Manuscripts and Collections.
Minnesota Historical Society Newsletters.
Minnesota in the Civil and Indian Wars, 1861–1862. Vol. 1 and Vol. 11. State Government Board of Commissioners.
The Official Records of the Union and Confederate Armies in the War of the Rebellion. Washington, D.C.: U.S. Govt. Printing Office, 1894–1922.
South Dakota Historical Society Collections, Vol. IV (1908), Vol. V (1910), Vol. VIII (1916), edited by Doane Robinson.
U.S. Senate Records of Sioux War Trials of 1862. Record Group 46, National Archives, Washington, D.C..
Walter Stanley Campbell Collections (Stanley Vestal), University of Oklahoma.

Newspapers

Central Republican
Daily Dispatch
Frank Leslie's Illustrated Newspaper
Free Press
Frontier Scout
Harper's Monthly Magazine
Harper's Weekly
Minneapolis State Atlas
St. Paul Pioneer
St. Paul Daily Press
Star Tribune

Books

Anderson, Gary C. *Little Crow: Spokesman for the Sioux*. St. Paul: Minnesota Historical Society Press, 1986.
Anderson, Gary C., and Alan R. Woolworth, eds. *Through Dakota Eyes: Narrative Accounts of the Minnesota Indian War of 1862*. St. Paul: Minnesota Historical Society, 1998.
Andrews, C.C., ed. *Minnesota in the Civil and Indian Wars*. St. Paul Pioneer Press, 1899.
Atkins, Annette. *Creating Minnesota: A History from the Inside Out*. St. Paul: Minnesota Historical Society Press, 2007.
Barnes, Jeff. *The Great Plains Guide to Custer: 85 Forts, Fights and Other Sites*. Mechanicsburg, PA: Stackpole Books, 2011.

Beck, Paul N. *Columns of Vengeance: Soldiers, Sioux, and the Punitive Expeditions 1863–1864*. Norman: University of Oklahoma Press, 2013.
Berg, Scott W. *38 Nooses: Lincoln, Little Crow, and the Beginnings of The Frontier's End*. New York: Vintage Books, 2013.
Bergemann, Kurt D. *Brackett's Battalion: Minnesota Cavalry in the Civil War and Dakota War*. Nepean, Canada: Borealis Books, 2004.
Berghold, Alexander. *The Indians' Revenge, or Days of Horror: Some Appalling Events in the History of the Sioux*. Roseville: Edinborough Press, 2007.
Brake, Andrew S. *Man in the Middle: The Reforms and Influence of Henry Benjamin Whipple, the First Episcopal Bishop of Minnesota*. Lanham, MD: University Press of America, 2005.
Brown, Dee. *Bury My Heart at Wounded Knee: An Indian History of the American West*. London: Vintage, 1991.
_____. *The Galvanized Yankees*. Norman: University of Nebraska Press, 1986 (reprint).
Brown, Samuel J. *In Captivity: The Experiences, Privations and Dangers of Sam'l J. Brown, and Others, While Prisoners of the Hostile Sioux, During the Massacre and Indian War of 1862*. New York: Garland Publishing Co., 1900.
Bryant, Charles S., and Abel B. Murch. *A History of the Great Massacre by the Sioux Indians in Minnesota, Including the Personal Narratives of Many Who Escaped*. Cincinnati: Rickey and Carroll, Publishers, 1864.
Buck, Daniel. *Indian Outbreaks*. St. Paul: The Pioneer Press, 1904.
Buck, Solon J., ed. *Minnesota History Bulletin*, Vol. 1. St. Paul: Minnesota Historical Society, 1915.
Carley, Kenneth. *The Dakota War of 1862: Minnesota's Other Civil War*. St. Paul: Minnesota Historical Society, 1976.
Chaky, Doreen. *Terrible Justice: Sioux Chiefs and U.S. Soldiers on the Upper Missouri, 1854–1868*. Norman: University of Oklahoma Press, 2012.
Chomsky, Carol. "The United States–Dakota War Trials: A Study in Military Injustice." *Stanford Law Review* 43, No. 1 (November 1990): 13–98.
Clodfelter, Micheal. *The Dakota War: The United States Army Versus the Sioux, 1862–1865*. Jefferson, NC: McFarland, 1998.
Connolly, Alonzo P. *A Thrilling Narrative of the Minnesota Massacre and the Sioux War of 1862–63*. Chicago: A.P. Connolly, 1896.
Cox, Hank H. *Lincoln and the Sioux Uprising of 1862*. Nashville: Cumberland House, 2005.
Curtiss-Wedge, Franklyn, ed. *The History of Redwood County, Minnesota*. Chicago: H.C. Cooper & Co., 1916.
_____. *The History of Renville County, Minnesota*. Chicago: H.C. Cooper & Co., 1916.
Custer, Elizabeth B. *"Boots and Saddles" or, Life in Dakota With General Custer*. Norman: University of Oklahoma Press, 1987 (first published 1885).
Custer, George A. *My Life on the Plains: Or Personal Experiences with Indians*. New York: Sheldon & Co., 1874.
Daniels, Asa W. *Reminiscences of the Little Crow Uprising*. St. Paul: Minnesota Historical Society, 1910.
Drimmer, Frederick, ed. *Captured by the Indians: 15 Firsthand Accounts, 1570–1780*. Mineola, NY: Dover Publications, 1985.
Eggleston, Edward. *The Kit Carson of the Northwest*. St. Paul: Minnesota Historical Society, 1953.
Eggleston, Michael A. *The Tenth Minnesota Volunteers, 1862–1865: A History of Action in the Sioux Uprising and the Civil War*. Jefferson, NC: McFarland, 2012.
English, Abner M. *Dakota's First Soldiers: History of the First Dakota Cavalry, 1862–1865*. Bismarck, ND: D. Robinson, 1900.

Bibliography 243

Flandrau, Charles, E. *A History of Minnesota and Tales of the Frontier.* St. Paul: E.W. Potter, 1900.
Folwell, William W. *A History of Minnesota.* St. Paul: Minnesota Historical Society, 1924.
Gardner, Abbie, *A History of the Spirit Lake Massacre and the Captivity of Miss Abbie Gardner.* Des Moines: Iowa Printing Co., 1885.
Gilman, Rhoda R. *Henry Hastings Sibley: Divided Heart.* St. Paul: Minnesota Historical Society Press, 2004.
Glanville, Amos E. *I Saw the Ravages of an Indian War.* St. Paul: J. Granville, 1988.
Goodwin, Doris Kearns. *Team of Rivals: The Political Genius of Abraham Lincoln.* New York: Simon & Schuster, 2005.
Haymond, John A. *The Infamous Dakota War Trials of 1862: Revenge, Military Law, and the Judgment of History.* Jefferson, NC: McFarland, 2016.
Heard, Isaac V.D. *History of the Sioux War and Massacres of 1862 and 1863.* New York: Harper and Brothers, 1863.
Hoffert, Sylvia D. *Jane Grey Swisshelm: An Unconventional Life, 1815-1884.* Chapel Hill: University of North Carolina Press, 2004.
Holcombe, Return I. *Minnesota in Three Centuries.* Mankato: Publishing Society of Minnesota, 1908
Humphrey, John A. *Boyhood Remembrances of Life Among the Dakotas and the Massacre of 1862.* St. Paul: Minnesota Historical Society, 1910.
Hutton, Paul A. *Phil Sheridan and His Army.* Lincoln: University of Nebraska Press, 1985.
Jackson, Helen H. *A Century of Dishonor: A Sketch of the United States Government's Dealings with Some of the Indian Tribes.* New York: Harper & Brothers, 1881.
Jones, Robert H. *The Civil War in the Northwest: Nebraska, Wisconsin, Iowa, Minnesota, and the Dakotas.* Norman: University of Oklahoma Press, 1960.
Judd, A.N. *Campaigning Against the Sioux.* Bismarck, ND: S. Lewis, 1973.
Kelly, Fanny. *Narrative of My Captivity Among the Sioux Indians.* Hartford: Mutual Publishing Co., 1872.
Keneally, Thomas. *Abraham Lincoln: A Life.* Melbourne: Penguin Books, 2008.
Leonhart, Rudolph. *Memories of New Ulm: My Experiences During the Indian Uprising in Minnesota, 1862.* Roseville, MN: Edinborough Press, 2005.
Lounsberry, Clement A. *Early History of North Dakota.* Washington, D.C.: Liberty Press, 1919.
Mardock, Robert Winston. *The Reformers and the American Indian.* Columbia: University of American Press, 1971.
McClure, Nancy. *The Story of Nancy McClure: Captivity Among the Sioux.* St. Paul: Minnesota Historical Society, 1894.
McConkey, Harriet E.B. *Dakota War Whoop or Indian Massacres and War in Minnesota, 1862-3.* New York: Wm. J. Moses Press, 1864.
McPherson, James M. *Battle Cry of Freedom: The American Civil War.* London: Penguin Books, 1994.
Michno, Gregory F. *Dakota Dawn: The Decisive First Week of the Sioux Uprising, August 17-24, 1862.* New York: Savas Beattie, 2011.
_____. *Encyclopedia of Indian Wars: Western Battles and Skirmishes, 1850-1890.* Missoula, MT: Mountain Press, 2003.
Michno, Gregory, and Susan Michno. *A Fate Worse Than Death: Indian Captives in the West, 1830-1885.* Caldwell, ID: Caxton Press, 2007.
Moe, Richard. *The Last Full Measure: The Life and Death of the First Minnesota Volunteers.* New York: Avon Books, 1993.
Myers, Frank. *Soldiering in Dakota Among the Indians, 1863-4-5.* Pierre: South Dakota State Historical Society, 1936 (reprint).

Namias, June. *White Captives: Gender and Ethnicity on the American Frontier.* Chapel Hill: University of North Carolina Press, 1993.
Naparsteck, Martin. *Sex and Manifest Destiny: The Urge That Drove Americans Westward.* Jefferson, NC: McFarland, 2012.
Nichols, David A. *Lincoln and the Indians: Civil War Policy & Politics.* Urbana: University of Illinois Press, 2000.
Nix, Jacob. *The Sioux Uprising in Minnesota, 1862: Jacob Nix's Eyewitness History.* Manchester, NH: NCSA Literature, 2016 (originally published in 1887).
Oneroad, Amos E., and Alanson B. Skinner. *Being Dakota: Tales and Traditions of the Sisseton and Wahpeton.* St. Paul: Minnesota Historical Society Press, 2003.
Ostler, Jeffrey. *The Plains Sioux and U.S. Colonialism from Lewis and Clarke to Wounded Knee.* Cambridge: Cambridge University Press, 2004.
Palmer, Jessica D. *The Dakota Peoples: A History of the Dakota, Lakota, and Nakota through 1863.* Jefferson, NC: McFarland, 2008.
Pattee, John. *Reminiscences of John Pattee.* Pierre: South Dakota Historical Society, 1910.
Pfaller, Louis. *Sully's Expedition of 1964 Featuring the Killdeer Mountain and Badland Battles.* Bismarck: State Historical Society of North Dakota, 1964 (reprint).
Pond, Samuel W. *Dakota Life in the Upper Midwest.* St. Paul: Minnesota Historical Society Press, 1986.
Prucha, Francis P. *American Indian Treaties: The History of a Political Anomaly.* Berkley: University of California Press, 1994.
Reilly, Hugh J. *The Frontier Newspapers and the Coverage of the Plains Indian Wars.* Santa Barbara, CA: Praeger, 2010.
Renville, Mary B. *A Thrilling Narrative of Indian Captivity: Dispatches From the Dakota War.* Minneapolis: Atlas Company's Book and Job Printing Office, 1863.
Riggs, Stephen R. *History of the Dakotas: James W. Lynd's Manuscript (Classic Reprint.)* London: Forgotten Books, 2018.
_____. *Mary and I: Forty Years with the Sioux.* Chicago: W.B. Holmes, 1880.
Satterlee, Marion P. *Outbreak and Massacre by the Dakota Indians in Minnesota in 1862.* Westminster, MD: Heritage Books, 2009.
Schultz, Duane. *Over the Earth I Come: The Great Sioux Uprising of 1862.* New York: Thomas Dunne Books, 1992.
Schwandt, Mary. *The Story of Mary Schwandt: Her Captivity During the Sioux "Outbreak" 1862.* St. Paul: Minnesota Historical Society, 1894.
Silver, Peter. *Our Savage Neighbors: How Indian Warfare Transformed Early America.* New York: W.W. Norton, 2008.
Tarble, Helen M. *The Story of My Capture and Escape During the Minnesota Indian Massacre of 1862.* St. Paul: Abbot Printing Co., 1904.
Thrapp, Dan L. *Encyclopedia of Frontier Biography.* Lincoln: University of Nebraska Press, 1991.
Utley, Robert M. *Frontiersmen in Blue: The United States Army and the Indian, 1848–1865.* Lincoln: University of Nebraska Press, 1981.
_____. *The Indian Frontier of the American West, 1864–1890.* Albuquerque: University of New Mexico Press, 1894.
Vestal, Stanley. *Sitting Bull: Champion of the Sioux.* Norman: University of Oklahoma Press, 1957 (originally published 1932).
Wakefield, Sarah. *Six Weeks in the Sioux Tepees: A Narrative of Indian Captivity.* Norman: University of Oklahoma Press (reprint of 1864 original), 1997.
Wall, Oscar G. *Recollections of the Sioux Massacre: An Authentic History.* Lake City: The Home Printery, 1909
Wellman, Paul I. *Death on the Prairie: The Terrible Struggle for the Western Plains.* London: W. Foulsham & Co., 1962.

West, Nathaniel, D.D. *The Ancestry, Life and Times of Hon. Henry Hastings Sibley, LL.D.* St. Paul: Pioneer Press, 1889.

Williams, Paul. *Custer and the Sioux, Durnford and the Zulus: Parallels in the American and British Defeats at the Little Bighorn (1876) and Isandlwana (1879).* Jefferson, NC: McFarland, 2015.

———. *Frontier Forts Under Fire: The Attacks on Fort William Henry (1757) and Fort Phil Kearney (1866).* Jefferson, NC: McFarland, 2017.

———. *Rebel Guerrillas: Mosby, Quantrill and Anderson.* Jefferson, NC: McFarland, 2018.

Wilson, James. *The Earth Shall Weep: A History of Native America.* New York: Grove Press, 1998.

Wooster, Robert. *The Military & United States Indian Policy: 1865–1903.* Lincoln: University of Nebraska Press, 1995.

Wright, James A. *No More Gallant a Deed: A Civil War Memoir of the First Minnesota Volunteers.* St. Paul: Minnesota Historical Society Press, 2008.

Online Sources

"Big Eagle," Digital History, www.digitalhistory.uh.edu/disp_textbook.cfm?smtid=3&psid=695.

"Dustin Massacre," *Herald Journal*, www.herald-journal.com/archives/2013/stories/hl-dustins.html.

"Deadliest Attack on a Western Town," History Net, www.historynet.com/new-ulm-deadliest-indian-attack-western-town.htm.

George E.H. Day to Abraham Lincoln, U.S. Dakota War of 1862, www.usdakotawar.org›History›Multimedia.

Image 1 of Causes of the Massacre, https://www.loc.gov/resource/lhbum.0866g_0307_0326/?st=text.

Itinerary of Delegates, Peabody Museum, Harvard U. https://www.peabody.harvard.edu›Online Exhibitions›Breaking the Silence.

"Julia Wright Was a Forgotten Survivor," *Star Tribune*, http://www.startribune.com/julia-wright-was-a-forgotten-survivor-of-the-u-s-dakota-war/397198831/.

Letters regarding the 1862 Lake Shetek Massacre, Minnesota Historical Society, www.mnhs.org/library/findaids/00914/pdfa/00914-000001.pdf.

"Little Crow's Death," https://athrillingnarrative.com/2012/05/07/lamsons-daughter-tells-the-story-of-little-crows-death/.

Sheehan, Timothy J., "The U.S.–Dakota War of 1862," www.usdakotawar.org/history/timothy-j-sheehan.

The Siege of Fort Abercrombie, Friends of, www.ftabercrombie.org/the-siege-of-fort-abercrombie.html.

"The Spirit Lake Massacre," History Net, www.historynet.com/spirit-lake-massacre.htm.

"There Once was a Kaposia Village," St. Paul Historical Society, saintpaulhistorical.com/items/show/115.

"Timeline: The U.S. Dakota War of 1862," www.usdakotawar.org/timeline.

"Time Passages: Quiet Heroine of Fort Ridgely," https://www.srperspective.com/2014/07/time-passages-quiet-heroine-of-fort-ridgely.

Transcript of L. Taliaferro journal, Vol. 15, p. 48, Collections, collections.mnhs.org/cms/web5/media.php?pdf=1&irn=10056132.

"Urania S. White's Story," Renville County, genealogytrails.com/minn/renville/uprising_survivors_white.html.

"The U.S.–Dakota War/Battle of Acton," *Tri-County News*, www.kimballarea.com/index.php?option=com...s...battle-of-acton...

White, Helen McCann, "Captain Fisk Goes to Washington," *Minnesota Historical Society Magazine* 228, collections.mnhs.org/MNHistoryMagazine/articles/38/v38i05p216-230.pdf.

Index

Acton 37–38, 91, 110, 144, 229, 236, 246
Akepa 44
Aldrich, Leonard 84
Alone (steamboat) 166, 169, 201
Anawangmant, Simon 44
Anderson, Joseph 86–88, 91, 245
Andre, Alexis 141, 151
Anderson, Mary 51–52
Assiniboine (steamboat) 160
Atlanta 226
Auge, James 89–90
Austin, Horace 60, 94
Ayer, Otis 61

Badlands, Battle of 194, 196–197, 199–200, 206, 230
Baker, Howard 36–37
Baker, James 23, 157–158
Baker, Mrs. 36–38
Bear's Rib 208
Beaver, Frederick 154–155, 159–*161*, 163
Beaver Creek 87, 122, 213
Beckerman, Lieutenant 221
Belden, George 172, 174
Bell, Adrian 45–*46*
Belle Peoria (steamboat) 166, 169
Beltz, John 197
Benjamin, John 145
Big Eagle, Chief 9, 25, 27, 29, 36, 38, 41, 64, 71, 104–107, 233–234, 245
Big Head, Chief 172
Big Mound, Battle of 152, 154–155, 163, 170, 230
Big Thunder (Little Crow's father) 17
Big Thunder (later Santee chief) 35, 39, 215
Big Woods 22, 36, 44, 85–86, 114–145
Birch Coulee, Battle of 87, 91, 94–95, 105, 123, 229
Bishop, Harriet 21, 129
Bishop, John 7–12, 68, 71, 223
Bismarck 158, 242–244
Black Hawk War 126
Black Hills 129, 144, 185, 225
Black Kettle 226

Blackmer, Frank 70
"blanket" Indians 23–27
Bleum, Margaret 59
Bleum, Martin 59
Blodgett, William 8–9, 11, 41
Blue Face 44
Blue Sky Woman 40
Boardman, L.M. 60
Bonaparte, Napoleon 13
Bowler, Sergeant 106
Boyer, Peter 90
Brackett, Alfred 183
Brackett, George 189, 192–193, 239, 242
Brandt, Frederick 127–128, 130
Breaking Up 36
Brennan, Private 10
Brings Plenty 209, 211–212
Brisbois, Elizabeth 43
Brisbois, Louis 43
Broburg, John 55
Brockmann, H. 58, 60
Brown, Joseph 16, 48, 86, 104, 135, 138, 148, 176
Brown, Samuel 49, 55, 104–105, 107, 109, 114, 119, 128, 176
Brown, Sarah 53
Brown, Susan 48
Brown Wing 36
Bruce, Amos 19
Bruch, Harlan 201
Bruerger, Emil 100
Buell, Salmon 77, 80
Bull Run, Battles of 6, 23, 93, 97, 105, 164–165, 226
Burch, Andrew 220
Burnt Boat Island 159
Busse, Wilhelmina 34

Camp Atchison 151
Camp Hayes 150
Camp Lincoln 128, 130–131
Camp Pope 147, 150
Camp Release 114, 116–*118*, 124, 138, 148, 230
Campbell, Antoine "Joe" 20, 95, 108–111, 113, 152, 156

248 Index

Campbell, Cecilia 8
Campbell, Jack 214, 239
Campbell, William 195
Cardinal, Margaret 53
Carroll, William 59–61, 242
Carrothers, Althea 49
Carrothers, Helen 24, 49, 72, 83–84
Carrothers, James 24, 49
Carter, Theodore 159
Cedar City 46
Champlin, Ezra 105–107, 133
Charleston Harbour 22
Chaska 44, 103, 113, 115–117, 122–123, 135–136, 138–139
Chaskaydon 135
Chaskays 134
Cheyennes 164, 208, 215, 219, 226
Childs, Albert 179
Chippewa (Ojibwe) 13, 22, 25, 30, 32, 34, 39, 45, 47, 49, 64, 98, 101, 143, 151, 201, 216
Chippewa Falls (steamboat) 201
Chivington, John 213
Civil War 22–23, 26, 34, 97, 98, 105, 165, 175, 214, 222, 224, 226, 242–245
Clapp, George 153
Clark, William 92, 139
Cole, Edwin 11
Comanches 77, 226
Company B 31, 35, 65
Company C 35, 64–65
Confederates 6, 64, 75, 94, 105, 178, 186, 208–209, 222
Congress 26, 82, 130, 141, 211–212, 215, 225, 230, 238–239, 241
Connolly, A.P. 143, 148, 150, 156, 158, 162, 238, 242
Connor, Patrick 214, 221–222
Cook, John 164
Coursolle, Joseph 66, 69, 71, 89, 102, 108
Cox, Eugene St. Julien 79, 84, 242
Crawford, Charles 128
Crawler 209, 211–212
Crees 143
Crooks, William 88, 90, 122, 148, 150–151, 155, 159–160, 238
Crow Creek Reservation 167, 176, 225
Cullen, William 16, 20, 22
Culver, Charlie 5
Culver, Lieutenant 6, 35, 65
Custer, Elizabeth B. 242
Custer, George A. 168–169, 170, 199, 212, 222, 225–226, 238, 240–242, 245
cut-hair farmer 41; *see* "cut-hairs" 21, 28, 39, 53, 102
Cut Nose 48–49, 53, 12248–49, 53, 122

Dagenais, George 67
Dallas, Alexander G. 142–143, 230
Daniels, Asa 61, 76–77, 79
Daniels, Jared 86–87, 235, 242

Danielson, John 154
Davey, Peter 156
Davis, Jefferson 214
Day, George E.H. 22
Dead Buffalo Lake, Battle of 154–156, 163, 230
De Camp, Joseph 68–69
Demarias, Joseph 100
Denver, James 16, 20
Devil's Lake 141, 144, 147, 152, 169 0 170, 214, 218–219, 225, 227
Dickinson, Joseph 5
Dickinson, Lathrop 51
Dill, Daniel 185, 204, 207
Dilts, Jefferson 204–207, 230
Dimon, Charles 215–*218*
Dodd, William 76
Dole, William 133, 178, 181, 229, 237
Doud, George 84, 184
Duley, Belle 55
Duley, Jefferson 54–55
Duley, Laura 55
Duley, William 54–55
Dunn, James 10–11
Dustin, Amos 144, 238, 245

Earle, Ezmon 66, 68–70
Eastlick, Frederick 54
Eastlick, Lavina 54–55
Edmunds, Newton 178, 215
Egan, James 88–91
1856 census 23
Endreson, Anna 55
Endreson, Brita 55
Endreson, Guri 55
Endreson, Gurid 55
Endreson, Lars 55
English, Abner 242
Estes, Benjamin 184
Excel, Christian 150

Faribault, David 42–43
Faribault, Nancy 23, 42–43; house 8
Fenske, John 11, 41
Fields, Lieutenant 151
Fifth Minnesota Volunteers 6
Fire Cloud 20–21
Fisk, James 191, 204–207, 212, 240, 246
Flandrau, Charles 16, 61, 73–80, 85, 235, 243
Flora (township) 47
Forbes, William 29, 95
Forest City 37, 55, 85, 91–93
Fort Abercrombie 99–100, 140, 150, 180–181, 229, 236, 245
Fort Abraham Lincoln 168
Fort Benton 180, 201
Fort Berthold 163, *203*, 208, 217, 219, 221–222, 231
Fort Buford 202
Fort Dilts 204, 206–207, 230
Fort Dodge 225

Index

Fort Garry 141–*142*, 146, 163. 230
Fort Laramie 186, 222, 225
Fort Michilimackinac 32
Fort Mims 64
Fort Phil Kearny 245
Fort Pierre 141, 167–*168*, 169–170, 176
Fort Randall 164, 166–167, 170, 176, 208
Fort Rankin 213
Fort Reno 222, 224
Fort Rice *185*–187, 202–204, 206–208, 214–*218*, 219, 221–222, 230–231
Fort Ridgely 5–6, 8, 11, 15, 16, 20, 25, 28, 30, 32–33, 35, 41–47, 50–52, 56, 58, 61, *62*, 63–65, 81, 84–87, 89–90, 95, 99, 102, 104, 123, 126, 178; first battle 65–68; second battle 69–73; *see also* New Ulm
Fort Ripley 35, 81
Fort Snelling 6, 12–13, *14*, 17, 35, 42, 45, 49, 63, 82, 119, 126, 128–129, 143, 162, 167, 176, 181, 224
Fort Sully 176–*177*, *178*, 208–212
Fort Sumter 22
Fort Thompson *167*
Fort Totten 219, 227
Fort Union 201–*202*, *203*, 208
Fort Wadsworth 208
Foster, James 31
Four Horns 192
Frazer, Jack 31
Freeman, Ambrose 154, 163
Frémont, Charles 219
Frontier Scout (army newspaper) 221, 240–241
Furnas, Robert 172, 174, 238

Galbraith, Thomas 6, 23, 26–35, 45–46, 63–65, 86–87, 95, 119, 126
Gall 190
Gardner, Abbie 44, 187, 243
Garvie, Stewart 45–46
Gere, Thomas 6–7, 30–31, 33, 62–64
German Land Company 57
Gettysburg 144, 151, 167
Gleeson, George 44, 104, 116, 122, 136
Gibbon, John 165
Gibbons, Richard 88
Glanville, Amos 150, 238, 243
Gleeson, George 44, 104, 116, 122, 136
Gluth, Henry 74
Godfrey, Edward 226
Godfrey, Joseph 52, 121
Good Thunder 116
Good Voiced Hail 30
Gorman, James 35, 65
Gorman, John 72, 106
Grant, Hiram 86–91, 117-118, 123
Grant, Ulysses S. 151, 214
Grattan, John 12, 177
Gray Bird 86
Gray Eagle, Chief 156

Groetch, John 99
Gros Ventre 141, 203

Hakewaste, Robert (aka Good Fifth Son) 29
Hall, Charles 175, 239
Hall, Turner 78
Halleck, Henry 81, 97–*98*, 101, 120–121, 123, 133, 146–147, 164, 180–181, 205, 208, 214, 238–239
Harney, William 166, 177
Hart, William 88
Hatch, Edwin 147, 181
Hayden, Mary 11, 43
Hazzard, W.H. 75, 78, 235
Heard, Isaac 52, 121
Heart River 181, 185, 188, 195, 196
Henderson, Clarissa 49, 72
Henderson, Stephen 49–50, 90
Henderson township 11, 128
Hendricks, Captain 107
Hern, Margaret 70–71
Hesselberger, G.A. 210–211
Hilger, Nicholas 196, 198–200
Hinman, Samuel 5, 36, 41, 126, 167, 238
Hobbs, Sergeant 220–221
Hodgson, Thomas 194, 207
Hoffman, Sergeant 220–221
Homestead Act 23, 229
Houghton, Newell 78
House, Albert 171
Huey, William 73, 79
Hufstudler, James 220–221
Huggan, Nancy 107, 114
Huggins, Amos 45
Humphrey, John 7–10, 233, 243
Humphrey, Philander 7
Hunt, Thomas 154
Hunter, Alexander 41
Hurley, Mary 186
Hutchison (township) 85, 92–93, 144–145, 150
Hutchison, John 180
Hutchison, Private 11

Indian Territory 225–226
Ingalls 49
Ingerman, Ole 37
Inkpaduta 15–17, 20–21, 30, 129, 152, 155, 171, 185, 189–190, 203, 225, 229, 233
Island City (steamboat) 201
Island Cloud 38
Ives, Luther 59

Jackson, Andrew 164, 243
Jewett Family 214
Jimeno, Manuela 164
Jones, Ann 36–37
Jones, Clara 36–37
Jones, John 32, *65*–67, 70–72, 148, 156–157, 160, 180, 190, 192–193, 197–198, 200, 236
Jones, Maria 66

Index

Jones, Robinson 36-37, 9136-37, 91
Julesburg 213
Jumping Bear 209-210

Kaposia (village) 17, 19, 233, 245
Kelly, Fanny 2, 186-*187*, *188*, 193-194, 197, 206-213, 239-240, 243
Kelly, Josiah 186
Killdeer Mountain, Battle of 189, 190, 194, 204, 206, 212-213, 222, 230, 244
Killing Ghost 36
Kinney, Newcome 159
Kiowas 226
Kitzman, Paul 47, 87
Knife River 188-189, 217, 219, 221
Kreiger, Frederick 47
Kreiger, Justina 47-48, 87, 90

LaBathe, Francois 125
LaBoo, Captain 170
La Croix, Louis 6-7
La Framboise, Joe 171, 190
Lake Herman 20
Lake Shetek 54, 138, 234-235, 245
Lake Traverse 150, 208, 225
Lakota Dakotas 111, 155, 162, 166, 180-181, 185, 189, 203, 205, 208-209, 224-225; *see also* Tetons
Lamb, John 41
Lamson, Mary 85, 92, 145, 245
Lamson, Nathan 144, 230
Larimer, Sarah 187, 193
Larned, William 207
Latimer, Mr. 187
La Tour, Joseph 67
Lea, Luke 14
Lean Bear 44, 152
Lean Grizzly Bear 54; wife 54
Leavitt, Lieutenant 174
Lee, Corwin 172, 174
Lee, Robert E. 93
Leonhart, Rudolph 34, 58, 74-75, 78-79, 243
Le Sueur 60
Le Sueur Tigers 75
Lightning Blanket 66-69, 71
Lincoln, Abraham 22-23, 34, 47, 58, 93, 95, 121, 124-*126*, 128-132, 134, 137, 139, 147, 151, 224, 229, 230, 233, 235, 237, 242-245
Little Box Elder Creek 186, 209, 212
Little Crow (Taoyateduta) 17, *18*, 19-21, *27*, 29, 32-33, 36, 38-41, 43, 49-50, 58, 61, 64-69, 71-73, 81, 84-87, 91-96, 101-114, 119-120, 122-123, 140-141, *142*-146, 150-152, 176, 224, 230, 233, 241-242, 245
Little Paul 44
Little Soldier, Chief 172
Logan, Captain 210
Lone Dog 190-191
Louisiana Purchase 13

Lower Bands 15; Episcopal Church 27, 36; *see also* Mdewakanton; Wahpekute
Lower Dakota (Redwood) Agency 5, 23
Lundborg, Andreas 55
Luse, J.C. 173
Lynd, James 15; Episcopal Church 27, 36; *see also* Mdewakanton; Wahpekute
Lyons, Earl 147

Mackinaw boat 163, 170-171
Magil, John 7
Magner, Edward 6
Magner, John 6-7
Malros, Oscar 95
Man-Who-Never-Walked (Bear Heart) 192
Mandan 141, 185, 203
Mankato (township) 15, 38, 59, 78-80, 83, 107, 118, 126, 128, 130-131, 133, 178, 124, 230, 243
Mankato, Chief 38, 64, 107
Marsh, John 5-10, 11, 25, 29-30, 32-33, 35, 43-44, 53; death 62-64
Marshall, William 107, 126, 128, 148, 151, 153-154, 157
Martell, Oliver 5-7, 42, 233
Massopust, Franz 51, 127
Massopust, John 127
Maximilian, Prince Alexander P. 160
May, Sebastian 59
Mayo, William 61
Mazakutemani, Paul 85, 104, 111, 115
McAuliffe, Samuel 59
McClellan, George 93
McClure, James 42; wife Winona 42
McFall, Orlando 66, 68, 70-71
McGrew, James 65-66, 70-71
McKenzie, John 181
McLaren, Robert 107, 154, 156, 188, 194
McMahon, Henry 77
McPhail, Samuel 83, 89, 90-91, 153-154, 157, 159
Mdewakanton 15, 17, *18*, 23, 26, 82
Meagher, John 76
Medicine Bottle (Indian) 103
Meeker County 37, 91
Messmer, Joe 51, 57
Milford (township) 51, 57
Miller, John 163
Miller, Nicolas 159-160
Miller, Stephen 130-131, 135, 137
Minnesota River *4*, 5, 8, 10, 13, 14-15, 20-24, 34, 45, 57, 61, 73, 79, 81, 86-87, 97, 102, 106, 111, 117, 229; Territory 14-15, 19; Valley 47, 105
Mississippi River 13, 129
Missouri River Battle 111, 141, 147, 151, 155, 158, *161*-162, 164, 170, 180, 183, 196, 202, 208, 230
Mix, Charles 20-12
Moreland, Abraham 166, 220
Morton, Thomas 152

Mosby, John 120, 245
Much Hail 40
Muller, Alfred 62, 70, 72
Muller, Eliza 70
Murphy, John 154
Murray, Alexander 16
My Life on the Plains (book) 170, 238, 242
Myers, Frank 188, 193, 201, 239, 243
Myrick, Andrew 29, 33, 40–41, 43, 87, 95

Nairn, John 41; Mrs. Nairn 41
New Ulm 22, 34, 41, 51, 54, 56–61, 64, 67, 70–75, 78–79, 83–85, 93–94, 104, 123, 127, 130, 138, 229, 243, 245
New York 25, 160
New York Regiment 165
Nicolay, John 47
Nix, Jacob 35, 57, 73, 78, 60, 234, 244
Nordstrom, Charles 34
Northrup, George 190

Ojibwe 13; *see also* Chippewa
Old Fool Dog 196
Old Pawn 54–55
Olin, Lieutenant 107
Olssen, Nels 37
O'Shea, Dennis 65, 67, 70–71
Other Day, John 17, 44–47, 102, 125, 225
Ottawa 186

Paine, James 204
Parsley, Thomas 11
Patch, Edward 162
Patoile, Francis 51
Patoile, Peter 45
Pattee, John 166, 186, 191–192, 197–199, 208, 216–**218**, 219–222, 239, 244
Paulie, Emilie 60
Paulson, Ole 152
Pell, John 208–209, 240
Pembina 141, 147, 181
Perry, Robert 178
Pickett, Eli 148
Pierce, Henry 169
Pike, Zebulon 13
Platt, John 163
Platte Bridge Station 214
Ponca Creek Massacre 166
Pope, John 93–**94**, 95, 97–101, 105, 117, 120–126, 132, 139, 144, 146–148, 162, 164–**165**, 169, 170, **173**, 176–178, 180–181, 205, 208, 214–215, 217, 223, 226–227, 223, 238–239; Camp Pope 150
Pope, Nathanial 183, 190–191–192, 198, 200
Porter, Fitz John 266
Potter, Theodore 74, 77–78, 243
Pratt, John 156
Prescott, Philander 102–103
Puffy Eyes 166

"Quaker" cannon 195
Quinn, George 108
Quinn, Peter 6, 8–9, 28, 33, 44

Ramer, James 150
Ramsey, Alexander 11, 14–15, 81, **82**, 93, 97–96, 98–99, 100, 108, 124, 128, 132–133, 144
Randall, Ben 5–6, 65, 70
Ravoux, Augustin 136–137
Red Blanket Woman 82
Red Cloud 222
Red Iron 108
Red Middle Voice 38, 110
Red Plume, Chief 155
Redwood Ferry, Battle of 5–6, 8, 12, 25, 42, 44, 58, 60, **62**, 87, 299
Renville, Gabriel 104, 152
Renville County 47, 233–234, 245
Renville Rangers 6, 34–35, 63, 65–66, 72, 106
Rhodes, Mr. 54
Rice, Ebenezer 184
Rice, Henry 146
Rice, Thomas 129, 237
Rice Creek 38, 110
Richards, Elkanah 171–172
Richardson, Eliphalet 69
Riggs, Martha 46
Riggs, Stephen 23, 32, 45, **46**, 52, 85, 95, 116, 120, 122, 135–135, 138, 148, 237, 244
Roaring Cloud 6, 16
Robinson, Doane 209, 211, 241
Roos, Charles 57–58, 60, 94
Rose, A.H. 92
Rose, Ezekiel 11
Rothammer, Siegmund 166–168
Round Wind 137
Runs Against Something When Crawling 36
Rupert's Land 112, 141–**142**, 144, 146, 180–181

St. Cloud 45, 84, 100, 132
St. Croix River 13
St. Paul 11, 17, 25, 37, 47, 60, 63, 79, 83–84, 91, 93, 97–99, 116, 122, 128–129, 131–132, 136, 139, 143, 160–161, 225, 229, 233–236, 241–245
Sand Creek Massacre 213
Santees 5, 141, **167**, 171, 176, 180, 185, 213,215, 224–225, 230
Scarlet Plume 152
Schneider, Creszentia 76
Schwandt, Karolina 51–52
Schwandt, Mary 51–**53**, 110, 116, 121, 234, 237, 244
Second Artillery 20
"Sesesh" 26
Sewell, Captain 220
Shakopee (chief) 38, 46, 110, 181
Sheehan, Timothy 6, 28, 30, **31**, 32–33, 35, 64–68, 71–72, 83, 89, 235
Sheridan, Philip 34
Sherman, Thomas 16–17, 20

252 Index

Shillock, Daniel 75
Shoemaker, James 76
Shreveport (steamboat) 166
Sibley, Henry H. 29, 79, 81–82, **83**–86, 90–91, 94–97, 100–102, 104–111, 113–121, 123–125, 127–128, 131–132, 136, 139–141, 144–148, **149**–160, **161**–162, 164–167, 169–171, 176–177, 180–**182**, 183–184, 187, 204–205, 208, 214, 225, 229–230, 236–239, 243, 245
Sibley County 79, 225
Sioux City 143, 147, 158, 166, 170, 176, 181, 183–184, 208, 214–215, 217, 230
Sisseton 14, 23, 26, 48, 68, 100, 141, 152, 162, 181
Sitting Bull 2–3, 190–192, 199, 201–202, 205, 211–212, 219, 221, 225, 239–240, 244
Smith, A.E. 38
Smith, Henry 54
Smith, John 159
Smith, Lieutenant 204–207
Smith, T.D. 99
Smitz, John 22
Snana (Maggie) 116
Snellin, Josiah 13
Soldiers' Lodge 14, 23, 26, 48, 68, 100, 141, 152, 162, 181
Spencer, George 53, 115
Spencer, Milton 166, 169, 174–175, 179, 238–239
Spirit Lake Massacre 15, 20, 25, 33, 30, 33, 38, 187, 203, 229, 233, 239, 243,245
Springfield, Minnesota 16, 83, 191
Standing Buffalo 16, 140–141, 151–152, 155
Stanton, Edwin 93, 95, 97, 132, 204
Stay, Cecelia Campbell 8
Steele, James 82
Steele, Sarah 82
Stevens, Salon 153
Stewart, George 75
Stony Lake, Battle of 156, 230
Strout, Richard 91–92
Stufft, Christian 189, 193
Sturgis, William 63
Sully, Alfred 2–3, 147, **149**, 158, 160–161, 164–**165**, 166–168, 169–**173**, 174–**177**, **178**, 181–**182**, 183–**185**, 187–198, 200–212, 215–**218**, 219, 221 223, 225–227, 230–231, 238–240
Sully, Thomas 164
Sutherland, William 11
Svendson, Ole 10–11
Swan Lake 184
Sweet Corn (Chief) 100, 155
Swisshelm, Jane 94, 132, 134, 243

Taliaferro, Lawrence 13, 233, 245
Tall Crown 153
Taylor, Captain 156
Tazoo 52, 137
Tehehdonecha 53
Teton Dakotas 104, 111, 158, 216; *see also* Lakota Dakotas

Thomas, Minor 181, 191
Thomas, Ralph 59, 60
Thompson, Clark 25
Thunder Blanket 12, 73
Traveling Hail 27, 32, 38
Treasury 26
Treaty of Mendota 14, 19
Treaty of Traverse des Sioux 14
Trent (ship) 147
Trescott, Solon 9,31
Trip, William 200
Turnbull, George 88
Two Bears (Chief) 215

Union Army 6, 82, 190, 226
Upper Bands 14–15, 44
Upper Dakota (Yellow Medicine) Agency 6, 8, 16, 20, 23, 26, 28–30, 32–33, 41, 44, 48, 54, 98–99, 104, 119
Usher, John Palmer 63, 124

Van Buren, Private 10
Vander Horck, John 99
Van Horhes A.J. 132
Van Minden, H. 202
Vestal, Stanley 211–212, 239–241, 244
Vicksburg 107, 151, 167

Wabasha, Chief 27–28, 38–39, 136
Wacouta, Chief 39, 52
Wagner, August 41
Wahpekute 15, 17, 23, 26
Wahpeton 14, 17, 23, 26, 68, 108, 140–141, 244
Wakan Tanka 19, 190, 197
Wakefield, John 44–45, 187
Wakefield, Mr. 187
Wakefield, Sarah 29, 31, 33, 53, 68, 70, 97, 103–104, 113, 115, 117, 136, 139, 234–237, 244
Walks on Iron 108
Wall, Oscar 151
Washburn, Edward 15
Washington D.C. 3, 21, 44, 81, 93, 118, 134–135, 147, 226, 240–241, 243, 246
Washita, Battle of the 226
Webster, Rosa Ann 36–38
Webster, Viranus 36–37
Weiser, Joseph 153–154, 163, 170
Welch, Abraham 97, 105–107, 133
Welles, Gideon 123–124
Weschke, Carl 61
West Lake 55
Whipple, Henry 76, 133–134, 167, 225, 238, 242
Whipple, John 65, 66–67, 157
White, Asa 77
White, Nathan 22
White, Urania 22, 26, 34, 103, 107
White Bull 191–192, 199, 205, 239
White Dog 8–9, 136
White Lodge 44, 152

White Spider 41
Whitestone Hill, Battle of 171, *173*, 174, 177–181, 239
Wieneke, Henry 193
Wilkinson, James 13
Wilkinson, Morton 146
Williams, Alpheus 93
Williams, Mattie 51–52, 121
Williamson, John 33, 125–126
Williamson, Thomas 19, 33, 45, 119, 137
Wilson, David 193
Wilson, Eugene 156
Windmill defense 75, 78
Winget, Private 194
Winnebagos 49, 73, 96, 101, 124, 141, *167*, 225
Wohler, Frances 49

Wolfe, Lewis 172
Wood, Major 191
Wood Lake, Battle of 103–105, 107, 114, 121, 123, 126, 133, 140, 230
Workman, Harper 55
Wounded Knee 1, 225, 237, 240, 242, 244
Wowinapa 140, 143–145, 152, 224
Wright, Julia 54–55, 235; husband John 55

Yankton Dakotas 111, 141, 146–147, 176
Yanktonai Dakotas 28, 162, 111, 146–147, 155, 171, 177, 180–181, 185, 190, 199, 215
Yellow Medicine Mission 45
Yellow Medicine River 16, 23, 30
Yomahah 35